Certified Flight Instructor
Oral Exam Guide

by Michael D. Hayes

Fifth Edition

The comprehensive
guide to prepare you
for the FAA Oral Exam

Aviation Supplies & Academics, Inc.
Newcastle, Washington

Certified Flight Instructor Oral Exam Guide
Fifth Edition

Aviation Supplies & Academics, Inc.
7005 132nd Place SE
Newcastle, Washington 98059-3153

Visit ASA's website often (**www.asa2fly.com**) to find updates posted there due to FAA regulation revisions that may affect this book.

Printed in the United States of America

2014   2013   2012   2011   9 8 7 6 5 4 3

ASA-OEG-CFI5

ISBN   1-56027-690-8
           978-1-56027-690-6

Library of Congress Cataloging-in-Publication Data:

Hayes, Michael D.
  Certified flight instructor oral exam guide : the comprehensive guide to prepare you for the FAA oral exam / by Michael D. Hayes.
     p.   cm.
  Includes bibliographical references.
  1. Flight training—Examinations, questions, etc.—Study guides.
2. Airplanes—Piloting—Examinations—Study guides. 3. United States, Federal Aviation Administration—Examinations—Study guides. I. Title
TL712.H39 1994   94-42322
629.132'52'0715—dc20   CIP

This guide is dedicated to the many talented students, pilots, and flight instructors I have had the opportunity to work with over the years. Also special thanks to Mark Hayes, David Sickler, the staff at Howell Aircraft Service, and the many others who supplied the patience, encouragement, and understanding necessary to complete the project.

—M.D.H.

Contents

Continued

4 Takeoffs and Climbs

5 Fundamentals of Flight

6 Slow Flight, Stalls, and Spins

7 Basic Instrument Maneuvers

8 Performance Maneuvers

9 Ground Reference Maneuvers

10 Approaches and Landings

11 Emergency Operations

Introduction

The *Certified Flight Instructor Oral Exam Guide* is a comprehensive guide designed for commercial pilots who are involved in training for the initial Flight Instructor Certificate.

This guide was originally designed for use in a Part 141 school but has quickly become popular with those training under 14 CFR Part 61 who are not affiliated with an approved school. It will also prove beneficial to flight instructors who wish to refresh their knowledge or who are preparing to renew their flight instructor certificate.

The *Flight Instructor Practical Test Standards—Airplane* book (FAA-S-8081-6C) specifies the areas in which knowledge and skill must be demonstrated by the applicant before issuance of a flight instructor certificate with the associated category and class ratings. The *Certified Flight Instructor Oral Exam Guide* contains questions on the procedures and maneuvers in the Private Pilot, Commercial Pilot, and Instrument Rating Practical Test Standards. The performance standards for those procedures and maneuvers are also included; these standards should be mostly up to the skill level expected of the Commercial Pilot (FAA-S-8081-12B), unless the maneuver only appears in the *Private Pilot Practical Test Standards—Airplane* (FAA-8081-14A). In the latter case, the skill level expected of the flight instructor applicant is supposed to be "more precise" than that of a private pilot applicant, determined at the discretion of the examiner (FAA-S-8081-6B).

During the exam, an FAA examiner will attempt to determine that the applicant is able to make a practical application of the fundamentals of instructing and is competent to teach the subject matter, procedures, and maneuvers included in the standards to students with varying backgrounds and levels of experience and ability. Through very intensive post-CFI-checkride de-briefings, we have provided you with the questions most consistently asked along with the information or the appropriate reference necessary for a knowledgeable response.

Continued

This guide may be supplemented with other comprehensive study materials as noted in parentheses after each question; for example: (FAA-H-8083-9). The abbreviations for these materials and their titles are listed below. Ensure that the latest revision of these references is used when reviewing for the test. Also, check the ASA website at **www.asa2fly.com** for the latest updates to this book; all the latest changes in FAA procedures and regulations that affect these questions will be listed there. In addition to the regular question-and-answer sessions in each chapter, questions for further review have been included at the end of sections. These additional questions are designed to be good study aids for the references below, upon which they are based.

14 CFR Part 47	*Aircraft Registration*
14 CFR Part 61	*Certification: Pilots and Flight Instructors*
14 CFR Part 67	*Medical Standards and Certification*
14 CFR Part 91	*General Operating and Flight Rules*
14 CFR Part 97	*Standard Instrument Approach Procedures*
49 CFR Part 1552	*Transportation Security Administration: Flight Schools*
NTSB Part 830	*Notification and Reporting of Aircraft Accidents and Incidents*
AC 00-2	*Advisory Circular Checklist*
AC 00-6	*Aviation Weather*
AC 00-45	*Aviation Weather Services*
AC 61-65	*Certification: Pilots and Flight Instructors*
AC 61-67	*Stall and Spin Awareness Training*
AC 61-98A	*Currency and Additional Qualification Requirements for Certificated Pilots*
AC 61-134	*General Aviation Controlled Flight Into Terrain Awareness*
AC 65-15	*Airframe & Powerplant Mechanics: Airframe Handbook*
AC 90-48	*Pilots' Role in Collision Avoidance*
AC 91-63	*Temporary Flight Restrictions*
AC 91-67	*Minimum Equipment Requirements for General Aviation Operations under Part 91*

FAA-H-8083-1	*Aircraft Weight and Balance Handbook*
FAA-H-8083-3	*Airplane Flying Handbook*
FAA-H-8083-9	*Aviation Instructor's Handbook*
FAA-H-8083-15	*Instrument Flying Handbook*
FAA-H-8083-25	*Pilot's Handbook of Aeronautical Knowledge*
FAA-P-8740-50	*On Landings – Part III*
FAA-S-8081-4	*Instrument Rating Practical Test Standards*
FAA-S-8081-6	*Flight Instructor Practical Test Standards (Airplane Single- and Multi-Engine)*
FAA-S-8081-12	*Commercial Pilot Practical Test Standards*
FAA-S-8081-14	*Private Pilot Practical Test Standards*
Order 8700.1	*General Aviation Operations Inspector's Handbook*
AIM	*Aeronautical Information Manual*
A/FD	*Airport/Facility Directory*
POH/AFM	*Pilot Operating Handbooks and FAA-Approved Flight Manuals*

Most of the publications listed above are reprinted by ASA and are available from aviation retailers worldwide.

A review of the information and references presented within this guide should provide the necessary preparation for the FAA initial Certified Flight Instructor certification check.

Were you asked a question during your checkride that was not covered in this book? If so, please send the question to ASA. We are constantly striving to improve our publications to meet the industry needs.

email: asa@asa2fly.com
Fax: 425.235.0128

7005 132nd Place SE
Newcastle, WA 98059-3153

Fundamentals of Instructing

1

A. The Learning Process

1. Briefly define the term "learning." (FAA-H-8083-9)

Learning can be defined as a change in behavior as a result of experience.

2. What are the basic characteristics of learning? (FAA-H-8083-9)

Learning is purposeful—Each student is a unique individual whose past experience affects readiness to learn and understanding of the requirements involved.

Learning is a result of experience—Learning is an individual process from individual experience. Knowledge cannot be poured into the student's head.

Learning is multifaceted—It may involve verbal, conceptual, perceptual, or emotional elements, and elements of problem solving all taking place at once.

Learning is an active process—For students to learn, they must react and respond.

3. What are the principles (laws) of learning? (FAA-H-8083-9)

They are rules and principles that apply generally to the learning process. The first three are the basic laws; the last three are the result of experimental studies.

R eadiness
E xercise
E ffect
P rimacy
 I ntensity
R ecency

4. What is the law of readiness? (FAA-H-8083-9)

Individuals learn best when they are ready to learn, and they do not learn if they see no reason for it or lack motivation. If students have a strong purpose, a clear objective, and a well-fixed reason for learning something, they make more progress.

5. What is the law of exercise? (FAA-H-8083-9)

Those things most often repeated are best remembered. It is the basis of practice and drill.

6. What is the law of effect? (FAA-H-8083-9)

It states that learning is strengthened when accompanied by a pleasant or satisfying feeling, but weakened when associated with an unpleasant feeling.

7. What is the law of primacy? (FAA-H-8083-9)

Primacy, the state of being first, often creates a strong, almost un-shakable, impression. What is taught must be right the first time.

8. What is the law of intensity? (FAA-H-8083-9)

A vivid, dramatic, or exciting learning experience teaches more than a routine or boring experience.

9. What is the law of recency? (FAA-H-8083-9)

The things most recently learned are best remembered.

10. What is the basis of all learning? (FAA-H-8083-9)

All learning comes from perceptions that are directed to the brain by one or more of the five senses (sight, hearing, touch, smell, and taste).

11. How do people learn? (FAA-H-8083-9)

All learning involves the following:

Perception — Initially all learning comes from perceptions which are directed to the brain by one or more of the five senses (sight, hearing, touch, smell and taste).

Insight — The grouping of perceptions into a meaningful whole.

Motivation — The most dominant force governing the student's progress and ability to learn.

12. What are the four basic levels of learning?
(FAA-H-8083-9)

Rote learning—The ability to repeat back something which one has been taught, without understanding or being able to apply what has been learned.

Understanding—Perceiving and learning what has been taught.

Application—Achieving the skill to apply what has been learned and to perform correctly.

Correlation—Associating what has been learned with other things previously learned or encountered.

13. State several principles used in learning a skill.
(FAA-H-8083-9)

a. *Physical skills involve more than muscles:* Perceptions change as the physical skill becomes easier.

b. *Desire to learn:* Shorter initial learning time and more rapid progress take place when a desire to learn exists.

c. *Patterns to follow:* The best way to prepare a student is to provide a clear step-by-step example.

d. *Perform the skill:* The student needs coordination between muscles and visual and tactile senses.

e. *Knowledge of results:* It is important for students to be aware of their progress.

f. *Progress follows a pattern:* Learning a skill usually follows a pattern. There is rapid improvement in the early stages, followed by a "leveling off" or "learning plateau."

g. *Duration and organization of the lesson:* In planning for student performance, the length of time devoted to practice is very important.

h. *Evaluation versus critique:* In the initial stages, practical suggestions are more valuable than a grade.

i. *Application of skill:* Students must use what has been learned—they must learn the skill so well that it becomes easy to perform.

14. Why do individuals forget what has been learned? (FAA-H-8083-9)

Disuse—A person forgets things that are not used.

Interference—A certain experience has overshadowed it, or the learning of something similar has interfered.

Repression—The submersion of ideas into the unconscious mind; they may unintentionally repress unpleasant material, or that which produces anxiety.

15. What actions can the instructor take to assist individuals in remembering what has been learned? (FAA-H-8083-9)

a. Praise stimulates remembering.

b. Recall is prompted by association.

c. Favorable attitudes aid retention—people learn and remember only what they wish to know.

d. Learning with all our senses is most effective—the best perception results from all senses working together.

e. Meaningful repetition aids recall.

16. Does positive or negative transfer of learning occur when a student learns a maneuver through learning a different maneuver? (FAA-H-8083-9)

This is positive transfer of learning.

Additional Study Questions

1. What are several factors that affect an individual's ability to perceive? (FAA-H-8083-9)

2. Define "insight." Why is stimulating insight in a student one of the instructor's major responsibilities? (FAA-H-8083-9)

3. What are the three domains of learning? (FAA-H-8083-9)

4. **What is the difference between negative motivation and positive motivation?** (FAA-H-8083-9)

5. **How can an instructor ensure that a student develops proper habits and correct techniques during flight training?** (FAA-H-8083-9)

B. Human Behavior and Effective Communication

1. **Control of human behavior involves understanding human needs. Name the five basic needs.** (FAA-H-8083-9)

   a. Physical
   b. Safety
   c. Social
   d. Egoistic
   e. Self-fulfillment

2. **What are defense mechanisms?** (FAA-H-8083-9)

   Certain behavior patterns are called defense mechanisms because they are subconscious defenses against the realities of unpleasant situations.

3. **What are eight common defense mechanisms?** (FAA-H-8083-9)

   Compensation — Students often attempt to disguise the presence of a weak or undesirable quality by emphasizing a more positive one.

   Projection — Students relegate the blame for their own shortcomings and mistakes to others, or attribute their motives, desires, and characteristics to others.

   Rationalization — Justifying actions that otherwise would be unacceptable; substitution of excuses for reasons.

   Denial of Reality — Students may ignore or refuse to acknowledge disagreeable realities.

   Continued

Reaction Formation—Developing a who-cares-how-other-people-feel attitude to cover up feelings of loneliness and a hunger for acceptance.

Flight—Escaping from frustrating situations by taking flight, physically or mentally; examples are faked illness or daydreaming.

Aggression—Students may ask irrelevant questions, refuse to participate, etc., when they cannot deal directly with the cause of their frustration.

Resignation—Students may become so frustrated that they lose interest and give up.

4. What are the three basic elements of communication? (FAA-H-8083-9)

The source—sender, speaker, transmitter, or instructor.

The symbols—words or signs.

The receiver—listener, reader, or student.

5. What are the four barriers to effective communication? (FAA-H-8083-9)

a. Lack of common experience
b. Confusion between the symbol and the symbolized object
c. Overuse of abstractions
d. Interference

6. Why is it important that an instructor be a good listener? (FAA-H-8083-9)

Instructors must know something about their students in order to communicate effectively, and must determine the abilities of the students and understand the students to properly communicate. One way to become better acquainted with students is to be a good listener.

7. **How can an instructor teach his students to be good listeners?** (FAA-H-8083-9)

   Teach them to apply the following steps for effective listening:

   a. Take notes.
   b. Listen for main ideas.
   c. Guard against daydreaming.
   d. Be emotionally calm.
   e. Listen to understand, not refute.
   f. Be responsible for listening.
   g. Be ready to listen.

8. **Why is good questioning by the instructor an important tool for determining if effective communication has taken place?** (FAA-H-8083-9)

   Good questioning can determine how well the student understands. It also shows the student that the instructor is paying attention, and that the instructor is interested in the student's response.

Additional Study Questions

1. **Give several examples of abnormal reactions to stress by students during flight training.** (FAA-H-8083-9)

2. **How would an instructor teach a student to counteract fear and anxiety?** (FAA-H-8083-9)

3. **If an instructor has used personal contact and good advice to correct an observed pilot's unsafe operations and still cannot correct the situation, what should he/she do?** (FAA-H-8083-9)

4. **What is the greatest single barrier to effective communication between an instructor and student?** (FAA-H-8083-9)

C. The Teaching Process

1. What are the four basic steps involved in the teaching process? (FAA-H-8083-9)

a. Preparation
b. Presentation
c. Application
d. Review and evaluation

2. What responsibilities does the flight instructor have in the "preparation" stage of a lesson? (FAA-H-8083-9)

For each lesson or instructional period, the instructor must prepare a lesson plan. This plan includes:

a. A statement of lesson objectives.

b. The procedures and facilities to be used during the lesson.

c. The specific goals to be attained.

d. The means to be used for review and evaluation.

The lesson plan should also include home study or other special preparation to be done by the student. The instructor should make certain that all necessary supplies, materials, and equipment needed for the lesson are readily available and that the equipment is operating properly.

3. What are the elements of performance-based objectives? (FAA-H-8083-9)

Performance-based objectives consist of three parts:

a. *Description of the skill or behavior*—Desired outcome of training stated in concrete terms that can be measured.

b. *Conditions*—The framework under which the skill or behavior will be demonstrated.

c. *Criteria*—The standard which will be used to measure the accomplishment of the objective.

4. What are the three most common methods of presentation? (FAA-H-8083-9)

a. Lecture method

b. Demonstration/performance method

c. Guided discussion

Additional Study Questions

1. Should the instructor always use the same method for presentations? (FAA-H-8083-9)

2. Why is immediate application of knowledge beneficial to the student? (FAA-H-8083-9)

3. What should the evaluation of a student's performance be based on? (FAA-H-8083-9)

D. Teaching Methods

1. What three main steps are involved when organizing the material for a particular lesson? (FAA-H-8083-9)

a. Introduction

b. Development

c. Conclusion

2. What are the basic elements of the introduction step? (FAA-H-8083-9)

Attention—Gain the student's attention and focus it on the subject involved.

Motivation—Should appeal to each student personally and accentuate their desire to learn.

Overview—Tell the student what is to be covered; give a clear presentation of the objectives and key ideas; provide a road map of the route to be followed.

3. Discuss the development step of a presentation. (FAA-H-8083-9)

This is the main part of the lesson. The instructor develops the subject matter in a manner that helps the student achieve desired objectives, and logically organizes the material to show the relationships of the main points.

4. Discuss the conclusion step of a presentation. (FAA-H-8083-9)

An effective conclusion retraces the important elements of the lesson and relates them to the objective. This review and wrap-up of ideas reinforces the student's learning and improves the retention of what has been learned.

5. What are the five most common teaching methods? (FAA-H-8083-9)

a. Lecture method
b. Guided discussion method
c. Demonstration/performance method
d. Cooperative or group learning
e. Computer-based training

6. Discuss the lecture method of teaching. (FAA-H-8083-9)

The lecture is used primarily to introduce students to a new subject, but it is also a valuable method for summarizing ideas, showing relationships between theory and practice, and re-emphasizing main points.

7. Describe the cooperative or group learning method of teaching. (FAA-H-8083-9)

It is an instructional strategy that organizes students into small groups which work together to maximize their own and each other's learning. The most significant characteristic of group learning is that it continually requires active participation of the student.

8. What is the guided discussion method of teaching? (FAA-H-8083-9)

This method relies on the students to provide ideas, experiences, opinions, and information. Through the skillful use of "lead-off" type questions, the instructor "draws out" what the student knows, rather than spending the entire class period telling them.

9. What are the different types of questions that may be used in a guided discussion? (FAA-H-8083-9)

Overhead—Directed at entire group; used to stimulate thought and response; good lead-off question.

Rhetorical—Used to stimulate thought; usually asked and answered by the instructor.

Direct—Used to get a response from a specific individual.

Reverse—Instructor redirects student's question in an effort to let the student provide the answer.

Relay—Instructor redirects student's question to the group for an answer instead of to the individual.

10. What is the demonstration/performance method of teaching? (FAA-H-8083-9)

This method of teaching is based on the simple yet sound principle that we learn by doing.

11. What are the five essential phases of the demonstration/performance method of teaching? (FAA-H-8083-9)

a. Explanation
b. Demonstration
c. Student performance
d. Instructor supervision
e. Evaluation

12. Discuss the computer-based training method of teaching. (FAA-H-8083-9)

Computer-based training (CBT) is the use of the personal computer as a training device (sometimes called computer-based instruction, CBI). One of the major advantages of CBT is that students can progress at a rate that is comfortable for them, and are often able to access the CBT at their own convenience rather than that of the instructor.

13. What are some limitations of computer-based training? (FAA-H-8083-9)

Improper or excessive use of CBT should be avoided. For example, a flight instructor should not rely exclusively on a CBT program on traffic patterns and landings to do the ground instruction for a student pilot, then expect the student to demonstrate patterns and landings in the aircraft.

Computer-based training should not be used by the instructor as stand-alone training any more than a textbook or video. Like video or a textbook, CBT is an aid to the instructor. The instructor must be actively involved with the students when using instructional aids. This involvement should include close supervision, questions, examinations, quizzes, or guided discussions on the subject matter.

14. What is Scenario-Based Training (SBT)? (Order 8700.1)

This is a training system that uses a highly-structured script of real-world experiences to address flight evaluation in an operational environment. The scenarios should be adapted to the flight characteristics of the specific aircraft and the likely flight environment, and require the pilot to make real-time decisions in a realistic setting. SBT gives the pilot an opportunity to practice for situations that require sound aeronautical decision-making. Therefore it is an effective method for the development of judgment and decision-making skills.

15. Explain the term "Technically Advanced Aircraft (TAA)." (Order 8700.1)

A TAA is an aircraft that contains a GPS navigator with a moving map and any additional systems. Many new TAAs have advanced engine management, integrated cockpit systems, and "glass cockpit" avionics (i.e., primary flight displays and multifunctional displays). Typically, new TAAs also have a greater performance envelope (speed, range, altitude) than "legacy" aircraft.

Additional Study Questions

1. What are the different ways an instructor may develop the main points of a lesson? (FAA-H-8083-9)

2. When presenting a particular subject or idea, what are some of the advantages and disadvantages associated with the lecture method? (FAA-H-8083-9)

3. When using the lecture method, what are some of the common types of presentations? (FAA-H-8083-9)

4. What are some of the characteristics of an effective question? (FAA-H-8083-9)

E. Critique and Evaluation

1. What is the basic purpose of a critique? (FAA-H-8083-9)

A critique should improve students' performance and provide them with something constructive with which to work and upon which they can build.

2. What are the characteristics of an effective critique? (FAA-H-8083-9)

A critique should be:

a. *Objective*—Focused on student performance; should not reflect the personal opinions of the instructor.

b. *Flexible*—Fit in tone, technique, and content to the occasion and to the student.

c. *Acceptable*—Students must first accept the instructor. Effective critiques are presented with authority, conviction, sincerity, and from a position of recognizable competence.

d. *Comprehensive*—Cover a few major points or a few minor points as well as the student's overall strengths and weaknesses.

e. *Constructive*—Provide positive guidance for correcting the faults and strengthening the weaknesses.

f. *Well-organized*—Follow some pattern of organization.

g. *Thoughtful*—Geared toward the student's need for self-esteem, recognition, and approval from others.

h. *Specific*—Comments and recommendations should not be so general that the student can find nothing to hold on to.

3. Name several useful methods for critique of a student's performance. (FAA-H-8083-9)

a. *Instructor/Student critique*—instructor leads a group discussion in which members of the class are invited to offer criticism of a performance.

b. *Student-led critique*—instructor asks a student to lead the critique.

c. *Small group critique*—a class is divided into small groups and each group is assigned a specific area to analyze.

d. *Individual student critique by another student*—another student presents the entire critique.

e. *Self-critique*—student is required to critique personal performance.

f. *Written critique*—several advantages; the instructor can devote more time and thought to it than to an oral critique in the classroom; students can keep written critiques and refer to them whenever they wish; when the instructor requires all the students to write a critique of a performance, the student/performer has the permanent record of the suggestions, recommendations, and opinions of all the other students.

4. What are the "ground rules" for critiquing? (FAA-H-8083-9)

a. Except in rare and unusual instances, do not extend the critique beyond its scheduled time and into the time allotted for other activities. A point of diminishing returns can be reached quickly.

b. Avoid trying to cover too much. A few well-made points will usually be more beneficial than a large number of points that are not developed adequately.

c. Allow time for a summary of the critique to reemphasize the most important things a student should remember.

d. Avoid dogmatic or absolute statements, remembering that most rules have exceptions.

e. Avoid controversies with the class, and do not get into the delicate position of taking sides with group factions.

f. Never allow yourself to be maneuvered into the unpleasant position of defending criticism. If the criticism is honest, objective, constructive, and comprehensive, no defense should be necessary.

g. If part of the critique is written, make certain that it is consistent with the oral portion.

5. **What types of oral questions should the instructor avoid?** (FAA-H-8083-9)

   a. "Puzzle" type questions with many parts and subparts.

   b. "Oversize" questions that are too general, covering a wide area.

   c. "Toss-up" questions where there is more than one correct answer.

   d. "Bewilderment" questions that are not clear as to their content.

   e. "Trick" questions that cause students to think they are engaged in a battle of wits.

   f. "Irrelevant" questions that are unrelated to what is being discussed.

6. **As an instructor, what should you do and/or say if asked a question you do not know the answer to?** (FAA-H-8083-9)

   You should indicate to the student you do not know the answer, but will help the student find the correct answer.

7. **What are the six characteristics of a good written test?** (FAA-H-8083-9)

   Reliability—it yields consistent results.

   Validity—it measures what should be measured.

   Usability—it is easy to understand and grade.

   Comprehensiveness—it must sample whatever is being measured.

   Discrimination—it will detect small differences.

   Objectivity—the non-subjective method of scoring a test (that is, it doesn't reflect the biases of the person grading the test). The test will be graded the same regardless of who is grading it.

8. **Where can a flight instructor find the performance standards for evaluation of a particular maneuver?** (FAA-H-8083-9)

   The FAA publishes "Practical Test Standards" which establish the minimum standards for the certification of pilots. They are available from ASA and the GPO (Government Printing Office).

Additional Study Questions

1. What are some of the basic characteristics of an "effective" question? (FAA-H-8083-9)

2. What are several important considerations when answering questions from students? (FAA-H-8083-9)

3. What are several ways an instructor may evaluate a student's progress? (FAA-H-8083-9)

4. Why should an instructor use oral quizzing for evaluation of a student's performance? (FAA-H-8083-9)

5. What are two basic types of oral questions? (FAA-H-8083-9)

F. Flight Instructor Characteristics

1. What are the four main responsibilities for aviation instructors? (FAA-H-8083-9)

   a. Helping students learn

   b. Providing adequate instruction

   c. Demanding adequate standards

   d. Emphasizing the positive

2. How can an instructor provide a more positive and efficient learning experience? (FAA-H-8083-9)

   a. Devise a plan of action

   b. Create a positive student-instructor relationship

   c. Present information and guidance effectively

   d. Transfer responsibility to the student as learning occurs

   e. Evaluate student learning and thereby measure teaching effectiveness

3. Faulty performance of a maneuver due to student overconfidence should be corrected in which way? (FAA-H-8083-9)

Students who are fast learners may develop overconfidence that could result in faulty performance. For such students, the instructor should constantly raise the standard of performance for each lesson, demanding greater effort.

4. Why is it important for an instructor to continuously evaluate standards of performance? (FAA-H-8083-9)

Instructors fail to provide competent instruction when they permit their students to get by with a substandard performance, or without learning thoroughly an item of knowledge pertinent to safe piloting. More importantly, such deficiencies may in themselves allow hazardous inadequacies in student performance later on.

5. Discuss the significance of always emphasizing the positive when providing flight instruction. (FAA-H-8083-9)

Aviation instructors have a tremendous influence on their students' perception of aviation. The way instructors conduct themselves, the attitudes they display, and the way they develop their instruction all contribute to either positive or negative impressions by their students. Much of the success of the instructor depends on the ability to present instruction so that students develop a positive image of aviation.

6. What are several examples of additional responsibilities that all flight instructors have? (FAA-H-8083-9)

a. Evaluation of student piloting ability

b. Pilot supervision

c. Practical Test recommendations

d. Flight Instructor endorsements

e. Additional training and endorsements

f. Pilot proficiency

7. What are important personal characteristics that a flight instructor should possess? (FAA-H-8083-9)

a. *Sincerity*—should be straightforward and honest.

b. *Acceptance of the student*—should accept students as they are including all their faults and problems.

c. *Personal appearance and habits*—should be neat, clean and appropriately dressed.

d. *Demeanor*—should be calm, thoughtful, and disciplined.

e. *Safety practices and accident prevention*—practices emphasized by instructors have a lasting effect on students.

f. *Proper language*—should speak normally, without inhibitions, and develop the ability to speak positively and descriptively without excesses of language.

g. *Self-improvement*—should be constantly alert for ways to improve their qualifications, effectiveness, and the services they provide to students.

8. Describe several methods to minimize student frustrations. (FAA-H-8083-9)

a. Keep students motivated.

b. Keep students informed.

c. Approach students as individuals.

d. Give credit when due.

e. Criticize constructively.

f. Be consistent.

g. Admit errors.

9. **What major considerations and qualifications are included in the definition of professionalism?** (FAA-H-8083-9)

   Professionalism:

   a. Exists only when a service is performed for someone, or for the common good.

   b. Is achieved only after extended training and preparation.

   c. True performance as a professional is based on study and research.

   d. Professionals must be able to reason logically and accurately.

   e. Requires the ability to make good judgmental decisions. Professionals cannot limit their actions and decisions to standard patterns and practices.

   f. Demands a code of ethics. Anything less than truth and a sincere performance is quickly detected, and immediately destroys their effectiveness.

Additional Study Questions

1. **How can an instructor determine that a student is ready to solo?** (FAA-H-8083-9)

2. **14 CFR Part 61 covers rules for endorsements. Which Advisory Circular should the flight instructor be familiar with as well?** (FAA-H-8083-9)

3. **What is FAA Form 8710-1 used for?** (FAA-H-8083-9)

G. Techniques of Flight Instruction

1. Describe the "telling-and-doing" technique. (FAA-H-8083-9)

This is a variation of the demonstration–performance method. It follows the four steps of demonstration–performance except that the first step is preparation. This long-used method is very effective in teaching physical skills.

2. What are the five steps of the "telling-and-doing" technique? (FAA-H-8083-9)

a. *Preparation*—accomplished prior to the flight lesson with a discussion of lesson objectives and completion standards.

b. *Instructor Tells • Instructor Does*—the carefully planned demonstration and accompanying verbal explanation of the procedure or maneuver.

c. *Student Tells • Instructor Does*—student plays the role of instructor, telling the instructor what to do and how to do it.

d. *Student Tells • Student Does*—the application step; student describes the maneuver but also performs it. This is where learning takes place and where performance habits are formed.

e. *Student Does • Instructor Evaluates*—the instructor reviews what has been covered during the instructional flight and determines to what extent the student has met the objectives outlined during the preflight discussion.

3. **What are several examples of obstacles to learning a student may encounter when receiving flight instruction?** (FAA-H-8083-9)

   Certain obstacles are common to flight instruction and may apply directly to the student's attitude, physical condition, and psychological makeup. These are:

   a. Feeling of unfair treatment;

   b. Impatience to proceed to more interesting operations;

   c. Worry or lack of interest;

   d. Physical discomfort, illness, and fatigue;

   e. Apathy due to inadequate instruction; and

   f. Anxiety.

4. **Why is it important that the instructor and student understand the "positive exchange of flight controls" concept as it relates to flight training?** (FAA-H-8083-9)

   During flight training, there must always be a clear understanding between students and flight instructors of who has control of the aircraft. There should be a preflight briefing that includes the procedure for the exchange of flight controls. A positive three-step process in the exchange of flight controls between pilots is a proven procedure, and is strongly recommended.

5. **Describe the three-step process used for the positive exchange of flight controls.** (FAA-H-8083-9)

   a. When the flight instructor wants the student to take control of the aircraft, the instructor says to the student: "You have the flight controls."

   b. The student acknowledges immediately by saying: "I have the flight controls."

   c. The flight instructor again says: "You have the flight controls."

   Note: During this procedure, a visual check is recommended to see that the other person actually has the flight controls. When returning the controls to the instructor, the student should follow the same procedure the instructor used.

6. What is the purpose of using distractions during flight training? (FAA-H-8083-9)

To determine that the student possesses the skills required to cope with distractions while maintaining the degree of aircraft control required for safe flight. Pilots at all skill levels should be aware of the increased risk of entering into an inadvertent stall or spin while performing tasks that are secondary to controlling the aircraft.

7. How should the instructor incorporate the use of distractions into his or her flight instruction? (FAA-H-8083-9)

The instructor should tell the student to divide his/her attention between the distracting task and maintaining control of the aircraft. The following are examples of distractions that can be used for this training:

a. Drop a pencil. Ask the student to pick it up.

b. Ask the student to determine a heading to an airport using a chart.

c. Ask the student to get something from the back seat.

d. Ask the student to compute true airspeed with a flight computer.

e. Ask the student to identify terrain or objects on the ground.

f. Ask the student to identify a field suitable for a forced landing.

8. Define the term "aeronautical decision making." (FAA-H-8083-9)

Aeronautical decision making is the systematic approach to the mental process used by aircraft pilots to consistently determine the best course of action in response to a given set of circumstances.

9. During flight, decisions must be made regarding events that involve interactions between the four risk elements. What are they? (FAA-H-8083-9)

Pilot-in-command—the aircraft—the environment—the operation.

Remember: PAVE

Pilot – **A**ircraft – En**V**ironment – **E**xternal pressures

10. The DECIDE model for decision making involves which elements? (FAA-H-8083-9)

D etect a change needing attention.

E stimate the need to counter or react to change.

C hoose the most desirable outcome for the flight.

I dentify actions to successfully control the change.

D o something to adapt to the change.

E valuate the effect of the action countering the change.

11. Name the five hazardous attitudes and their antidotes that negatively impact a pilot's judgment and ability to make competent decisions. (FAA-H-8083-9)

Attitude	Antidote
Anti-authority	Follow the rules, they are usually right.
Impulsivity	Think first—not so fast.
Invulnerability	It could happen to me.
Macho	Taking chances is foolish.
Resignation	I can make a difference, I am not helpless.

12. What does the term "single-pilot resource management" refer to? (FAA-S-8081-6C)

It refers to the effective use of *all* available resources: human resources, hardware, and information. Similar to crew resource management (CRM) procedures emphasized in multi-crewmember operations, with SRM only one crewmember (the pilot) is involved. Human resources include all other groups routinely working with the pilot who are involved in decisions required for safe flight operation, such as dispatchers, weather briefers, maintenance personnel, and air traffic controllers.

13. What are the elements of single-pilot resource management? (FAA-S-8081-6C)

a. Proper arranging and securing of essential materials and equipment in the cockpit.

b. Proper use and/or adjustment of cockpit items such as safety belts, shoulder harnesses, rudder pedals, and seats.

c. Occupant briefing on emergency procedures and use of safety belts.

d. Proper utilization of all resources required to operate a flight safely, dispatchers, weather briefers, maintenance personnel, and air traffic control.

14. What common errors can occur with single-pilot resource management? (FAA-S-8081-6C)

a. Failure to place and secure essential materials and equipment for easy access during flight.

b. Failure to properly adjust cockpit items, such as safety belts, shoulder harnesses, rudder pedals, and seats.

c. Failure to provide proper adjustment of equipment and controls.

d. Failure to provide occupant briefing on emergency procedures and use of safety belts.

e. Failure to utilize all resources required to operate a flight safely.

15. What is situational awareness? (FAA-H-8083-9)

The accurate perception and understanding of all the factors and conditions within the four fundamental risk elements affecting safety before, during, and after the flight.

16. Situational awareness takes into consideration which four elements? (FAA-H-8083-9)

The four elements to be taken into consideration with situational awareness are:

Pilot—Aircraft—Environment—Type of Operation—and their interaction with each other.

17. Why are pilots encouraged to use checklists? (FAA-H-8083-9)

Checklists provide a logical and standardized method to operate a particular make and model airplane. Following a checklist reinforces the use of proper procedures throughout all major phases of flight operations.

18. What are the two primary methods of checklist usage? (FAA-H-8083-9)

a. *Read and Do*—The pilot picks up a checklist, refers to an item, and sets the condition. The items for any particular phase of flight would all be accomplished before the checklist is set aside.

b. Do and Verify—In this method, the condition of the items for a particular phase of operation are set from memory or flow pattern. Then, the checklist is read to verify that the appropriate condition for each item in that phase has been set. It is not wise for a pilot to become so reliant upon a flow pattern that he or she fails to verify with a checklist. Checking important items solely from memory is not an acceptable substitute for checklists.

Additional Study Questions

1. Define the term "integrated flight instruction."
   (FAA-H-8083-9)

2. What does the term "poor judgment chain" or "error chain" refer to? (FAA-H-8083-9)

3. What are the major factors affecting judgment and decision making? (FAA-H-8083-9)

4. What are operational pitfalls? Give several examples of this which pilots have been known to experience. (FAA-H-8083-9)

5. What are some of the elements, both inside and outside the aircraft, that a pilot must consider in order to maintain situational awareness? (FAA-H-8083-9)

H. Planning Instructional Activity

1. Define the following terms. (FAA-H-8083-9)

Curriculum—a set of courses in an area of specialization offered by an educational institution. A curriculum for a pilot school usually includes courses for the various pilot certificates and ratings.

Training syllabus—a summary or outline of a course of study; a syllabus defines the unit of training, states what the student is expected to accomplish during the unit, shows an organized plan for instruction, and dictates the evaluation process.

Training course outline—within a curriculum, may be described as the content of a particular course. It normally includes statements of objectives, descriptions of teaching aids, definitions of evaluating criteria, and indications of desired outcome.

2. How are the objectives and standards developed for a course of training? (FAA-H-8083-9)

The overall objectives of an aviation training course are usually well established, and the general standards are included in various rules and related publications. Eligibility, knowledge, proficiency, and experience requirements for pilots and maintenance students are stipulated in the regulations, and the standards are published in the applicable practical test standards (PTS).

3. Why is it so important to develop and assemble learning blocks in their proper relationship? (FAA-H-8083-9)

Training for any such complicated and involved task as piloting or maintaining an aircraft requires the development and assembly of many segments or blocks of learning in their proper relationships, because a student can master the segments or blocks individually and can progressively combine these with other related segments. The result is such that the student meets the overall training objectives.

4. What should each lesson of a training syllabus include? (FAA-H-8083-9)

a. The objective.
b. The content.
c. The completion standards.

5. Would it be acceptable for an instructor to depart from the order specified in the training syllabus? (FAA-H-8083-9)

The syllabus must be flexible and used primarily as a guide. When necessary, the order of training can and should be altered to suit the progress of the student and the demands of special circumstances (such as weather variations, aircraft availability, etc). For example, previous experience or different rates of learning often will require some alteration or repetition to fit individual students.

6. What is a lesson plan? (FAA-H-8083-9)

A lesson plan is an organized outline for a single instructional period. It is a necessary guide for the instructor in that it tells what to do, in what order to do it, and what procedure to use in teaching the material of a lesson.

7. What is the purpose of lesson plans? (FAA-H-8083-9)

They are designed to ensure each student receives the best possible instruction under the existing conditions. An adequate lesson plan:

a. Ensures a wise selection of material and the elimination of unimportant details.

b. Makes certain that due consideration is given to each part of the lesson.

c. Aids the instructor in presenting a suitable sequence for efficient learning.

d. Provides an outline of the teaching procedure to be used.

e. Serves as a means of relating the lesson to the objectives of the course of training.

f. Gives the inexperienced instructor confidence.

g. Promotes uniformity of instruction regardless of the instructor or the date on which the lesson is given.

8. What are characteristics of a good lesson plan? (FAA-H-8083-9)

a. *Unity*—Each lesson should be a unified segment of instruction.

b. *Content*—Each lesson should contain new material as well as a short review of earlier lessons.

c. *Scope*—Each lesson should be reasonable in scope.

d. *Practicality*—Each lesson should be planned in terms of the conditions under which the training is to be conducted.

e. *Flexibility*—Although the lesson plan provides an outline and training sequence, it should allow some flexibility.

f. *Relation to Course of Training*—Each lesson should be planned and taught so that its relation to the course objectives are clear to each student.

g. *Instructional Steps*—Each lesson, when adequately developed, falls logically into the four steps of the teaching process: preparation, presentation, application, and review and evaluation.

Additional Study Questions

1. Explain the proper use of a lesson plan. Once a lesson plan has been developed, should it ever be adapted or changed? (FAA-H-8083-9)

2. What is the basic reason for use of the "building block" method of instruction? (FAA-H-8083-9)

3. What are some of the main elements of all lesson plans? (FAA-H-8083-9)

I. Preflight Lesson on a Maneuver

An FAA examiner will determine that the applicant exhibits instructional knowledge of the elements related to the planning of instructional activity. This will be accomplished by requiring the applicant to develop a lesson plan for any one of the required maneuvers. The following is an example of a lesson plan for a 90-minute flight instruction period.

Lesson   *Stalls*

Student _____

Date   _____

Objective	To familiarize the student with the stall warnings and handling characteristics of the airplane as it approaches a stall. To develop the student's skill in recognition and recovery from stalls.
Content	Configuration of airplane for power-on and power-off stalls.
	Observation of airplane attitude, stall warnings, and handling characteristics as it approaches a stall.
	Control of airplane attitude, altitude, and heading.
	Initiation of stall recovery procedures.
Schedule	Preflight Discussion :10
	Instructor Demonstrations :25
	Student Practice :45
	Postflight Critique :10
Equipment	Chalkboard or notebook for preflight discussion
Instructor's Actions	*Preflight*—Discuss lesson objective. *Inflight*—Demonstrate elements. Demonstrate power-on and power-off stalls and recovery procedures. Coach student practice.

Postflight	Critique student performance and assign study material.
Student's Actions	*Preflight*—Discuss lesson objective and resolve questions.
	Inflight—Review previous maneuvers including slow flight. Perform each new maneuver as directed.
	Postflight—Ask pertinent questions.
Completion Standards	Student should demonstrate competency in controlling the airplane at airspeeds approaching a stall. Student should recognize and take prompt corrective action to recover from power-on and power-off stalls.

Flight Instructor
Responsibilities

2

Note: Flight instructors should consult the most current edition of 49 CFR Part 1552 and 14 CFR Part 61 for the *full* text of the regulations on security awareness and pilot certification.

A. Aviation Security

1. As an active flight instructor, what does the TSA require you to do before you start flight training a U.S. flight student? A foreign flight student? (49 CFR 1552.3)

U.S. students:

You must determine whether an individual is a citizen or national of the United States prior to providing flight training to the individual.

Foreign students:

You must first submit background information and receive clearance from the TSA before beginning flight training.

2. Who is required to complete security awareness training? (49 CFR 1552.23)

a. A flight instructor or ground instructor certificated under 14 CFR Parts 61, 141, or 142;

b. A chief instructor certificated under 14 CFR Part 141;

c. A director of training certificated under 14 CFR Part 142;

d. Any other person employed by a flight school, including an independent contractor, who has direct contact with a flight school student. This includes independent flight instructors certificated under 14 CFR Part 61.

3. When must "initial" security awareness training be completed? (49 CFR 1552.23)

a. Each flight school employee or independent instructor employed on January 18, 2005 receives initial security awareness training in accordance with the regulations by January 18, 2005; and

b. Each flight school employee or flight instructor hired after January 18, 2005 receives initial security awareness training within 60 days of being hired.

4. How often must recurrent security awareness training be accomplished? (49 CFR 1552.23)

Every 12 months.

B. General

1. What is 14 CFR Part 61? (14 CFR 61.1)

Part 61 prescribes the requirements for issuing pilot, flight instructor, and ground instructor certificates and ratings, the conditions under which those certificates and ratings are necessary, and their associated privileges and limitations.

2. What are the various certificates issued under Part 61? (14 CFR 61.5)

a. Pilot certificates—student pilot, sport pilot, recreational pilot, private pilot, commercial pilot, airline transport pilot;

b. Flight instructor certificates; and

c. Ground instructor certificates.

3. What are the various ratings that may be placed on a pilot certificate (other than student pilot)? (14 CFR 61.5)

These ratings are placed on a pilot certificate (other than student pilot) when an applicant satisfactorily accomplishes the training and certification requirements for the rating sought:

a. Aircraft category ratings—Airplane, Rotorcraft, Glider, Lighter-than-air, Powered-lift, Powered parachute, Weight-shift control aircraft.

b. Airplane class ratings—Single-engine land, Multi-engine land, Single-engine sea, Multi-engine sea.

c. Rotorcraft class ratings—Helicopter, Gyroplane.

d. Lighter-than-air class ratings—Airship, Balloon.

e. Weight-shift-control aircraft class ratings—Weight-shift control aircraft land, Weight-shift control aircraft sea.

f. Powered parachute class ratings—Powered parachute land, Powered parachute sea.

g. Aircraft type ratings—Large aircraft other than lighter-than-air, Turbojet-powered airplanes, Other aircraft type ratings specified by the Administrator through the aircraft type certification procedures, Second-in-command pilot type rating for aircraft that is certificated for operations with a minimum crew of at least two pilots.

h. Instrument ratings (on private and commercial pilot certificates only)—Instrument – Airplane • Instrument – Helicopter • Instrument – Powered-lift.

4. What are the various ratings that may be placed on a flight instructor certificate? (14 CFR 61.5)

These ratings are placed on a flight instructor certificate when an applicant satisfactorily accomplishes the training and certification requirements for the rating sought:

a. Aircraft category ratings—Airplane, Rotorcraft, Glider, Powered-lift.

b. Airplane class ratings—Single-engine, Multi-engine.

c. Rotorcraft class ratings—Helicopter, Gyroplane.

d. Instrument ratings—Instrument Airplane, Instrument Helicopter, Instrument Powered-lift.

5. A temporary pilot certificate that has been recently issued will remain effective for what length of time? (14 CFR 61.17)

120 days.

6. What is the duration of a flight instructor certificate? (14 CFR 61.19)

A flight instructor certificate is effective only while the holder has a current pilot certificate, and it expires 24 calendar months from the month in which it was issued or renewed.

7. What are the required medical certificates for the various pilot certificates? (14 CFR 61.23)

a. Must hold a first-class medical certificate when exercising the privileges of an airline transport pilot certificate;

b. Must hold at least a second-class medical certificate when exercising the privileges of a commercial pilot certificate; or

c. Must hold at least a third-class medical certificate when exercising the privileges of a private pilot, a recreational pilot, a student pilot, or a flight instructor certificate (except for a flight instructor certificate with a glider category rating or sport pilot rating, if the person is acting as the pilot-in-command or is serving as a required crewmember); or except for a glider category rating or a balloon class rating, prior to taking a practical test that is performed in an aircraft for a certificate or rating at the recreational, private, commercial, or airline transport pilot certificate level.

8. Give several examples of operations that do not require a medical certificate. (14 CFR 61.23)

a. When exercising the privileges of a flight instructor certificate if not acting as pilot-in-command or serving as a required crewmember;

b. When exercising the privileges of a ground instructor certificate;

c. When serving as an examiner or a check airman during the administration of a test or check for a certificate, rating, or authorization conducted in a flight simulator or flight training device; or

d. When taking a test or check for a certificate, rating, or authorization conducted in a flight simulator or flight training device.

9. **In the event an airman certificate, medical certificate, or knowledge test report is lost or destroyed, what procedure should be followed?** (14 CFR 61.29)

   a. An application for the replacement of a lost or destroyed certificate or report is made by letter to the Department of Transportation, FAA;

   b. A person who has lost a certificate or report may obtain a facsimile from the FAA confirming that it was issued. The facsimile may be carried as a certificate for a period not to exceed 60 days pending receipt of a duplicate certificate.

10. **When is a type rating required?** (14 CFR 61.31)

    A type rating is required when acting as pilot-in-command of:

    a. Large aircraft (except lighter-than-air);

    b. Turbojet-powered airplanes;

    c. Other aircraft (specified through aircraft type certificate procedures).

11. **According to regulations, what additional training is required to act as pilot-in-command of a complex airplane?** (14 CFR 61.31)

    No person may act as pilot-in-command of a complex airplane (an airplane with retractable landing gear, flaps, and controllable-pitch propeller, or in the case of a seaplane, flaps, and controllable-pitch propeller), unless the person has:

    a. Received and logged ground and flight training from an authorized instructor in a complex airplane, or in a flight simulator or flight training device (representative of a complex airplane), and has been found proficient in its operation and systems;

    b. Received a one-time logbook endorsement from an authorized instructor certifying the person is proficient to operate a complex airplane.

    Note: This is not required if the person has logged flight time as pilot-in-command of a complex airplane, or in a flight simulator or flight training device prior to August 4, 1997.

12. According to regulations, what additional training is required to act as pilot-in-command of a high-performance airplane? (14 CFR 61.31)

No person may act as pilot-in-command of a high-performance airplane (an engine of more than 200 horsepower), unless the person has:

a. Received and logged ground and flight training from an authorized instructor in a high-performance airplane, or in a flight simulator or flight training device (representative of a high-performance airplane), and has been found proficient in its operation and systems;

b. Received a one-time logbook endorsement from an authorized instructor certifying the person is proficient to operate a high-performance airplane.

Note: This is not required if the person has logged flight time as pilot-in-command of a high-performance airplane, or in a flight simulator or flight training device representative of a high-performance airplane prior to August 4, 1997.

13. Describe the minimum required elements of instruction for transition to a tailwheel aircraft. (14 CFR 61.31)

No person may act as pilot-in-command of a tailwheel airplane unless that person has received and logged flight training from an authorized instructor in a tailwheel airplane, and has received a logbook endorsement from an authorized instructor who found the person proficient in the operation of a tailwheel airplane, to include at least these maneuvers and procedures: normal and crosswind takeoffs and landings, wheel landings (unless the manufacturer has recommended against such landings), and go-around procedures. This is not required if the person logged pilot-in-command time in a tailwheel airplane before April 15, 1991.

14. To be eligible to take an FAA knowledge test, what must an applicant accomplish? (14 CFR 61.35)

An applicant must have received an endorsement from an authorized instructor certifying that the applicant accomplished a required ground-training or a home-study course for the certificate or rating sought, and is prepared for the knowledge test; and must have proper identification at the time of application that contains the applicant's photograph, signature, date of birth (which shows the applicant meets or will meet the age requirements of this part for the certificate sought before the expiration date of the airman knowledge test report), and actual residential address (if different from the applicant's mailing address).

15. What various methods may be used by a student to show evidence of ground school or home study course completion? (AC 61-65)

a. A certificate of graduation from a pilot training course by an FAA-certificated pilot school.

b. An endorsement from an appropriately rated FAA-certificated ground or flight instructor.

c. A certificate of graduation or statement of accomplishment from a ground school course (high school, college, adult education program, etc.).

d. A certificate of graduation from an industry-provided aviation home study course.

e. An endorsement from an appropriately rated FAA-certificated ground or flight instructor for completion of an individually developed home study course.

16. What actions is an applicant required to have accomplished in order to be eligible for a practical test for a certificate or rating issued under 14 CFR Part 61? (14 CFR 61.39)

a. Pass the required knowledge test within the 24-calendar-month period preceding the month the applicant completes the practical test, if a knowledge test is required;

b. Present the knowledge test report at the time of application for the practical test, if a knowledge test is required;

c. Have satisfactorily accomplished the required training and obtained the aeronautical experience prescribed by this part for the certificate or rating sought;

d. Hold at least a current third-class medical certificate, if a medical certificate is required;

e. Meet the prescribed age requirement of this part for the issuance of the certificate or rating sought;

f. Have a logbook or training record endorsement, if required by this part, signed by an authorized instructor who certifies that the applicant: has received and logged training time within 60 days preceding the date of application in preparation for the practical test; is prepared for the required practical test; and has demonstrated satisfactory knowledge of subject areas in which the applicant was deficient on the knowledge test; have a completed and signed application form.

17. Other than the Practical Test Standards, what general guidelines will an examiner follow when judging the ability of an applicant for a pilot certificate or rating? (14 CFR 61.43)

The examiner will judge based on that applicant's ability to safely:

a. Perform the tasks specified in the areas of operation for the certificate or rating sought within approved standards;

b. Demonstrate mastery of the aircraft with the successful outcome of each task performed never seriously in doubt;

c. Demonstrate satisfactory proficiency and competency within approved standards;

d. Demonstrate sound judgment; and

e. Demonstrate single-pilot competence if the aircraft is type certificated for single-pilot operations.

18. An applicant for a knowledge or practical test who fails that test may only reapply when what actions have been accomplished? (14 CFR 61.49)

An applicant who fails may only reapply for the test after the applicant has received:

a. The necessary training from an authorized instructor, who has determined that the applicant is proficient to pass the test; and

b. An endorsement from an authorized instructor who gave the applicant the additional training.

19. What type of flight time must be documented and recorded by all pilots? (14 CFR 61.51)

a. Training and aeronautical experience used to meet the requirements for a certificate, rating, or flight review.

b. The aeronautical experience required for meeting the recency of flight experience requirements of Part 61.

20. What regulatory guidelines are established concerning the logging of instrument time? (14 CFR 61.51)

a. A person may log instrument flight time only for that flight time when the person operates the aircraft solely by reference to instruments under actual or simulated instrument flight conditions.

b. An authorized instructor may log instrument flight time when conducting instrument flight instruction in actual instrument flight conditions.

c. For the purposes of logging instrument flight time to meet the recent instrument experience requirements of §61.57(c) the following information must be recorded in the person's logbook: the location and type of each instrument approach accomplished; and the name of the safety pilot, if required.

d. A flight simulator or flight training device may be used by a person to log instrument flight time, provided an authorized instructor is present during the simulated flight.

21. When entering time in a logbook, what time is considered as "training time"? (14 CFR 61.51)

a. A person may log training time when that person receives training from an authorized instructor in an aircraft, flight simulator, or flight training device.

b. The training time must be logged in a logbook and must be endorsed in a legible manner by the authorized instructor; and include a description of the training given, the length of the training lesson, and the instructor's signature, certificate number, and certificate expiration date.

22. What requirements must be met when conducting a flight review? (14 CFR 61.56)

A flight review consists of a minimum of 1 hour of flight training and 1 hour of ground training, including a review of the current general operating and flight rules of Part 91 and a review of those maneuvers and procedures that, at the discretion of the person giving the review, are necessary for the pilot to demonstrate the safe exercise of the privileges of the pilot certificate.

23. What logbook entries should be made by the flight instructor if a pilot demonstrates unsatisfactory performance during a flight review? (AC 61-98A)

The instructor should sign the logbook to record the instruction given, and then recommend additional training in the areas of the review that were unsatisfactory. The instructor should not make record of an unsatisfactory review in the logbook.

24. When is a flight review not required? (14 CFR 61.56)

Pilots who have satisfactorily completed within the preceding 24 calendar months before the month in which they act as pilot-in-command:

a. A pilot proficiency check conducted by the FAA, an approved pilot check airman, or U.S. Armed Forces, for a pilot certificate, rating, or operating privilege.

b. Completed one or more phases of an FAA-sponsored pilot proficiency award program.

Also, a flight instructor who holds a current flight instructor certificate and has satisfactorily completed renewal of a flight instructor certificate need not accomplish the 1 hour of ground instruction.

Note: The flight review may be accomplished in combination with the requirements of §61.57 and other applicable recency-of-experience requirements at the discretion of the instructor.

25. What are the "recency-of-experience" requirements for acting as pilot-in-command of an aircraft carrying passengers? (14 CFR 61.57)

No person may act as a pilot-in-command of an aircraft carrying passengers, or as a required pilot onboard an aircraft that requires more than one pilot flight crewmember, unless that person has made at least three takeoffs and three landings within the preceding 90 days, and:

a. The person acted as the sole manipulator of the flight controls;

b. The required takeoffs and landings were performed in an aircraft of the same category, class, and type (if a type rating is required), and if the aircraft to be flown is an airplane with a tailwheel, the takeoffs and landings must have been made to a full stop in an airplane with a tailwheel.

For the purpose of meeting these requirements, a person may act as a pilot-in-command of an aircraft under day VFR or day IFR, provided no persons or property are carried onboard the aircraft, other than those necessary for the conduct of the flight.

26. When acting as PIC of an aircraft carrying passengers at night, what recent night experience must the pilot have accomplished? (14 CFR 61.57)

No person may act as pilot-in-command of an aircraft carrying passengers during the period beginning 1 hour after sunset and ending 1 hour before sunrise, unless within the preceding 90 days that person:

a. Has made at least three takeoffs and three landings to a full stop during the period beginning 1 hour after sunset and ending 1 hour before sunrise;

b. Has acted as sole manipulator of the flight controls; and

c. Has performed the required takeoffs and landings in an aircraft of the same category, class and type (if a type rating is required).

C. Aircraft Rating and Special Certification

1. If a pilot wants to add an additional category rating to his or her pilot certificate, what is required? (14 CFR 61.63)

This person must:

a. Have received the required training and possess the prescribed aeronautical experience that applies to the pilot certificate for the aircraft category and, if applicable, class rating sought;

b. Have an endorsement in his or her logbook or training record from an authorized instructor, attesting that the applicant has been found competent in the appropriate aeronautical knowledge areas, and has been found proficient in the areas of operation appropriate to the pilot certificate for the aircraft category and, if applicable, class rating sought;

c. Pass the required practical test appropriate to the pilot certificate for the aircraft category and, if applicable, class rating sought.

This person need not take an additional knowledge test, provided that he or she holds an airplane, rotorcraft, powered-lift, or airship rating at that pilot certificate level.

2. If a pilot wants to add on an additional class rating to his or her pilot certificate, what is required? (14 CFR 61.63)

This person must:

a. Have an endorsement in his or her logbook or training record from an authorized instructor and that endorsement must attest that the applicant has been found competent in the aeronautical knowledge areas and proficient in the areas of operation, appropriate to the pilot certificate for the aircraft class rating sought;

b. Must pass the required practical test that is appropriate to the pilot certificate for the aircraft class rating sought.

This person need not meet the specified training time requirements that apply to the pilot certificate for the aircraft class rating sought, nor take an additional knowledge test, provided he or she holds an airplane, rotorcraft, powered-lift, or airship rating at that pilot certificate level.

3. For an applicant training under Part 61, what minimum aeronautical experience, is required before application for an instrument rating may take place? (14 CFR 61.65)

A person who applies for an instrument rating must have logged the following:

a. At least 50 hours of cross-country flight time as pilot-in-command, of which at least 10 hours must be in airplanes for an Instrument Airplane rating; and

b. A total of 40 hours of actual or simulated instrument time on the Part 61 areas of operation, to include at least 15 hours of instrument flight training from an authorized instructor in the aircraft category for which the instrument rating is sought; at least 3 hours of instrument training that is appropriate to the instrument rating sought from an authorized instructor (in preparation for the practical test within the 60 days preceding the date of the test); and for an Instrument Airplane rating, instrument training on cross-country flight procedures specific to airplanes that includes at least one cross-country flight in an airplane under IFR, and consists of a distance of at least 250 NM along airways or ATC-directed routing, an instrument approach at each airport, and three different kinds of approaches with the use of navigation systems.

4. **In what minimum aeronautical knowledge areas must a person who applies for an instrument rating have received instruction from an authorized instructor or home-study course?** (14 CFR 61.65)

   a. Federal Aviation Regulations that apply to flight operations under IFR.

   b. Appropriate information from the AIM that applies to flight operations under IFR.

   c. Air traffic control system and procedures for instrument flight operations.

   d. IFR navigation and approaches by use of navigation systems.

   e. Use of IFR enroute and instrument approach procedure charts.

   f. Procurement and use of aviation weather reports and forecasts and the elements of forecasting weather trends based on that information and personal observation of weather conditions.

   g. Safe and efficient operation of aircraft under instrument flight rules and conditions.

   h. Recognition of critical weather situations and windshear avoidance.

   i. Aeronautical decision-making and judgment.

   j. Crew resource management, including crew communication and coordination.

5. **To be eligible for an instrument rating, in what minimum areas of operation must the applicant have received training?** (14 CFR 61.65)

   A person who applies for an instrument rating must receive and log training from an authorized instructor in an aircraft, or in an approved flight simulator or approved flight training device that includes the following areas of operation:

   a. Preflight preparation;
   b. Preflight procedures;
   c. Air traffic control clearances and procedures;
   d. Flight by reference to instruments;
   e. Navigation systems;
   f. Instrument approach procedures;
   g. Emergency operations; and
   h. Postflight procedures.

D. Student Pilots

1. What are the eligibility requirements for a student pilot certificate? (14 CFR 61.83)

An applicant must:

a. Be at least 16 years of age for other than the operation of a glider or balloon.

b. Be at least 14 years of age for the operation of a glider or balloon.

c. Be able to read, speak, write, and understand the English language.

If the applicant is unable to meet one of these requirements due to medical reasons, then the Administrator may place such operating limitations on that applicant's pilot certificate as are necessary for the safe operation of the aircraft.

2. How can a person obtain a student pilot certificate? (14 CFR 61.85)

An application for a student pilot certificate is made on a form and in a manner provided by the Administrator and is submitted to:

a. A designated aviation medical examiner if applying for an FAA medical certificate under 14 CFR Part 67;

b. An examiner; or

c. A Flight Standards District Office.

3. What minimum aeronautical knowledge must be demonstrated by a student pilot before solo privileges are permitted? (14 CFR 61.87)

A student pilot must demonstrate satisfactory aeronautical knowledge on a knowledge test.

a. The test must address the student pilot's knowledge of:

- Applicable sections of 14 CFR Parts 61 and 91;
- Airspace rules and procedures for the airport where the solo flight will be performed; and
- Flight characteristics and operational limitations for the make and model of aircraft to be flown.

Continued

b. The student's authorized instructor must:
- Administer the test; and
- At the conclusion of the test, review all incorrect answers with the student before authorizing that student to conduct a solo flight.

4. What minimum flight training must a student pilot receive before solo privileges are permitted? (14 CFR 61.87)

Prior to conducting a solo flight, a student pilot must have:

a. Received and logged flight training for the Part 61 maneuvers and procedures appropriate to the make and model of aircraft to be flown; and

b. Demonstrated satisfactory proficiency and safety, as judged by an authorized instructor, on the Part 61 maneuvers and procedures in the make and model of aircraft or similar make and model of aircraft to be flown.

A student pilot training for a single-engine airplane rating must receive and log flight training for the following maneuvers and procedures:

a. Proper flight preparation procedures, including preflight planning and preparation, powerplant operation, and aircraft systems;

b. Taxiing or surface operations, including runups;

c. Takeoffs and landings, including normal and crosswind;

d. Straight-and-level flight, and turns in both directions;

e. Climbs and climbing turns;

f. Airport traffic patterns, including entry and departure procedures;

g. Collision avoidance, windshear avoidance, and wake turbulence avoidance;

h. Descents, with and without turns, using high and low drag configurations;

i. Flight at various airspeeds from cruise to slow flight;

j. Stall entries from various flight attitudes and power combinations with recovery initiated at the first indication of a stall, and recovery from a full stall;

k. Emergency procedures and equipment malfunctions;

l. Ground reference maneuvers;

m. Approaches to a landing area with simulated engine malfunctions;

n. Slips to a landing; and

o. Go-arounds.

5. What basic requirements must a student pilot meet before being allowed to conduct solo flight at night? (14 CFR 61.87)

a. Flight training at night on night-flying procedures, including takeoffs, approaches, landings, and go-arounds at night at the airport where the solo flight will be conducted;

b. Navigation training at night in the vicinity of the airport where the solo flight will be conducted;

c. An endorsement in the student's logbook for the specific make and model aircraft to be flown for night solo flight, by an authorized instructor who gave the training within the 90-day period preceding the date of the flight.

6. What limitations are imposed upon student pilots operating an aircraft in solo flight? (14 CFR 61.87)

A student pilot may not operate an aircraft in solo flight unless they received:

a. An endorsement from an authorized instructor on his or her student pilot certificate for the specific make and model aircraft to be flown; and

b. An endorsement in the student's logbook for the specific make and model aircraft to be flown by an authorized instructor, who gave the training within the 90 days preceding the date of the flight.

7. What limitations are imposed upon flight instructors authorizing student pilot solo flights? (14 CFR 61.87)

No instructor may authorize a student pilot to perform a solo flight unless that instructor has:

a. Given that student pilot training in the make and model of aircraft or a similar make and model of aircraft in which the solo flight is to be flown;

b. Determined the student pilot is proficient in the Part 61 prescribed maneuvers and procedures;

c. Determined the student pilot is proficient in the make and model of aircraft to be flown;

d. Ensured that the student pilot's certificate has been endorsed by an instructor authorized to provide flight training for the specific make and model aircraft to be flown; and

e. Endorsed the student pilot's logbook for the specific make and model aircraft to be flown, and that endorsement remains current for solo flight privileges, provided an authorized instructor updates the student's logbook every 90 days thereafter.

The flight training required by this section must be given by an instructor authorized to provide flight training who is appropriately rated and current.

8. State the general limitations which apply to all student pilots. (14 CFR 61.89)

A student pilot may not act as pilot-in-command of an aircraft:

a. Carrying a passenger;

b. Carrying property for compensation or hire;

c. For compensation or hire;

d. In furtherance of a business;

e. On an international flight, (with exceptions—see §61.89)

f. With a flight or surface visibility of less than 3 statute miles during daylight hours or 5 statute miles at night;

g. When the flight cannot be made with visual reference to the surface; or

h. In a manner contrary to any limitations placed in the pilot's logbook by an authorized instructor.

A student pilot may not act as a required pilot flight crewmember on any aircraft for which more than one pilot is required by the type certificate of the aircraft or regulations under which the flight is conducted, except when receiving flight training from an authorized instructor onboard an airship, and no person other than a required flight crewmember is carried on the aircraft.

9. What requirements must be met before a flight instructor can allow a student pilot to make repeated specific solo cross-country flights without each flight being logbook endorsed? (14 CFR 61.93)

Repeated specific solo cross-country flights may be made to another airport within 50 NM of the airport from which the flight originated, provided:

a. The authorized instructor has given the student flight training in both directions over the route, including entering and exiting the traffic patterns, takeoffs, and landings at the airports to be used;

b. The authorized instructor who gave the training has endorsed the student's logbook certifying the student is proficient to make such flights;

c. The student has current solo flight endorsements in accordance with §61.87; and

d. The student has current solo cross-country flight endorsements in accordance with §61.87(c); however, for repeated solo cross-country flights to another airport within 50 NM from which the flight originated, separate endorsements are not required to be made for each flight.

10. Before a student pilot is permitted solo cross-country privileges, they must have received several endorsements. What are they? (14 CFR 61.93)

Student pilot certificate endorsement:

A student pilot must have a solo cross-country endorsement from the authorized instructor who conducted the training, and that endorsement must be placed on that person's student pilot certificate for the specific category of aircraft to be flown.
Logbook endorsement:

a. A student pilot must have a solo cross-country endorsement from an authorized instructor placed in the student pilot's logbook for the specific make and model of aircraft to be flown.

b. A certificated pilot who is receiving training for an additional aircraft category or class rating must have an endorsement in his or her logbook or training record from an authorized instructor, and that endorsement must attest that the applicant has been found competent in the areas of aeronautical knowledge and operation that are appropriate to the pilot certificate for the aircraft category and, if applicable, class rating sought.

c. For each cross-country flight, the authorized instructor who reviews the cross-country planning must make an endorsement in the person's logbook after reviewing that person's cross-country planning, as specified in §61.93(d). The endorsement must specify the make and model of aircraft to be flown, state that the student's preflight planning and preparation is correct and that the student is prepared to make the flight safely under the known conditions, and state that any limitations required by the student's instructor are met.

11. Before solo cross-country privileges are permitted, what minimum cross-country flight training requirements must a student pilot satisfy? (14 CFR 61.93)

The student pilot must receive and log flight training in the following maneuvers and procedures:

a. Aeronautical charts for VFR navigation using pilotage and dead reckoning with aid of a magnetic compass;

b. Use of aircraft performance charts for cross-country flight;

c. Procurement and analysis of aeronautical weather reports and forecasts, recognizing critical weather situations and estimating visibility while in flight;

d. Emergency procedures;

e. Traffic pattern procedures that include area departure, area arrival, entry into the traffic pattern, and approach;

f. Collision avoidance, wake turbulence precautions, and wind-shear avoidance;

g. Recognition, avoidance, and operational restrictions of hazardous terrain features in the geographical area where the cross-country flight will be flown;

h. Proper operation of the instruments and equipment installed in the aircraft to be flown;

i. Use of radios for VFR navigation and two-way communications;

j. Takeoff, approach, and landing procedures, including short-field, soft-field, and crosswind takeoffs, approaches, and landings;

k. Climbs at best angle and best rate; and

l. Control and maneuvering solely by reference to flight instruments, including straight-and-level flight, turns, descents, climbs, use of radio aids, and ATC directives.

12. Before a flight instructor can authorize a student pilot to conduct a solo cross-country flight, what requirements must be met? (14 CFR 61.93)

The instructor must have determined that:

a. The student's cross-country planning is correct for the flight;

b. Upon review, the current and forecast weather conditions show that the flight can be completed under VFR;

c. The student is proficient to conduct the flight safely; and

d. The student has the appropriate and current solo cross-country endorsement for the make and model of aircraft to be flown;

e. The student's solo flight endorsement is current for the make and model aircraft to be flown.

13. What actions must a flight instructor take to allow a student pilot to operate within Class B airspace? (14 CFR 61.95)

A student pilot may not operate an aircraft on a solo flight in Class B airspace unless:

a. The student pilot has received both ground and flight training from an authorized instructor on that Class B airspace area, and the flight training was received in the specific Class B airspace area for which solo flight is authorized;

b. The logbook of that student pilot has been endorsed by the authorized instructor who gave the student pilot flight training, and the endorsement is dated within the 90-day period preceding the date of the flight in that Class B airspace area; and

c. The logbook endorsement specifies that the student pilot has received the required ground and flight training, and has been found proficient to conduct solo flight in that specific Class B airspace area.

14. What action must a flight instructor take to allow a student pilot to operate to, from, or at an airport located within Class B airspace? (14 CFR 61.95)

A student pilot may not operate an aircraft on a solo flight to, from, or at an airport located within Class B airspace unless:

a. The student pilot has received both ground and flight training from an instructor authorized to provide training to operate at that airport, and the flight and ground training has been received at the specific airport for which the solo flight is authorized;

b. The logbook of that student pilot has been endorsed by an authorized instructor who gave the student pilot flight training, and the endorsement is dated within the 90-day period preceding the date of the flight at that airport; and

c. The logbook endorsement specifies that the student pilot has received the required ground and flight training, and has been found proficient to conduct solo flight operations at that specific airport.

E. Recreational Pilots

1. What are the eligibility requirements for a recreational pilot certificate? (14 CFR 61.96)

a. Be at least 17 years of age;

b. Be able to read, speak, write, and understand the English language;

c. Receive a logbook endorsement from an authorized instructor who conducted the training or reviewed the applicant's home study on the required aeronautical knowledge areas, and certified that the applicant is prepared for the required knowledge test;

d. Pass the required knowledge test on the aeronautical knowledge areas;

e. Receive flight training and a logbook endorsement from an authorized instructor who conducted the training on the required areas of operation, and certified that the applicant is prepared for the required practical test;

f. Meet the required aeronautical experience;

g. Pass the required practical test on the areas of operation that apply to the aircraft category and class rating sought.

2. What aeronautical experience must an applicant for a recreational pilot certificate have accomplished? (14 CFR 61.99)

An applicant must receive and log at least 30 hours of flight training time that includes at least:

a. 15 hours of flight training from an authorized instructor on the required areas of operation that consists of at least 2 hours of flight training en route to an airport more than 25 NM from the airport where the applicant normally trains, which includes at least three takeoffs and three landings at the airport, and 3 hours of flight training in the aircraft for the rating sought in preparation for the practical test within the 60 days preceding the date of the practical test; and

b. 3 hours of solo flying in the aircraft for the rating sought, on the areas of operation listed in §61.98 of this part that apply to the aircraft category and class rating sought.

3. What are the privileges that apply to recreational pilots? (14 CFR 61.101)

A recreational pilot may:

a. Carry no more than one passenger; and

b. Not pay less than the pro rata share of the operating expenses of a flight with a passenger, provided the expenses involve only fuel, oil, airport expenses, or aircraft rental fees.

c. Act as pilot-in-command of an aircraft on a flight within 50 NM from the departure airport, provided that person has:

- Received ground and flight training for takeoff, departure, arrival, and landing procedures at the departure airport;

- Received ground and flight training for the area, terrain, and aids to navigation that are in the vicinity of the departure airport;

- Been found proficient to operate the aircraft at the departure airport and the area within 50 NM from that airport; and

- Received from an authorized instructor a logbook endorsement, which is carried in the person's possession in the aircraft, that permits flight within 50 NM from the departure airport.

d. Act as pilot-in-command of an aircraft on a flight that exceeds 50 NM from the departure airport, provided that person has:

- Received ground and flight training from an authorized instructor on the required cross-country training that applies to the aircraft rating held;

- Been found proficient in cross-country flying; and

- Received from an authorized instructor a logbook endorsement, which is in the person's possession in the aircraft, that certifies the person has received and been found proficient in the required cross-country training that applies to the aircraft rating held.

4. What are the limitations that apply to all recreational pilots? (14 CFR 61.101)

A recreational pilot may not act as pilot-in-command of an aircraft:

a. That is certificated for more than four occupants, with more than one powerplant, with a powerplant of more than 180 horsepower, or with retractable landing gear.

b. That is classified as a multi-engine airplane, powered-lift, glider, airship, balloon, powered parachute, or weight-shift control aircraft;

c. That is carrying a passenger or property for compensation or hire;

d. For compensation or hire;

e. In furtherance of a business;

f. Between sunset and sunrise;

g. In Class A, B, C, and D airspace, at an airport located in Class B, C, or D airspace, or to, from, through, or at an airport having an operational control tower;

h. At an altitude of more than 10,000 feet MSL or 2,000 feet AGL, whichever is higher;

i. When the flight or surface visibility is less than 3 statute miles;

j. Without visual reference to the surface;

k. On a flight outside the United States, unless authorized by the country in which the flight is conducted;

l. To demonstrate that aircraft in flight to a prospective buyer;

m. That is used in a passenger-carrying airlift and sponsored by a charitable organization; and

n. That is towing any object.

A recreational pilot may not act as a pilot flight crewmember on any aircraft for which more than one pilot is required by the type certificate of the aircraft or the regulations under which the flight is conducted, except when receiving flight training from a person authorized to provide flight training onboard an airship, and no person other than a required flight crewmember is carried on the aircraft.

F. Private Pilots

1. What are the general eligibility requirements for a private pilot certificate? (14 CFR 61.103)

To be eligible for a private pilot certificate, a person must:

a. Be at least 17 years of age for a rating in other than a glider or balloon;

b. Be at least 16 years of age for a rating in a glider or balloon;

c. Be able to read, speak, write, and understand the English language;

d. Receive a logbook endorsement from an authorized instructor who conducted the training or reviewed the person's home study on the required aeronautical knowledge areas and certified that the person is prepared for the required knowledge test;

e. Pass the required knowledge test on the aeronautical knowledge areas;

f. Receive flight training and a logbook endorsement from an authorized instructor who conducted the training in the required areas of operation and certified that the person is prepared for the required practical test;

g. Meet the aeronautical experience requirements that apply to the aircraft rating sought before applying for the practical test;

h. Pass a practical test on the required areas of operation that apply to the aircraft rating sought.

2. In what areas of aeronautical knowledge must an applicant for a private pilot certificate have received instruction? (14 CFR 61.105)

a. Federal Aviation Regulations that relate to private pilot privileges, limitations, and flight operations;

b. NTSB accident reporting requirements;

c. Use of the *Aeronautical Information Manual* and FAA ACs;

d. Aeronautical charts for VFR navigation using pilotage, dead reckoning, and navigation systems;

e. Radio communication procedures;

f. Recognition of critical weather situations from the ground and in flight, windshear avoidance, and the procurement and use of aeronautical weather reports and forecasts;

g. Safe and efficient operation of aircraft, including collision avoidance, and recognition and avoidance of wake turbulence;

h. Effects of density altitude on takeoff and climb performance;

i. Weight and balance computations;

j. Principles of aerodynamics, powerplants, and aircraft systems;

k. Stall awareness, spin entry, spins, and spin recovery techniques for the airplane and glider category ratings;

l. Aeronautical decision making and judgment; and

m. Preflight action that includes how to obtain information on runway lengths at airports of intended use, data on takeoff and landing distances, weather reports and forecasts, and fuel requirements, and how to plan for alternatives if the planned flight cannot be completed or delays are encountered.

3. In what pilot operations must an applicant for a private pilot certificate have received instruction?
(14 CFR 61.107)

a. Preflight preparation

b. Preflight procedures

c. Airport and seaplane base operations

d. Takeoffs, landings, and go-arounds

e. Performance maneuvers

f. Ground reference maneuvers

g. Navigation

h. Slow flight and stalls

i. Basic instrument maneuvers

j. Emergency operations

k. Night operations

l. Postflight procedures

4. What minimum aeronautical experience must be accumulated by a student pilot before application for a private pilot certificate? (14 CFR 61.109)

Total Time: 40 hours of flight time which consists of at least—
Dual: 20 hours of flight training with an instructor on the Private Pilot areas of operation that includes:

a. 3 hours of cross-country flight training in a single-engine airplane;

b. 3 hours of night flight training in a single-engine airplane, that includes at least:

- 1 cross-country flight of over 100 NM total distance; and
- 10 takeoffs and 10 landings to a full stop, each involving a flight in the traffic pattern.

c. 3 hours of flight training by reference to instruments in a single-engine airplane; and

d. 3 hours of flight training in a single-engine airplane within the preceding 60 days prior to the practical test.

Solo: 10 hours of solo flying in a single-engine airplane on the Private Pilot areas of operation, that includes:

a. 5 hours of solo cross-country flying;

b. 1 solo cross-country flight of at least 150 NM total distance with full stop landings at a minimum of 3 points and one segment of at least 50 NM between takeoff and landing; and

c. 3 takeoffs and landings to full stop (with each landing involving a flight in the traffic pattern) at a controlled airport.

5. How much time in a flight simulator or flight training device may be credited toward the flight training required for a private pilot certificate? (14 CFR 61.109)

A maximum of 2.5 hours of training (5 hours if under Part 142) in a flight simulator or flight training device representing the category, class, and type, if applicable, of aircraft appropriate to the rating sought, may be credited toward the flight training time required by this section, if received from an authorized instructor.

6. May a student pilot take the private pilot practical test without completing the 3 hours of night flying instruction? (14 CFR 61.110)

No, with one exception: student pilots who receive flight training in and reside in the state of Alaska are not required to comply with the night flight training requirements.

7. What privileges and limitations apply to private pilots? (14 CFR 61.113)

a. No person who holds a private pilot certificate may act as pilot-in-command of an aircraft carrying passengers or property for compensation or hire.

b. A private pilot may, for compensation or hire, act as pilot-in-command of an aircraft in connection with any business or employment if the flight is only incidental to that business or employment, and the aircraft does not carry passengers or property for compensation or hire.

c. A private pilot may not pay less than the pro rata share of operating expenses of a flight with passengers, provided the expenses involve only fuel, oil, airport expenditures, or rental fees.

d. A private pilot may act as pilot-in-command of an aircraft used in a passenger-carrying airlift sponsored by a charitable organization described in 14 CFR §61.113(d)(7) for which the passengers make a donation to the organization, when the requirements of §61.113(d) are met.

e. A private pilot may be reimbursed for aircraft operating expenses directly related to search and location operations, provided the expenses involve only fuel, oil, airport expenditures, or rental fees, and the operation is sanctioned and under the direction and control of a local, State, or Federal agency, or an organization that conducts search and location operations.

f. A private pilot who is an aircraft salesman and who has at least 200 hours of logged flight time may demonstrate an aircraft in flight to a prospective buyer.

g. A private pilot who meets the requirements of §61.69 may act as pilot-in-command of an aircraft towing a glider.

G. Commercial Pilots

1. What are the general eligibility requirements for a commercial pilot certificate? (14 CFR 61.123)

a. Be at least 18 years of age;

b. Be able to read, speak, write, and understand the English language;

c. Receive a logbook endorsement from an authorized instructor who conducted the required ground training or reviewed the person's home study on the required aeronautical knowledge areas that apply to the aircraft category and class rating sought, and certified that the person is prepared for the required knowledge test;

d. Pass the required knowledge test on the aeronautical knowledge areas;

e. Receive the required training and a logbook endorsement from an authorized instructor who conducted the training on the required areas of operation that apply to the aircraft category and class rating sought, and certified that the person is prepared for the required practical test;

f. Meet the required aeronautical experience before applying for the practical test;

g. Pass the required practical test on the required areas of operation;

h. Hold at least a private pilot certificate; and

i. Comply with the sections of Part 61 that apply to the aircraft category and class rating sought.

2. In what areas of aeronautical knowledge must an applicant for a commercial pilot certificate have received instruction? (14 CFR 61.125)

a. Federal Aviation Regulations that relate to commercial pilot privileges, limitations, and flight operations;

b. NTSB accident reporting requirements;

c. Basic aerodynamics and the principles of flight;

   d. Meteorology (recognition of critical weather situations, wind-shear recognition and avoidance, and the use of aeronautical weather reports and forecasts);

   e. Safe and efficient operation of aircraft;

   f. Weight and balance computations;

   g. Use of performance charts;

   h. Significance and effects of exceeding aircraft performance limitations;

   i. Use of aeronautical charts and a magnetic compass for pilotage and dead reckoning;

   j. Use of air navigation facilities;

   k. Aeronautical decision making and judgment;

   l. Principles and functions of aircraft systems;

   m. Maneuvers, procedures, and emergency operations appropriate to the aircraft;

   n. Night and high-altitude operations;

   o. Procedures for operating within the National Airspace System; and

   p. Procedures for flight and ground training for lighter-than-air ratings.

3. In what pilot operations must an applicant for a commercial pilot certificate have received instruction? (14 CFR 61.127)

   a. Preflight preparation
   b. Preflight procedures
   c. Airport and seaplane base operations
   d. Takeoffs, landings, and go-arounds
   e. Performance maneuvers
   f. Ground reference maneuvers
   g. Navigation
   h. Slow flight and stalls
   i. Emergency operations
   j. High-altitude operations
   k. Postflight procedures

4. What minimum aeronautical experience must be accumulated by a private pilot training under Part 61 before application for a commercial pilot certificate? (14 CFR 61.129)

Total Time: 250 hours of flight time as a pilot that consists of at least —

100 hours in powered aircraft, of which 50 hours must be in airplanes.

100 hours of pilot-in-command flight time, that includes at least:

a. 50 hours in airplanes; and

b. 50 hours in cross-country flying of which at least 10 hours must be in airplanes.

Dual: 20 hours of flight training on the Commercial Pilot areas of operation that includes at least:

a. 10 hours of instrument training of which at least 5 hours must be in a single-engine airplane;

b. 10 hours of training in a complex airplane or a turbine-powered airplane;

c. 1 cross-country of 2 hours in a single-engine airplane in day VFR conditions of a total straight-line distance greater than 100 NM from the departure point;

d. 1 cross-country of 2 hours in a single-engine airplane in night VFR conditions of a total straight-line distance greater than 100 NM from the departure point;

e. 3 hours of flight training in a single-engine airplane within the preceding 60 days prior to the practical test.

Solo: 10 hours of solo flight in a single-engine airplane on the Commercial Pilot areas of operation, including:

a. One cross-country flight of not less than 300 NM with landings at a minimum of 3 points, one of which is a straight-line distance of at least 250 NM; and

b. 5 hours in night VFR conditions with 10 takeoffs and landings (each landing must involve flight in the traffic pattern) at a controlled airport.

5. What privileges and limitations apply to commercial pilots? (14 CFR 61.133)

Commercial pilot general privileges are as follows: a person who holds a commercial pilot certificate may act as pilot-in-command of an aircraft carrying persons or property for compensation or hire, provided the person is qualified in accordance with 14 CFR Part 61, and for compensation or hire, provided the person is qualified in accordance with Part 61 and applicable parts of the regulations that apply to the operation.

As for limitations, a person who applies for a commercial pilot certificate with an airplane category or powered-lift category rating and does not hold an instrument rating in the same category and class will be issued a commercial pilot certificate that contains the limitation, "The carriage of passengers for hire in (airplanes) (powered-lifts) on cross-country flights in excess of 50 nautical miles or at night is prohibited." The limitation may be removed when the person satisfactorily accomplishes the requirements listed in §61.65 for an instrument rating in the same category and class of aircraft listed on the person's commercial pilot certificate.

H. Airline Transport Pilots

1. What are the general eligibility requirements for an airline transport pilot certificate? (14 CFR 61.153)

a. Be at least 23 years of age;

b. Be able to read, speak, write, and understand the English language;

c. Be of good moral character;

d. Meet at least one of the following requirements:

- Hold at least a commercial pilot certificate and an instrument rating;

- Meet the military experience requirements under §61.73 to qualify for a commercial pilot certificate, and an instrument rating if the person is a rated military pilot or former rated military pilot of an Armed Force of the United States; or

Continued

- Hold either a foreign airline transport pilot or foreign commercial pilot license and an instrument rating if the person holds a pilot license issued by a contracting State to the Convention on International Civil Aviation;

e. Meet the aeronautical experience requirements applicable to the aircraft category and class rating sought before applying for the practical test;

f. Pass a knowledge test on the required aeronautical knowledge areas that apply to the aircraft category and class rating sought;

g. Pass the practical test on the required areas of operation that apply to the aircraft category and class rating sought; and

h. Comply with the sections of Part 61 that apply to the aircraft category and class rating sought.

2. **What minimum aeronautical experience must be accumulated by a person applying for an Airline Transport Pilot certificate with an airplane category and class rating?** (14 CFR 61.159)

Total Time: 1,500 hours that includes —

a. 500 hours of cross-country flying;

b. 100 hours of night flight time;

c. 75 hours of instrument time, actual or simulated; and

d. 250 hours in an airplane as a PIC, or as SIC performing the duties of PIC, or any combination thereof, that includes at least:

- 100 hours of cross-country flying; and
- 25 hours of night flight time.

I. Flight Instructors

1. In what areas of aeronautical knowledge must an applicant for a flight instructor certificate have received instruction? (14 CFR 61.185)

The fundamentals of instructing, including:

a. The learning process;
b. Elements of effective teaching;
c. Student evaluation and testing;
d. Course development;
e. Lesson planning; and
f. Classroom training techniques.

Also, the aeronautical knowledge areas for a recreational, private, and commercial pilot certificate applicable to the aircraft category for which flight instructor privileges are sought; and the aeronautical knowledge areas for the instrument rating applicable to the category for which instrument flight instructor privileges are sought.

2. In what areas of operation must an applicant for a flight instructor certificate have received instruction? (14 CFR 61.187)

a. Fundamentals of instructing
b. Technical subject areas
c. Preflight preparation
d. Preflight lesson on a maneuver to be performed in flight
e. Preflight procedures
f. Airport and seaplane base operations
g. Takeoffs, landings, and go-arounds
h. Fundamentals of flight
i. Performance maneuvers
j. Ground reference maneuvers
k. Slow flight, stalls, and spins
l. Basic instrument maneuvers
m. Emergency operations
n. Postflight procedures

3. What are the required records a flight instructor must retain? (14 CFR 61.189)

a. A flight instructor must sign the logbook of each person to whom that instructor has given flight training or ground training.

b. A flight instructor must maintain a record in a logbook or a separate document that contains the name of each person whose logbook or student pilot certificate that instructor has endorsed for solo flight privileges, and the date of the endorsement; and the name of each person that instructor has endorsed for a knowledge test or practical test, and the record shall also indicate the kind of test, the date, and the results.

c. Each flight instructor must retain the required records for at least 3 years.

4. What are the various endorsements a flight instructor is authorized to give? (14 CFR 61.193)

A person who holds a flight instructor certificate is authorized within the limitations of that person's flight instructor certificate and ratings to give training and endorsements that are required for, and relate to:

a. A student pilot certificate;
b. A pilot certificate;
c. A flight instructor certificate;
d. A ground instructor certificate;
e. An aircraft rating;
f. An instrument rating;
g. A flight review, operating privilege, or recency of experience requirement;
h. A practical test; and
i. A knowledge test.

5. What limitations on endorsements apply to all flight instructors? (14 CFR 61.195)

A flight instructor may *not* endorse:

a. A student pilot's certificate or logbook for solo flight privileges, unless that flight instructor has given that student the required flight training and has determined that the student is prepared to conduct the flight safely under known circumstances, subject to any limitations that the instructor considers necessary for the safety of the flight;

b. A student pilot's certificate and logbook for a solo cross-country flight, unless that flight instructor has determined the student's flight preparation, planning, equipment, and proposed procedures are adequate for the proposed flight under the existing conditions and within any limitations that the instructor considered necessary for the safety of the flight;

c. A student pilot's certificate and logbook for solo flight in a Class B airspace area or at an airport within Class B airspace unless that flight instructor has given that student ground and flight training in that Class B airspace or at that airport; and determined that the student is proficient to operate the aircraft safely;

d. The logbook of a recreational pilot, unless that flight instructor has given that pilot the required ground and flight training; and determined that the recreational pilot is proficient to operate the aircraft safely;

e. The logbook of a pilot for a flight review, unless that instructor has conducted a review of that pilot in accordance with the requirements of §61.56(a);

f. The logbook of a pilot for an instrument proficiency check, unless that instructor has tested that pilot in accordance with the requirements of §61.57(d).

6. How many hours of flight training is a flight instructor limited to? (14 CFR 61.195)

In any 24-consecutive-hour period, a flight instructor may not conduct more than 8 hours of flight training.

7. What qualifications must a flight instructor possess before instrument flight training may be given for the issuance of an instrument rating or a type rating not limited to VFR? (14 CFR 61.195)

The flight instructor must hold an instrument rating on his or her flight instructor certificate and pilot certificate that is appropriate to the category and class of aircraft in which instrument training is being provided.

8. What is the minimum pilot-in-command time requirement for a flight instructor with multi-engine privileges to give instruction to a student for a multi-engine rating? (14 CFR 61.195)

That flight instructor must have at least 5 flight hours of pilot-in-command time in the specific make and model of multi-engine airplane, helicopter, or powered-lift, as appropriate.

9. How can a flight instructor certificate be renewed? (14 CFR 61.197)

A person who holds a current flight instructor certificate may renew that certificate for an additional 24 calendar months if the holder:

a. Has passed a practical test for one of the ratings listed on the current flight instructor certificate, or an additional flight instructor rating; or

b. Has presented to an authorized FAA Flight Standards Inspector a record of training students showing that, during the preceding 24 calendar months, the flight instructor has endorsed at least five students for a practical test for a certificate or rating, and at least 80 percent of those students passed that test on the first attempt; or has a record showing that, within the preceding 24 calendar months, the flight instructor served as a company check pilot, chief flight instructor, company check airman, or flight instructor in a Part 121 or Part 135 operation, or in a position involving the regular evaluation of pilots; or has a graduation certificate showing that, within the preceding 3 calendar months, the person has successfully completed an approved flight instructor refresher course consisting of ground or flight training, or a combination of both.

Additional Study Questions

1. **If requested, who may inspect your airman certificate, medical certificate, or logbook?** (14 CFR 61.51)

2. **Must an airman who serves as safety pilot have a current medical certificate in their possession?** (14 CFR 61.23, 91.109)

3. **For what reasons may an examiner discontinue a practical test?** (14 CFR 61.43)

4. **Concerning instructional flights with both an authorized flight instructor and a certificated pilot onboard, which person is allowed to log pilot-in-command time?** (14 CFR 61.51)

5. **Under Part 61, must the CFI have his/her instrument rating (CFII) to teach the 3 hours of instrument training required for Private Pilot certificate?** (14 CFR 61.109, 61.193)

6. **Are appropriate ground instructor ratings necessary for a flight instructor to teach a ground school course?** (14 CFR 61.193)

7. **Can dual instruction be given to a pilot seeking an instrument rating from a flight instructor who does not possess an instrument flight instructor rating?** (14 CFR 61.195)

8. **After renewing your CFI certificate, you notice you also need a Biennial Flight Review. Does the CFI renewal satisfy the Biennial Flight Review requirement?** (14 CFR 61.56)

9. **What additional training is required to act as pilot-in-command of a pressurized aircraft capable of operating at high altitudes?** (14 CFR 61.31)

Technical
Subject Areas

3

A. Aeromedical Factors

1. When should a student pilot obtain a medical certificate? (FAA-H-8083-25)

Prior to beginning flight training, a flight instructor should interview the prospective student about any health conditions and determine his or her ultimate goal as a pilot, and should advise the student to obtain the class of medical certificate required. Finding out first whether the student is medically qualified could save time and money.

2. Why is it important for students to obtain a medical certificate as soon as possible? (AIM 8-1-1)

Student pilots should visit an Aviation Medical Examiner as soon as possible in their flight training in order to avoid unnecessary training expenses should they not meet the medical standards.

3. What is a "statement of demonstrated ability (SODA)"? (14 CFR 67.401)

At the discretion of the Federal Air Surgeon, a Statement of Demonstrated Ability (SODA) may be granted, instead of an Authorization, to a person whose disqualifying condition is static or non-progressive and who has been found capable of performing airman duties without endangering public safety. A SODA does not expire and authorizes a designated aviation medical examiner to issue a medical certificate of a specified class if the examiner finds that the condition described on its face has not adversely changed.

4. State several medical conditions which might prevent the issuance of a medical certificate. (14 CFR Part 67)

a. Clinical diabetes

b. Coronary heart disease/heart attack

c. Epilepsy

d. Disturbance of consciousness

e. Alcoholism

f. Drug dependence

g. Psychosis

5. **What should students know about flight operations conducted while suffering from a medical deficiency?** (14 CFR 61.53)

   No person may act as pilot-in-command, or in any other capacity as a required flight crewmember, while having a known medical deficiency that would make him/her unable to meet the requirements for his/her current medical certificate.

Additional Study Questions

1. **What are the symptoms, effects, and corrective actions for the following: hypoxia, hyperventilation, middle ear and sinus problems, carbon monoxide poisoning?** (FAA-H-8083-25)

2. **What are the causes, effects, and corrective actions for the following: spatial disorientation, motion sickness?** (FAA-H-8083-25)

3. **Explain the effects of alcohol and drugs and their relationship to safety and flying.** (FAA-H-8083-25)

4. **Explain the effect of nitrogen excesses during scuba dives and how this affects a pilot during flight.** (FAA-H-8083-25)

5. **Explain the effects of fatigue on the safety of flight and the corrective actions to prevent it.** (FAA-H-8083-25)

B. Visual Scanning and Collision Avoidance

1. **What is the relationship between a pilot's physical or mental condition and vision?** (AIM 8-1-1)

   The two are closely related. Even a minor illness suffered in day-to-day living can seriously degrade performance of many piloting tasks including the pilot's ability to effectively use his/her vision. Use the IMSAFE checklist: I'm physically and mentally safe to fly, not being impaired by: Illness, Medication, Stress, Alcohol, Fatigue, Emotion.

2. Name several factors that can degrade a pilot's vision. (AIM 8-1-6, 8-1-8)

a. *Visibility conditions*—smoke, haze, dust, rain, and flying towards the sun can greatly reduce the ability to detect targets.

b. *Windshield conditions*—dirty or bug-smeared windshields can greatly reduce the ability to see other aircraft.

c. *Bright illumination*—reflected off clouds, water, snow, and desert terrain that produces glare resulting in eye strain and the inability to see effectively.

d. *Dim illumination*—small print and colors on aeronautical charts and aircraft instruments become unreadable.

e. *Dark adaptation*—eyes must have at least 20 to 30 minutes to adjust to reduced light conditions.

3. Describe some of the various optical illusions a pilot can experience in flight. (AIM 8-1-5)

The "leans"—An abrupt correction of a banked attitude, which has been entered too slowly to stimulate the motion sensing system in the inner ear, can create the illusion of banking in the opposite direction. Examples include: Coriolis illusion, graveyard spin, graveyard spiral, somatogravic illusion, inversion illusion, elevator illusion, false horizon and autokinesis.

Runway width illusion—A narrower-than-usual runway can create the illusion that the aircraft is at a higher altitude than it actually is. Unrecognized, the pilot may fly a lower approach, with the risk of striking objects along the approach path or landing short. A wider-than-usual runway can have the opposite effect, with the risk of leveling out high and landing hard or overshooting the runway.

Runway and terrain slope illusion—An upsloping runway, upsloping terrain or both, can create the illusion that the aircraft is at a higher altitude than it actually is. Unrecognized, the pilot may fly a lower approach. A downsloping runway, downsloping approach terrain, or both, can have the opposite effect.

Featureless terrain illusion—An absence of ground features, as when landing over water, darkened areas, and terrain made featureless by snow, can create the illusion that the aircraft is at a higher altitude than it actually is. Unrecognized, the pilot may fly a lower approach.

4. Explain the "see and avoid" concept. (14 CFR 91.113)

When weather conditions permit, regardless of whether the flight is conducted under instrument flight rules or visual flight rules, vigilance shall be maintained by each person operating an aircraft so as to see and avoid other aircraft.

5. Explain the practice of time sharing your attention inside and outside the cockpit. (AIM 8-1-6)

Studies show that the time a pilot spends on visual tasks inside the cabin should represent no more than 1/4 to 1/3 of the scan time outside, or no more than 4 to 5 seconds on the instrument panel for every 16 seconds outside.

6. What is a good visual scanning technique? (AIM 8-1-6)

Effective scanning is accomplished with a series of short, regularly spaced eye movements that bring successive areas of the sky into the central visual field. Each movement should not exceed 10 degrees, and each area should be observed for at least 1 second to enable detection. Although horizontal back and forth eye movements seem preferred, each pilot should develop a scanning pattern that is most comfortable and then adhere to it to ensure optimum scanning.

Additional Study Questions

1. Explain the relationship between aircraft speed differential and collision risk. (AC 90-48)

2. What situations involve the greatest collision risk? (AIM 8-1-8)

3. Explain the importance of knowing the aircraft's blind spots. (AIM 8-1-8)

4. How can a pilot determine the relative altitude/direction of flight of an aircraft on a possible collision course? (AIM 8-1-8)

5. What are proper clearing procedures? (FAA-H-8083-3)

C. Principles of Flight

1. What are the four dynamic forces that act on airplane during all maneuvers? (FAA-H-8083-25)

The airplane in straight-and-level unaccelerated flight is acted on by four forces:

Lift—the upward acting force
Gravity—or weight, the downward acting force
Thrust—the forward acting force
Drag—the backward acting force

2. Explain the following terms as they relate to the production of lift. (FAA-H-8083-25)

Bernoulli's principle—states in part that the internal pressure of a fluid (liquid or gas) decreases at points where the speed of the fluid increases. In other words, high speed flow (above the wing) is associated with low pressure, and low speed flow (below the wing) with high pressure.

Newton's Third Law—since for every action there is an opposite and equal reaction, an additional upward force is generated as the lower surface of the wing deflects air downward.

3. Define the following terms: (FAA-H-8083-25)

Airfoil—any surface designed to obtain reaction, such as lift, from the air through which it moves.

Angle of attack—the angle between the chord line of the wing and the direction of the relative wind.

Angle of incidence—the angle formed by the chord line of the wing and the longitudinal axis of the airplane.

Camber—the curvature of the airfoil from the leading edge to the trailing edge.

Chord line—an imaginary straight line drawn from the leading edge to the trailing edge of a cross section of an airfoil.

Wing planform—the shape or form of a wing as viewed from above. It may be long and tapered, short and rectangular, or various other shapes.

4. Explain the forces acting on an airplane when operating at an airspeed slower than cruise. (FAA-H-8083-25)

While maintaining straight-and-level flight at constant airspeeds slower than cruise, the opposing forces must still be equal in magnitude. In this flight condition the actual thrust no longer acts parallel and opposite to the flightpath and drag, but is instead inclined upward and now has two components: one acting perpendicular to the flightpath in the direction of lift, the other acting along the flightpath. Because it is inclined, its magnitude must be greater than drag if its component of thrust along the flightpath is equal to drag. So the actual thrust is greater than drag and wing lift is less than at cruise airspeed.

5. What causes an airplane to turn? (FAA-H-8083-25)

An object at rest or moving in a straight line will remain at rest or continue to move in a straight line until acted upon by some other force. An airplane requires a sideward force to make it turn; in a normal turn, this is done by banking the airplane so that lift is exerted inward as well as upward. This force of lift is separated into two components: one that acts vertically and opposite to weight (gravity) is called the "vertical component of lift"; the other that acts horizontally, toward the center of the turn, is called the "horizontal component of lift" or centripetal force. The latter is the force that pulls the airplane from a straight flightpath to make it turn. Centrifugal force is the "equal and opposite reaction" of the airplane to the change in direction and acts equal and opposite to the horizontal component of lift. This explains why, in a correctly executed turn, it is not rudder-supplied force that turns the airplane.

6. Define the term "stability" and name the two basic types. (FAA-H-8083-25)

Stability is the inherent characteristic designed into an airplane to correct for conditions that may disturb its equilibrium, and to return or to continue on the original flightpath. The two types of stability are static stability, which is the *initial* tendency that the airplane displays after its equilibrium is disturbed, and dynamic stability, which is the *overall* tendency the airplane displays after its equilibrium is disturbed.

7. Explain the effect of wing downwash on longitudinal stability. (FAA-H-8083-25)

In level flight, there will be a downwash of air from the wings that strikes the top of the horizontal stabilizer and produces a downward pressure, which at a certain speed will be just enough to balance the airplane's nose-heaviness. The faster the airplane is flying, the greater the downwash and the greater the downward force on the horizontal stabilizer. If the airplane's speed decreases, the speed of the airflow over the wing is decreased which reduces downwash, causing a lesser downward force on the horizontal stabilizer. In turn, nose-heaviness is accentuated, causing the airplane's nose to pitch down more. With the airplane in a nose-low attitude, this lessens the wings' angle of attack and drag, and allows the airspeed to increase. As the airplane continues in the nose-low attitude and its speed increases, the downward force on the horizontal stabilizer is once again increased. Consequently the tail is again pushed downward and the nose rises into a climbing attitude.

8. **What are the four factors that contribute to torque effect?** (FAA-H-8083-25)

   a. *Torque reaction of the engine and propeller:* For every action there is an equal and opposite reaction. The rotation of the propeller (from the cockpit) to the right, tends to roll or bank the airplane to the left.

   b. *Gyroscopic effect of the propeller:* Gyroscopic precession applies here, the resultant action or deflection of a spinning object when a force is applied to the outer rim of its rotational mass. If the axis of a propeller is tilted, the resulting force will be exerted 90 degrees ahead in the direction of rotation and in the same direction as the applied force. Most noticeable on takeoffs in taildraggers.

   Remember: Nose yaws to the right when nose is moving upwards (tail down). Nose yaws to the left when nose is moving downwards (tail up).

   c. *Corkscrewing effect of the propeller slipstream:* High speed rotation of an airplane propeller results in a corkscrewing rotation to the slipstream as it moves rearward. Most noticeable at high propeller speeds and low forward speeds, (as in a takeoff), the slipstream strikes the vertical tail surface on the left side pushing the tail to the right and yawing the airplane to the left.

   d. *Asymmetrical loading of the propeller (P-Factor):* When an airplane is flying with a high angle of attack, the bite of the downward-moving propeller blade is greater than the bite of the upward moving blade. This is due to the downward-moving blade meeting the oncoming relative wind at a greater angle of attack than the upward-moving blade. Consequently there is greater thrust on the downward moving blade on the right side, and this forces the airplane to yaw to the left.

9. **Explain the effects of speed on load factor.** (FAA-H-8083-25)

   The amount of excess load that can be imposed on the wing depends on how fast the airplane is flying. At slower speeds, the maximum allowable lifting force of the wing is only slightly greater than the amount necessary to support the weight of the airplane. Consequently, the load factor should not become excessive even if the controls are moved abruptly or the airplane encounters severe gusts. The reason for this is the airplane will stall before the load can become excessive. However, at high speeds, the lifting capacity of the wing is so great that a sudden movement of the elevator controls or a strong gust may increase the load factor beyond safe limits.

Additional Study Questions

1. **What are several factors which will affect both lift and drag?** (FAA-H-8083-25)

2. **Explain the distribution of forces in the following phases of flight: straight-and-level, climbs, descents, turns.** (FAA-H-8083-25)

3. **Explain ground effect.** (FAA-H-8083-25)

4. **Explain the relationship of center of gravity and center of pressure to longitudinal stability.** (FAA-H-8083-25)

5. **How does angle of incidence affect the control characteristics of your airplane?** (FAA-H-8083-25)

6. **What are several methods an aircraft manufacturer may employ to correct for turning tendency or torque effect in flight?** (FAA-H-8083-25)

7. **What are the limit load factors for normal, utility and acrobatic aircraft?** (FAA-H-8083-25)

8. **What are wingtip vortices and what flight precautions should be practiced?** (FAA-H-8083-25)

D. Airplane Flight Controls

1. What are elevators? Describe their function.
(FAA-H-8083-25)

The elevators are attached to the horizontal portion of the empennage — the horizontal stabilizer. The elevators provide control of the pitch attitude about the airplane's lateral axis.

2. What are ailerons? Describe their function.
(FAA-H-8083-25)

The movable portions of each wing are the ailerons. They are located on the trailing edge of each wing near the outer tips. When deflected up or down they, in effect, change the wing's camber (curvature) and its angle of attack, and therefore change the wing's lift/drag characteristics. Their primary use is to bank (roll) the airplane around its longitudinal axis.

3. What is a rudder and what is its function?
(FAA-H-8083-25)

The rudder is attached to the fixed vertical portion of the empennage — the vertical fin or vertical stabilizer. It is used to control direction (left or right) of yaw about the airplane's vertical axis.

4. What are movable trim devices and what is their function? (FAA-H-8083-25)

A trim tab is a small auxiliary control surface hinged at the trailing edge of a primary control surface (elevator, aileron, rudder). They are commonly used to relieve the pilot of maintaining continuous pressure on the primary controls when correcting for an unbalanced flight condition resulting from changes in aerodynamic forces or weight. A trim tab acts on the primary flight control surface, which in turn acts upon the entire airplane. A trim tab is a part of the control surface but may be moved up or down independently of the surface itself.

5. Describe the direction of movement of the elevator trim tab and elevator when the pilot is applying "up" or "down" elevator trim. (FAA-H-8083-25)

An upward deflection of the trim tab will force the elevator downward with the same result as moving the elevator downward with the elevator control, and conversely a downward deflection of the trim tab will force the elevator upward. The direction the trim tab is deflected will always cause the entire elevator to be deflected in the opposite direction.

6. What are flaps and what is their function? (FAA-H-8083-25)

The wing flaps are movable panels on the inboard trailing edges of the wings. They are hinged so that they may be extended downward into the flow of air beneath the wings to increase both lift and drag. Their purpose is to permit a slower airspeed and a steeper angle of descent during a landing approach. In some cases, they may also be used to shorten the takeoff distance.

7. Name four basic types of flaps. (FAA-H-8083-25)

Plain flap — the most simple design of the four types, which when extended increases the airfoil camber, resulting in a significant increase in the coefficient of lift as well as drag at a given angle of attack. This moves the center of pressure aft on the airfoil, resulting in a nose-down pitching moment.

Split flap — deflected from the lower surface of the airfoil, this flap produces a slight increase in lift compared to the plain flap. However, more drag is created because of the turbulent air pattern produced behind the airfoil.

Slotted flap — the most popular flap on airplanes today, which increases the lift coefficient significantly more than plain or spilt flaps. When the flap is lowered, it forms a duct between the flap well in the wing and the leading edge of the flap. In this way high-energy air from the lower surface is ducted to the flap's upper surface. The high-energy air from the slot accelerates the upper surface boundary layer and delays airflow separation, providing a higher coefficient of lift.

Continued

Fowler flap—a type of slotted flap that not only changes the camber of the wing, but also increases the wing area. It slides backwards on tracks in first portion of extension significantly increasing lift with little additional drag. As extension continues, the flap deflects downward, increasing drag with little additional increase in lift.

8. When lowering the flaps, why do some aircraft encounter a pitch change?

Use of flaps alters lift distribution and consequently causes the center of pressure to move aft. Because of this movement, a nose-down pitching moment may be experienced. Low-wing aircraft are more subject to this characteristic than high wing airplanes. With flap extension on a high-wing airplane, the center of pressure also moves aft, but the airflow from the wing is directed downward which pushes down on the horizontal stabilizer. This results in a counteracting nose-up pitching moment.

Additional Study Questions

1. Describe the system of control for the elevators, ailerons and rudder on your airplane. (AFM)

2. What is adverse yaw? (FAA-H-8083-3)

3. How does an aircraft manufacturer minimize adverse yaw on an airplane? (FAA-H-8083-25)

4. Describe the location, attachments, and system of control for the trim system on your airplane. (AFM)

5. Explain the proper technique for use of trim on your airplane. (AFM)

6. What are "fixed" trim tabs and where are they normally found on aircraft? (AFM)

7. Describe the wing flap system on your airplane. (AFM)

8. Explain the proper technique for use of flaps in an airplane. (AFM)

9. **Explain how the extension of flaps will affect stall speed.** (AFM)

10. **Explain the procedure for dealing with a "split" or asymmetric flap situation.** (AFM)

E. Airplane Weight and Balance

1. **Define the following weight and balance terms:**

   Arm; Basic Operating Weight; Center of Gravity; Center of Gravity Limits; Center of Gravity Range; Datum; Empty Weight; Fuel Load; Moment; Moment Index; Station; Useful Load. (FAA-H-8083-1)

   Arm—The horizontal distance in inches from the reference datum line to the center of gravity of an item.

   Basic Operating Weight—The weight of the aircraft, including the crew, ready for flight but without payload and fuel. This term is only applicable to transport aircraft.

   Center of Gravity—The point about which an aircraft would balance if it were possible to suspend it at that point, expressed in inches from datum.

   Center of Gravity Limits—The specified forward and aft or lateral points beyond which the CG must not be located during takeoff, flight or landing.

   Center of Gravity Range—The distance between the forward and aft CG limits indicated on pertinent aircraft specifications.

   Datum—An imaginary vertical plane or line from which all measurements of arm are taken. It is established by the manufacturer.

   Empty Weight—The airframe, engines, and all items of operating equipment that have fixed locations and are permanently installed in the aircraft. It includes optional and special equipment, fixed ballast, hydraulic fluid, unusable fuel, and undrainable oil.

   Fuel Load—The expendable part of the load of the aircraft. It includes only usable fuel, not fuel required to fill the lines or that which remains trapped in the tank sumps.

   Continued

Moment—The product of the weight of an item multiplied by its arm. Moments are expressed in pound-inches.

Moment Index—A moment divided by a constant such as 100, 1,000, or 10,000. The purpose of using a moment index is to simplify weight and balance computations of large aircraft where heavy items and long arms result in large, unmanageable numbers.

Station—A location in the aircraft which is identified by a number designating its distance in inches from the datum. The datum is, therefore, identified as station zero. The station and arm are usually identical. An item located at station +50 would have an arm of 50 inches.

Useful Load—The weight of the pilot, copilot, passengers, baggage, usable fuel and drainable oil. It is the empty weight subtracted from the maximum allowable takeoff weight. The term applies to general aviation aircraft only.

2. What performance characteristics will be adversely affected when an aircraft has been overloaded? (FAA-H-8083-1)

a. Higher takeoff speed

b. Longer takeoff run

c. Reduced rate and angle of climb

d. Lower maximum altitude

e. Shorter range

f. Reduced cruising speed

g. Reduced maneuverability

h. Higher stalling speed

i. Higher landing speed

j. Longer landing roll

k. Excessive weight on the nosewheel

3. What effect does a forward center of gravity have on an aircraft's flight characteristics? (FAA-H-8083-25)

Higher stall speed—Stalling angle of attack reached at a higher speed due to increased wing loading.

Slower cruise speed—Increased drag, greater angle of attack required to maintain altitude.

More stable—When angle of attack is increased, the airplane tends to reduce angle of attack; longitudinal stability is improved.

Greater back elevator pressure required—Longer takeoff roll, higher approach speeds and problems with the landing flare.

4. What effect does an aft center of gravity have on an aircraft's flight characteristics? (FAA-H-8083-25)

Lower stall speed—Less wing loading.

Higher cruise speed—Reduced drag, smaller angle of attack required to maintain altitude.

Less stable—Stall and spin recovery more difficult; when angle of attack is increased it tends to result in additional increased angle of attack.

5. What basic equation is used in all weight and balance problems to find the center of gravity location of an airplane and/or its components? (FAA-H-8083-25)

Weight x Arm = Moment

By rearrangement of this equation to the forms,
Weight = Moment ÷ Arm
Arm = Moment ÷ Weight
CG = Moment ÷ Weight

With any two known values, the third value can be found.

Additional Study Questions

1. **If the weight of an aircraft is within takeoff limits but the CG limit has been exceeded, what actions can the pilot take to correct the situation?** (FAA-H-8083-25)

2. **When a shift in weight is required, what standardized and simple calculations can be made to determine the new CG?** (FAA-H-8083-25)

3. **If the weight of an aircraft changes due to the addition or removal of cargo or passengers before flight, what formula may be used to calculate the new CG?** (FAA-H-8083-25)

4. **What simple and fundamental weight check can be made before all flights?** (FAA-H-8083-25)

F. Navigation and Flight Planning

1. **What are three common ways to navigate?** (FAA-H-8083-25)

   To navigate successfully, a pilot must know their approximate position at all times or be able to determine it whenever they wish. Position may be determined by:

   a. Pilotage (reference to visible landmarks);

   b. Dead reckoning (computing direction and distance from a known position); or

   c. Radio navigation (use of radio aids).

2. **Define the following terms:** (FAA-H-8083-25)

   Isogonic line—connect points of equal magnetic variation; found on most aeronautical charts and show amount and direction of variation.

   Magnetic variation—the error induced by the difference in location of true north and magnetic north. Expressed in east or west variation.

Magnetic deviation—the amount of deflection of the compass needle caused by magnetic influences within the airplane (electrical circuits, radios, lights, tools, engine magnetized metal parts, etc.)

Lines of latitude—circles parallel to the equator (lines running east and west); used to measure distance in degrees north or south of the equator.

Line of longitude—lines drawn from the north pole to the south pole and are at right angles to the equator. The Prime Meridian is used as the zero reference line from which measurement is made in degrees east or west to 180 degrees.

Course—the intended path of an aircraft over the earth; or the direction of a line drawn on a chart representing the intended aircraft path.

Heading—direction the nose of the airplane points during flight.

Track—the actual path made over the ground in flight.

Drift angle—the angle between heading and track.

Wind correction angle—correction applied to the course to establish a heading so track will coincide with course.

3. What is the basic formula for determining a compass heading? (FAA-H-8083-25)

TC +/- WCA = TH +/- VAR = MH +/- DEV = CH

4. Explain, as you would to a student, the procedure for planning a VFR cross-country.

  a. Get a preflight briefing consisting of the latest or most current weather, airport, and enroute NAVAID information.

  b. Draw course lines and mark checkpoints on the chart.

  c. Enter checkpoints on the log.

  d. Enter NAVAIDs on the log.

  e. Enter VOR courses on the log.

  f. Enter altitude on the log.

  g. Enter the wind (direction/velocity) and temperature on the log.

  h. Measure the true course on the chart and enter it on the log.

Continued

    i. Compute the true airspeed and enter it on the log.

    j. Compute the WCA and groundspeed and enter them on the log.

    k. Determine variation from chart and enter it on the log.

    l. Determine deviation from compass correction card and enter it on the log.

    m. Enter compass heading on the log.

    n. Measure distances on the chart and enter them on the log.

    o. Figure ETE and ETA and enter them on the log.

    p. Calculate fuel burn and usage; enter them on the log.

    q. Compute weight and balance.

    r. Compute takeoff and landing performance.

    s. Complete a Flight Plan form.

    t. File the Flight Plan with FSS.

5. Explain the procedure for diverting to an alternate. (FAA-H-8083-25)

    a. Mark your present position on the chart; write the current time next to your mark.

    b. Consider the relative distance to all suitable alternates; select the one most appropriate for emergency.

    c. Determine the magnetic course to the alternate and divert immediately.

    d. Wind correction, actual distance and estimated time/fuel can then be computed while en route to alternate.

Note: Use the radial of a nearby VOR or airway that most closely parallels the course to the alternate. Distances can be determined by placing a finger at the appropriate place on a straight edge of a piece of paper and then measuring the approximate distance on the mileage scale at the bottom of the chart.

Additional Study Questions

1. Explain the various terms and symbols on a sectional chart.

2. Explain the different types of airspace on a sectional chart.

3. What are several types of radio aids to use for navigation? (FAA-H-8083-25)

4. What is a VOR and explain, as you would to a student, how to use it for navigation. (FAA-H-8083-25)

5. Explain the purpose of and the procedure used in filing a flight plan. (FAA-H-8083-25)

6. What procedures will you teach your student to use, in the event they should become lost on a cross-country flight? (FAA-H-8083-25)

7. Explain the procedure for calculating fuel consumption. (FAA-H-8083-25)

8. Explain the importance of preparing and properly using a flight log. (FAA-H-8083-25)

G. Night Operations

1. What is the function of the rods and cones, and where are they located in the eye? (FAA-H-8083-3)

Rods—concentrated in a ring around the cones; primary function is peripheral vision. The process of night vision is placed almost entirely on the rods; about 30 minutes is needed for the rods to become adjusted to darkness; when adjusted they are about 100,000 times more sensitive to light.

Cones—located in the center of the retina and their function is to detect color, details, and faraway objects; after approximately 5 to 10 minutes, cones become adjusted to the dim light and the eyes become 100 times more sensitive.

2. What can the pilot do to improve the effectiveness of vision at night? (FAA-H-8083-3)

a. Adapt the eyes to darkness prior to flight and keep them adapted; usually 30 minutes is needed to adjust the eyes to maximum efficiency.

b. If oxygen is available, use it during night flying; a significant deterioration in night vision can occur at cabin altitudes as low as 5,000 feet.

c. Close one eye when exposed to bright light to help avoid the blinding effect.

d. Do not wear sunglasses after sunset.

e. Move the eyes more slowly than in daylight.

f. Blink the eyes if they become blurred.

g. Concentrate on seeing objects.

h. Force the eyes to view off center.

i. Maintain good physical condition.

j. Avoid smoking, drinking, and using drugs that may be harmful.

3. During preflight, what things should be done to adequately prepare for a night flight? (FAA-H-8083-3)

a. Study all weather reports and forecasts. Pay particular attention to temperature/dew point spreads to detect the possibility of fog formation.

b. Calculate wind directions and speeds along the proposed route of flight to ensure accurate drift calculations, as night visual perception of drift is generally inaccurate.

c. Obtain applicable aeronautical charts for both the proposed route as well as adjacent charts and clearly mark lighted checkpoints.

d. Review all radio navigational aids for correct frequencies and availability.

e. Check all personal equipment such as flashlights and portable transceivers for proper operation.

f. Do a thorough preflight inspection of the aircraft.

g. Check all aircraft position lights, as well as the landing light and rotating beacon, for proper operation.

h. Check ground areas for obstructions that may not be readily visible from the cockpit.

4. What are some guidelines to follow during the starting, taxiing, and run-up phases of a night flight? (FAA-H-8083-3)

a. The pilot should exercise extra caution on "clearing" the propeller arc area. The use of lights prior to engine startup can also alert persons in the area to the presence of the active aircraft.

b. During taxiing, avoid unnecessary use of electrical equipment which would put an abnormal load on the electrical system, such as the landing light.

c. Taxi slowly and follow any taxi lines.

5. What are some guidelines to follow during takeoff and departure phases of a night flight? (FAA-H-8083-3)

During takeoff the pilot should, on initial takeoff roll, use the distant runway edge lights as well as the landing light area to keep the aircraft straight and parallel with the runway on initial takeoff roll; and upon liftoff, keep a positive climb by referencing the attitude indicator along with positive rate of climb on the vertical speed indicator.

During climbout the pilot should not initiate any turns until reaching a safe maneuvering altitude, and should turn the landing light off as soon as possible.

6. What procedures should be followed during the approach and landing phase of a night flight?
(FAA-P-8740-50)

a. Allow plenty of time to do your pre-landing checklist before entering the pattern.

b. In the pattern, maintain the recommended speeds—don't exceed them. Give yourself plenty of time to prepare for the approach and landing.

c. A long, low final is to be avoided at all costs. Unseen obstacles around the airport are a prime reason to always check flight information publications for airport details before you launch.

d. On approach, make sure your glide path is high enough to stay well clear of all obstacles—not just the ones you can see.

e. Be sure your directional gyro is aligned with the magnetic compass. It will help you locate the runway you'll want to use. Also, set the heading bug on the DG (or heading indicator) if so equipped. The "bug" helps in flying a square pattern at night.

f. Set your altimeter. Remember, a one inch decrease in barometric pressure means your altimeter reading is about one thousand feet higher than your actual altitude.

g. On final, take advantage of VASI guidance where available. Never allow a "low" indication to appear at night. Get back up to your glide path immediately or take it around and try again.

Additional Study Questions

1. When approaching a well-lighted runway surrounded by a dark area with little or no features, what illusion should a pilot be alert for? (AIM 8-1-5)

2. If an engine failure occurs at night, what procedures should be followed? (FAA-H-8083-3)

3. Explain the procedure for conducting an approach and landing at night with no landing light. (FAA-H-8083-3)

4. What equipment is required on an aircraft for night flights? (14 CFR 91.205)

5. Explain the function and color of the following airport lighting: runway edge lights, runway end identifier lights (REIL), taxiway edge lights, taxiway centerline lights. (AIM 2-1-1 through 2-1-9)

6. What additional equipment should the pilot have in the cockpit for night flight operations? (FAA-H-8083-3)

H. High Altitude Operations

1. **What are the regulations concerning use of supplemental oxygen on board an aircraft?** (14 CFR 91.211)

   No person may operate a civil aircraft of U.S. registry:

   a. At cabin pressure altitudes above 12,500 feet MSL up to and including 14,000 feet MSL, unless, for that part of the flight at those altitudes that is more than 30 minutes, the required minimum flight crew is provided with and uses supplemental oxygen.

   b. At cabin pressure altitudes above 14,000 feet MSL, unless the required flight crew is provided with and uses supplemental oxygen for the entire flight time at those altitudes.

   c. At cabin pressure altitudes above 15,000 feet MSL, unless each occupant is provided with supplemental oxygen.

2. What is a "pressurized" aircraft? (FAA-H-8083-25)

In a "pressurized" aircraft, the cabin, flight compartment, and baggage compartments are incorporated into a sealed unit that is capable of containing air under a pressure higher than outside atmospheric pressure. On aircraft powered by turbine engines, bleed air from the engine compressor section is used to pressurize the cabin. Superchargers may be used on older model turbine powered airplanes to pump air into the sealed fuselage. Piston-powered airplanes may use air supplied from each engine turbocharger through a sonic venturi (flow limiter). Air is released from the fuselage by a device called an outflow valve. The outflow valve, by regulating the air exit, provides a constant inflow of air to the pressurized area.

3. What are the three types of oxygen systems normally in use? (FAA-H-8083-25)

Diluter demand system—supplies oxygen only when the user inhales through the mask.

Pressure demand system—similar to diluter demand oxygen equipment, except that oxygen is supplied to the mask under pressure at cabin altitudes above 34,000 feet.

Continuous flow system—system that is usually provided for passengers. Passenger mask typically has a reservoir bag, which collects oxygen from the continuous flow oxygen system during the time when the mask user is exhaling.

4. Can any kind of oxygen be used for aviator's breathing oxygen? (AC 65-15)

No, oxygen used for medical purposes or welding normally should not be used because it may contain too much water. The excess water could condense and freeze in the oxygen lines when flying at high altitudes. Specifications for "aviator's breathing oxygen" are 99.5% pure oxygen with not more than two milliliters of water per liter of oxygen.

5. What are the two types of decompression?
(FAA-H-8083-25)

Explosive decompression—Cabin pressure decreases faster than the lungs can decompress. Most authorities consider any kind of decompression which occurs in less than 1/2 second as explosive and potentially dangerous. This type of decompression could only be caused by structural damage, material failure, or by a door "popping" open.

Rapid decompression—A change in cabin pressure where the lungs decompress faster than the cabin. There is no likelihood of lung damage in this case. This type could be caused by a failure or malfunction in the pressurization system itself, or through slow leaks in the pressurized area.

Additional Study Questions

1. **What are the regulations pertaining to the use of supplemental oxygen on board a "pressurized" aircraft?** (14 CFR 91.211)

2. **Describe a typical cabin pressure control system.** (FAA-H-8083-25)

3. **What are the components of a cabin pressure control system?** (FAA-H-8083-25)

4. **How does a continuous-flow oxygen system operate?** (AC 65-15)

5. **What are the dangers of decompression?** (FAA-H-8083-25)

I. Federal Aviation Regulations and Publications

1. What is the purpose and general content of the following parts of the Federal Aviation Regulations?

14 CFR Part 61 .... Certification: Pilots, Flight Instructors, and Ground Instructors

14 CFR Part 91 .... General Operating and Flight Rules

14 CFR Part 141 .... Pilot Schools

2. What is the purpose and general content of NTSB Part 830?

Notification and reporting of aircraft accidents or incidents and overdue aircraft and preservation of aircraft wreckage, mail, cargo and records.

3. What is the *Aeronautical Information Manual*? (AIM)

A primary FAA publication whose purpose is to instruct airmen about operating in the National Airspace System of the U.S. It provides basic flight information, ATC procedures and general instructional information concerning health, medical facts, factors affecting flight safety, accident and hazard reporting, and types of aeronautical charts and their use.

4. What are Advisory Circulars? (AC 00-2)

The FAA issues advisory circulars to inform the aviation public in a systematic way of non-regulatory material. Unless incorporated into a regulation by reference, the contents of an advisory circular are not binding on the public. Advisory circulars are issued in a numbered-subject system corresponding to the subject areas of 14 CFR Chapter 1. An AC is issued to provide guidance and information in a designated subject area or to show a method acceptable to the FAA.

5. **Explain the purpose and general content of the Practical Test Standards.** (FAA-H-8083-3)

These are published by the FAA to establish the standards for the various practical tests administered for obtaining a pilot certificate or rating. The tests are conducted in compliance with these standards. They are available from the GPO or as reprints from commercial publishers.

6. **Explain availability, purpose, and general content of the** *Airport/Facility Directory* **(A/FD).** (FAA-H-8083-25)

It is a 7-volume booklet series containing data on airports, Seaplane bases, heliports, NAVAIDs, communications data, weather data sources, airspace, special notices, and operational procedures. Coverage includes the conterminous U.S., Puerto Rico, and the Virgin Islands. The A/FD shows data that cannot be readily depicted in graphic form; e.g. airport hours of operations, types of fuel available, runway widths, lighting codes, etc. Also provides a means for pilots to update visual charts between edition dates — it is published every 56 days while sectional and Terminal Area Charts are generally revised every six months.

Additional Study Questions

1. **How often are the regulations revised and how are pilots notified?**

2. **What is the purpose and general content of the following Parts of 14 CFR: 1, 23, 43, 67, and 135?**

3. **What advisory circular should be referenced for the appropriate endorsements when recommending an applicant for a practical test?**

4. **What are NOTAMs and where can they be found?** (FAA-H-8083-25)

5. **Explain the differences between FAA Approved Airplane Flight Manuals, Pilot Operating Handbooks, and Owner's Manuals.**

J. National Airspace System

1. What is Class A airspace? (AIM 3-2-2)

Generally, that airspace from 18,000 feet MSL up to and including FL600, including that airspace overlying the waters within 12 nautical miles of the coast of the 48 contiguous states and Alaska; and designated international airspace beyond 12 nautical miles of the coast of the 48 contiguous states and Alaska within areas of domestic radio navigational signal or ATC radar coverage, and within which domestic procedures are applied.

2. What is Class B airspace? (AIM 3-2-3)

Generally, that airspace from the surface to 10,000 feet MSL surrounding the nation's busiest airports in terms of IFR operations or passenger enplanements. The configuration of each Class B airspace area is individually tailored and consists of a surface area and two or more layers (some Class B airspace areas resemble upside down wedding cakes), and is designed to contain all published instrument procedures once an aircraft enters the airspace.

3. What is Class C airspace? (AIM 3-2-4)

Generally, that airspace from the surface to 4,000 feet above the airport elevation (charted in MSL) surrounding those airports that have an operational control tower, are serviced by a radar approach control, and that have a certain number of IFR operations or passenger enplanements.

4. What is Class D airspace? (AIM 3-2-5)

Generally, that airspace from the surface to 2,500 feet above the airport elevation (charted in MSL) surrounding those airports that have an operational control tower. The configuration of each Class D airspace area is individually tailored and when instrument procedures are published, the airspace will normally be designed to contain those procedures.

5. What is Class E (controlled) airspace? (AIM 3-2-6)

Generally, if the airspace is not Class A, Class B, Class C, or Class D, and it is controlled airspace, it is Class E airspace. Except for 18,000 feet MSL, Class E airspace has no defined vertical limit but rather it extends upward from either the surface or a designated altitude to the overlying or adjacent controlled airspace.

6. What is Class G (uncontrolled) airspace? (AIM 3-3-1)

Class G, or uncontrolled airspace is that portion of the airspace that has not been designated as Class A, B, C, D, and E airspace. Class G airspace begins at the surface and continues up to the overlying controlled (Class E) airspace, not to exceed 14,500 feet MSL.

7. Define the following types of special use airspace. (AIM 3-4-1 through 3-4-8)

Prohibited Area—For security or other reasons, aircraft flight is prohibited.

Restricted Area—Contains unusual, often invisible hazards to aircraft. Flights must have permission from the controlling agency if VFR. IFR flights will be cleared through or vectored around it.

Military Operations Area—Designed to separate military training from IFR traffic. Permission is not required but VFR flights should exercise caution. IFR flights will be cleared through or vectored around it.

Warning Area—Same hazards as a restricted area; extends from 3 nautical miles outward from the coast of the United States and contains activity that may be hazardous to nonparticipating aircraft; may be located over domestic or international waters or both.

Alert Area—Airspace containing a high volume of pilot training or an unusual type of aerial activity. No permission required but VFR flights should be particularly alert when flying in these areas. All activity shall be conducted in accordance with CFRs, without waiver. All pilots will be equally responsible for collision avoidance.

Continued

Controlled Firing Areas — CFAs contain activities which, if not conducted in a controlled environment, could be hazardous to non-participating aircraft. Activities are suspended immediately when spotter aircraft, radar or ground lookout positions indicate an aircraft might be approaching the area. CFAs are not charted.

National Security Areas — Airspace of defined vertical and lateral dimensions established at locations where there is a requirement for increased security and safety of ground facilities. Pilots are requested to voluntarily avoid flying through the depicted NSA. When it is necessary to provide a greater level of security and safety, flight in NSAs may be temporarily prohibited by regulation under the provisions of 14 CFR §99.7.

8. What is a TFR? (AC 91-63C)

Temporary Flight Restriction — a regulatory action issued via the U.S. Notice to Airmen (NOTAM) system to restrict certain aircraft from operating within a defined area, on a temporary basis, to protect persons or property in the air or on the ground.

9. What circumstances might cause the FAA to issue a TFR? (AC 91-63C)

While not an exhaustive list, a TFR may be issued for the following reasons: toxic gas leaks or spills; fumes from flammable agents which, if fanned by rotor or propeller wash, could endanger persons or property on the surface or in other aircraft; volcanic eruptions that could endanger airborne aircraft and occupants; hijacking incidents that may endanger persons or property on the surface, or airborne aircraft and occupants; aircraft accident/incident sites; aviation or ground resources engaged in wildfire suppression; aircraft relief activities following a disaster; aerial demonstrations or major sporting events; or reasons of national security.

10. How do I determine if a TFR has been issued for a specific area? (AC 91-63C)

National Airspace System (NAS) users or other interested parties should contact the nearest flight service station for TFR information. Additionally, you can find TFR information on automated briefings, NOTAM publications, and on the Internet at http://www.faa.gov. The FAA also distributes TFR information to aviation user groups and requests these groups to further disseminate the information to their members.

Additional Study Questions

1. **Explain the general dimensions for each class of airspace.** (AIM 3-2-1 through 3-2-6)

2. **Give examples of "other" airspace areas.** (AIM 3-5-1 through 3-5-7)

3. **What are the cloud clearance and visibility requirements to operate under VFR in controlled and uncontrolled airspace?** (14 CFR 91.155)

4. **Explain the requirements to operate under "Special VFR."** (14 CFR 91.157)

K. Navigation Aids and Radar Services

1. Name several types of radio aids to air navigation.

a. VOR (Very High Frequency Omnidirectional Range)
b. NDB (Nondirectional Radio Beacon)
c. RNAV (Area Navigation)
d. DME (Distance Measuring Equipment)
e. LORAN (Long Range Navigation)
f. GPS (Global Positioning Systems)

2. What is a VOR or VORTAC? (FAA-H-8083-25)

VORs are VHF radio stations that project radials in all directions (360°) from the station like spokes from the hub of a wheel. Each radial is denoted by its outbound magnetic direction. Almost all VOR stations will also be VORTACs (VOR-Tactical Air Navigation) which provide the standard bearing information of a VOR plus distance information to pilots of airplanes with DME. VOR transmitting frequencies of omnirange stations are in the VHF (very high frequency) band between 108 and 117.95 MHz, which are immediately below aviation communication frequencies.

3. What is an NDB? (AIM 1-1-2)

Nondirectional beacon—A low–medium frequency radio beacon transmits nondirectional signals whereby the pilot of a properly equipped aircraft can determine his bearing, then "home" or "track" to the station. NDBs normally operate in the frequency band of 190 to 535 kHz (immediately below AM broadcast bands) and transmit a continuous carrier with either 400 or 1020 Hz modulation. All radio beacons, except compass locators, transmit a continuous three-letter identification code.

4. What is ADF? (FAA-H-8083-25)

Automatic Direction Finder—Many GA airplanes are equipped with ADF radio receiving equipment which operates in the low–medium frequency bands. To navigate using the ADF, the pilot tunes the receiving equipment to an NDB. The most common use of ADF is that of "homing" by flying the needle to the station.

5. What is DME? (FAA-H-8083-25)

Distance measuring equipment (DME) is an ultra-high frequency (UHF) navigational aid present with VOR/DMEs and VORTACs. It measures, in nautical miles (NM), the slant range distance of an airplane from a VOR/DME or VORTAC (both hereafter referred to as a VORTAC). DME operates on frequencies in the UHF spectrum between 960 MHz and 1215 MHz. Reliable signals may be received at distances up to 199 NM at line-of-sight altitude.

6. What is RNAV? (P/CG)

Area Navigation (RNAV) is enhanced navigational capability for the pilot. RNAV equipment can compute the airplane position, actual track and ground speed, and then provide meaningful information relative to a route of flight selected by the pilot. Typical equipment provides distance, time, bearing, and crosstrack error relative to the selected "TO" or "active" waypoint and route. Several distinctly different navigational systems are capable of providing area navigational functions. Present day RNAV includes INS, LORAN, VOR/DME, and GPS systems.

7. Give a brief description of GPS. (AIM 1-1-19)

Global Positioning System— A satellite-based radio navigation system which broadcasts a signal that is used by receivers to determine precise position anywhere in the world. The receiver tracks multiple satellites and determines a pseudo-range measurement that is then used to determine the user location.

8. What is radar? (FAA-H-8083-3)

Radar is a device that detects objects that reflect back transmitted pulses. The reflected pulses are electronically processed to obtain information regarding distance and azimuth.

9. What are the types of radar systems? (FAA-H-8083-3)

Primary—A radar system in which a tiny portion of a radio pulse transmitted from a site is reflected by an object and then received back at the same site for processing and display at an ATC facility. In a primary system, large aircraft reflect better than small ones, and close aircraft reflect better than distant ones. Even the aircraft's structure (wood, fabric, aluminum, or composite) affects the strength of the reflected radio pulse.

Secondary—one in which the aircraft responds to a radio pulse (an interrogation) from a site with a distinctive transmission from its transponder. This reply transmission, rather than the directly reflected signal, is received at the site for processing and display. Secondary radar is typically used in conjunction with primary radar at most locations although some sites are equipped only with secondary radar. Sometimes referred to as the air traffic control radar beacon system (ATCRBS).

10. Can a hand-held GPS receiver be used as the primary means of navigation on a VFR cross-country flight? (AIM 1-1-19)

Types of receivers used for GPS navigation under VFR are varied, from a full IFR installation used to support a VFR flight, to a VFR only installation (in either a VFR or IFR capable aircraft), to a hand-held receiver. You need to understand the limitations of each type of installation in order to avoid misusing navigation information. In all cases, VFR pilots should never rely solely on one system of navigation. GPS navigation must be integrated with other forms of electronic navigation (when possible), as well as pilotage and dead reckoning. Only through the integration of these techniques can the VFR pilot ensure accuracy in navigation.

11. When considering the use of a VFR GPS or hand-held GPS receiver for VFR navigation, what operational limitations should a pilot be aware of? (AIM 1-1-19)

a. *RAIM capability*—VFR GPS receivers and all hand-held units have no RAIM alerting capability. This means that the pilot can't see information such as the loss of the required number of satellites in view, or the detection of a position error.

b. *Database currency* — In many receivers, an updatable database is used for navigation fixes, airports, and instrument procedures. These databases must be maintained to the current update for IFR operation, but no such requirement exists for VFR use.

c. *Antenna location* — In many VFR installations of GPS receivers, antenna location is more a matter of convenience than performance. In IFR installations, care is exercised to ensure that an adequate clear view is provided for the antenna to see satellites. If an alternate location is used, some portion of the aircraft may block the view of the antenna which means there is a chance you could lose navigation.

12. What are the two different types of ATC radar facilities? (FAA-H-8083-15)

a. *Terminal Radar Approach Control (TRACON)* — Considered terminal facilities because they provide the link between the departure airport and the enroute structure of the NAS. Terminal airspace normally extends 30 nautical miles (NM) from the facility, with a vertical extent of 10,000 feet; however, dimensions vary widely. Class B and Class C airspace dimensions are provided on aeronautical charts. All terminal facilities are approach controls, and should be addressed as "Approach" except when directed to do otherwise ("Contact departure on 120.4").

b. *Air Route Traffic Control Center (ARTCC)* — Responsible for maintaining separation between IFR flights in the enroute structure. Center radars (Air Route Surveillance Radar) acquire and track transponder returns using the same basic technology as terminal radars. Center airspace is divided into sectors and additionally divided by altitudes (high and low sectors). Each sector has a dedicated team of controllers and a selection of radio frequencies, because each Center has a network of remote transmitter/receiver sites. All Center frequencies are listed in the back of the A/FD and on IFR enroute charts.

Additional Study Questions

1. Each VOR indicator is composed of several elements. What are they? (FAA-H-8083-25)

2. When navigating by VOR, when will you have "reverse" sensing? (FAA-H-8083-25)

3. How are VOR NAVAIDs classified and what reception distances can be expected? (FAA-H-8083-25)

4. How will you teach your student to intercept and track a radial to or from a VOR station? (FAA-H-8083-25)

5. How will you teach your student to "home" to an NDB station? To track to an NDB station? (FAA-H-8083-25)

6. What are some advantages and disadvantages when using ADF for navigation? (FAA-H-8083-25)

7. The GPS system is composed of what three major elements? (FAA-H-8083-25)

8. How does a GPS system determine its position? (FAA-H-8083-25)

9. What is RAIM? (FAA-H-8083-15)

10. What are several limitations of ATC radar? (FAA-H-8083-25)

L. Logbook Entries and Certificate Endorsements

1. **As a CFI, what are the endorsements you will use for student pilots?** (AC 61-65)

   a. Pre-solo aeronautical knowledge

   b. Pre-solo flight training

   c. Pre-solo flight training at night

   d. Solo flight (each additional 90-day period)

   e. Solo takeoffs and landings at another airport within 25 NM

   f. Initial solo cross-country flight

   g. Solo cross-country flight

   h. Repeated solo cross-country flights not more than 50 NM from point of departure

   i. Solo flight in Class B airspace

   j. Solo flight to, from, or at an airport located in Class B airspace

2. **What are the required student pilot certificate endorsements and logbook entries required of you as CFI, before allowing a student pilot to conduct their first solo flight?** (AC 61-65)

   Prior to solo flight a student pilot is required to receive the following:

   a. An endorsement in their logbook for satisfactory completion of pre-solo aeronautical exam.

   b. An endorsement in their logbook for receiving required pre-solo training in make and model of aircraft.

   c. An endorsement on their student pilot certificate for the make and model of aircraft flown.

3. What are the required student pilot certificate endorsements and logbook entries required of you as CFI, before allowing a student pilot to conduct the initial solo cross-country flight? (AC 61-65)

Prior to the initial solo cross-country flight the student is required to receive:

a. An endorsement in their logbook from the instructor who has given the required solo cross-country training for the make and model of aircraft to be flown.

b. An endorsement on their student pilot certificate for the specific category to be flown.

c. An endorsement in their logbook for the specific solo cross-country flight to be flown.

Note: The CFI should also determine the student's solo flight endorsement is current for the make and model to be flown.

4. Your student is making the final preparations for a solo cross-country flight you have instructed them to make. You are not available to review the planning and preparation as required. Can another CFI conduct the review and provide the necessary endorsement? (AC 61-65)

Yes; before each cross-country flight, the student's logbook must be endorsed by an instructor, but this instructor need not be the instructor who provided the initial cross-country instruction to the student.

5. Give examples of additional endorsements you may give as a CFI. (AC 61-65)

Within the limitations of your flight instructor certificate and ratings, and your pilot certificate and ratings, you may give training and endorsements for:

a. Completion of a flight review

b. Completion of a phase of an FAA-sponsored pilot proficiency award program

c. Completion of an instrument proficiency check

d. To act as PIC in a complex airplane

e. To act as PIC in a high-performance airplane

f. To act as PIC in a pressurized aircraft capable of high altitude operations

g. To act as PIC in a tailwheel airplane

h. To act as PIC of an aircraft in solo operation when the pilot does not hold an appropriate category and class rating

i. Retesting after failure of a knowledge or practical test

6. Must the student pilot's certificate be endorsed every 90 days or is this endorsement required only in the student pilot's logbook? (AC 61-65)

The 90-day solo endorsement that is entered in the student's logbook is required every 90 days for continuing solo privileges. The endorsement on the student pilot certificate is a one-time endorsement.

Additional Study Questions

1. Your student recently soloed in a C-152. The student has expressed interest in transitioning to a C-172 for the remainder of the flight training and the checkride. What actions must you take to allow this student to solo a C-172? (14 CFR 61.87)

2. If a student pilot has their student pilot certificate endorsed to fly more than one model of aircraft in solo flight, is a logbook endorsement required for each one of these models? (14 CFR 61.87)

3. Another CFI has requested you review the preflight planning and preparation of their student for a solo cross-country flight. While conducting the review you notice that the 90-day solo endorsement has expired. Are you allowed to provide another 90-day solo endorsement or must you first fly with that student? (14 CFR 61.93)

Continued

4. **What distance from the point of departure is a student pilot allowed to fly, if his/her logbook has not been endorsed for cross-country flights?** (14 CFR 61.93)

5. **As a CFI-ASEL with no tailwheel experience, are you allowed to give a tailwheel endorsement?** (14 CFR 61.31 and 61.193)

M. Airworthiness Requirements

1. **What instruments and equipment are required for VFR day flight?** (14 CFR 91.205)

For VFR flight during the day, the following instruments and equipment are required:

T achometer for each engine

O il pressure gauge for each engine

M anifold Pressure gage for each altitude engine

A ltimeter

T emperature gage for each liquid-cooled engine

O il temperature gage for each air-cooled engine

F uel gage indicating the quantity in each tank

F lotation gear—if operated for hire over water beyond power off gliding distance from shore

L anding gear position indicator, if the airplane has retractable gear

A irspeed indicator

A nticollision light system—aviation red and white for small airplanes certificated after March 31,1996

M agnetic direction indicator

E mergency locator transmitter (if required by 14 CFR 91.207)

S afety belts (and shoulder harnesses for each front seat in aircraft manufactured after 1978)

2. What instruments and equipment are required for VFR night flight? (14 CFR 91.205)

Instruments and equipment required for VFR day flight and the following—

F uses—one spare set or three fuses of each kind required accessible to the pilot in flight.

L anding light—if the aircraft is operated for hire

A nticollision light system—approved aviation red or white

P osition lights—(navigation lights)

S ource of electrical energy—adequate for all installed electrical and radio equipment

3. Can a pilot conduct flight operations in an aircraft with known inoperative equipment? (AC 91-67, 14 CFR 91.213)

14 CFR Part 91 describes acceptable methods for the operation of an aircraft with certain inoperative instruments and equipment which are not essential for safe flight:

a. Operation of aircraft with a Minimum Equipment List (MEL), as authorized by 14 CFR 91.213(a).

b. Operation of aircraft without a MEL under 14 CFR 91.213(d).

4. What are Minimum Equipment Lists? (AC 91-67)

It is a precise list of instruments, equipment and procedures allowing an aircraft to be operated under specific conditions with inoperative equipment. The MEL is the specific inoperative equipment document for a particular make and model aircraft by serial and registration numbers; e.g., BE-200, N12345. The FAA-approved MEL includes only those items of equipment which the FAA finds may be inoperative and still maintain an acceptable level of safety.

5. What limitations apply to aircraft operations conducted using the deferral provision of 14 CFR §91.213(d)? (FAA-H-8083-25)

According to 14 CFR §91.213(d), when inoperative equipment is found during preflight or prior to departure, the decision should be to cancel the flight, obtain maintenance prior to flight, or to defer the item or equipment. Maintenance deferrals are not used for in-flight discrepancies; the manufacturer's AFM/POH procedures are to be used in those situations.

6. What limitations apply to aircraft operations being conducted using MELs? (FAA-H-8083-25)

The FAA considers an approved MEL to be a supplemental type certificate (STC) issued to an aircraft by serial number and registration number. It therefore becomes the authority to operate that aircraft in a condition other than originally type certificated. Once an operator requests an MEL, a Letter of Authorization (LOA) is issued by the FAA; then the use of the MEL becomes mandatory for that airplane. All maintenance deferrals must be accomplished in accordance with the terms and conditions of the MEL and the operator-generated procedures document.

7. What are the procedures for using the deferral provision of 14 CFR §91.213(d)? (FAA-H-8083-25)

The pilot determines whether the inoperative equipment is required by type design, the CFRs, or ADs. If the inoperative item is not required, and the airplane can be safely operated without it, the deferral may be made. The inoperative item shall be deactivated or removed and an INOPERATIVE placard placed near the appropriate switch, control, or indicator. If deactivation or removal involves maintenance (removal always will), it must be accomplished by certificated maintenance personnel. For example, if the position lights (installed equipment) were discovered to be inoperative prior to a daytime flight, the pilot would follow the requirements of §91.213(d).

8. What are Special Flight Permits? (FAA-H-8083-25)

A special flight permit is an authorization to operate an aircraft that may not currently meet applicable airworthiness requirements, but is safe for a specific flight. Before the permit is issued, an FAA inspector may personally inspect the aircraft or require it to be inspected by a certificated airframe and powerplant mechanic or repair station to determine its safety for the intended flight. The inspection must be recorded in the aircraft logbooks. It is issued to allow the aircraft to be flown to a base where repairs, alterations, or maintenance can be performed; for delivering or exporting the aircraft; or for evacuating an aircraft from an area of impending danger. A special flight permit may be issued to allow the operation of an overweight aircraft for flight beyond its normal range over water or land areas where adequate landing facilities or fuel is not available.

9. What is the procedure for obtaining a special flight permit? (FAA-H-8083-25)

If a special flight permit is needed, assistance and the necessary forms may be obtained from the local FSDO or Designated Airworthiness Representative (DAR).

10. What is an Airworthiness Directive? (FAA-H-8083-25)

An AD is the primary medium the FAA uses to notify aircraft owners and other interested persons of unsafe conditions and to prescribe the conditions under which the product may continue to be operated.

Airworthiness directives may be divided into two categories: (1) those of an emergency nature requiring immediate compliance upon receipt, and (2) those of a less urgent nature requiring compliance within a relatively longer period of time. Airworthiness directives are regulatory and must be complied with, unless specific exemption is granted.

11. What are the required tests and inspections of aircraft and equipment to be legal for both VFR and IFR flights? (14 CFR 91.171, 91.203, 91.207, 91.411, and 91.413)

a. The aircraft must have an annual inspection. If operated for hire or giving flight instruction for hire, it must also have a 100-hour inspection. A record must be kept in the aircraft logbooks.

b. The pitot/static system must be checked within the preceding 24 calendar months. A record must be kept in the aircraft logbook (for IFR).

c. The transponder must have been checked within the preceding 24 calendar months. A record must be kept in the aircraft logbook.

d. The altimeter must have been checked within the preceding 24 calendar months. A record must be kept in the aircraft logbook (for IFR).

e. The VOR must have been checked within the preceding 30 days. A record must be kept in a bound logbook (for IFR).

f. If operations require an emergency locator transmitter (ELT), it must be inspected within 12 calendar months after the last inspection.

12. If an aircraft, carrying passengers for hire, has been on a schedule of inspection every 100 hours, under what condition may it continue to operate beyond the 100 hours without a new inspection? (14 CFR 91.409)

The 100-hour limitation may be exceeded by not more than 10 hours while enroute to reach a place where the inspection can be done. The excess time used to reach a place where the inspection can be done must be included in computing the next 100 hours of time in service.

N. Special Emphasis Areas

1. What does the term "special emphasis areas" refer to? (PTS)

Special emphasis areas refer to a list of areas of aircraft operation that the FAA considers critical to flight safety. Examiners must place special emphasis on these areas and evaluate them during a practical test.

2. What are several examples of "special emphasis areas" in the current PTS? (FAA-S-8081-6C)

Positive aircraft control, positive exchange of the flight controls procedure; stall/spin awareness; collision avoidance; wake turbulence avoidance; LAHSO; runway incursion avoidance; CFIT; ADM and risk management; checklist usage; temporary flight restrictions (TFRs); special use airspace (SUA); and aviation security.

3. What is the definition of the term "runway incursion"? (FAA-H-8083-3A)

A runway incursion is any occurrence at an airport involving an aircraft, vehicle, person, or object on the ground that creates a collision hazard or results in a loss of separation with an aircraft taking off, landing, or intending to land.

4. Lack of preparation in what three major areas contribute to runway incursions? (FAA-H-8083-3A)

a. Communications,

b. Airport knowledge, and

c. Cockpit procedures for maintaining orientation.

Planning, clear communications, and enhanced situational awareness during airport surface operations will reduce the potential for surface incidents.

5. What role does a flight instructor play in preventing and/or reducing runway incursions? (FAA-H-8083-3A)

Safe aircraft operations can be accomplished and incidents eliminated if the pilot is properly trained early on and, throughout his/her flying career, accomplishes standard taxi operating procedures and practices. This requires the development of the formalized teaching of safe operating practices during taxi operations. The flight instructor is the key to this teaching.

6. What are several operating practices you can teach that will help prevent runway incursions? (FAA-H-8083-25)

a. Read back all runway crossing and/or hold instructions.

b. Review airport layouts as part of preflight planning and before descending to land, and while taxiing as needed.

c. Know airport signage.

d. Review Notices to Airmen (NOTAM) for information on runway/taxiway closures and construction areas.

e. Request progressive taxi instructions from ATC when unsure of the taxi route.

f. Check for traffic before crossing any Runway Hold Line and before entering a taxiway.

g. Turn on aircraft lights and the rotating beacon or strobe lights while taxing.

h. When landing, clear the active runway as soon as possible, then wait for taxi instructions before further movement.

i. Study and use proper phraseology in order to understand and respond to ground control instructions.

j. Write down complex taxi instructions at unfamiliar airports.

7. What is the definition of a "Controlled Flight Into Terrain" accident? (AC 61-134)

CFIT occurs when an airworthy aircraft is flown, under the control of a qualified pilot, into terrain (water or obstacles) with inadequate awareness on the part of the pilot of the impending collision.

8. What are the three basic categories of general aviation CFIT accidents? (AC 61-134)

a. CFIT by VFR pilots without an instrument rating operating in marginal VFR weather conditions or instrument meteorological conditions (IMC); commonly known as scud running.

b. CFIT by general aviation IFR operations in IMC conditions on an IFR flight.

c. CFIT by low-flying aircraft operating in VFR conditions.

9. Give two examples of how a CFIT accident might occur when a pilot continues to fly VFR into IMC.

a. Continued flight or maneuvers beneath a lowering ceiling, hitting an obstacle or terrain or impacting water. The accident may or may not be a result of a loss of control before the aircraft impacts the obstacle or surface; the pilot may or may not be instrument-rated.

b. Continued flight into reduced visual conditions compounded by night operations and/or overwater flight. VFR pilots in reduced visual conditions may develop spatial disorientation and lose control, possibly going into a graveyard spiral, or descend to an unsafe altitude while trying to maintain visual contact with the surface. The pilot then impacts terrain, the surface, or an obstacle while trying to maneuver.

10. Explain some of the operational practices you can teach that will help prevent CFIT accidents. (AC 61-134)

a. Non-instrument rated VFR pilots should not attempt to fly in IMC.

b. Know and fly above minimum published safe altitudes. VFR: Fly a minimum of 1,000 feet above the highest terrain in your immediate operating area in nonmountainous areas. Fly a minimum of 2,000 feet in mountainous areas.

c. Verify proper altitude, especially at night or over water, through use of a correctly set altimeter.

d. Maintain situational awareness both vertically and horizontally.

e. Comply with appropriate regulations for your specific operation.

f. Don't operate below minimum safe altitudes if uncertain of position or ATC clearance.

g. Be extra careful when operating outside the United States or in an area which you are not familiar.

h. Use current charts and all available information.

i. Use appropriate checklists.

j. Know your aircraft and its equipment.

11. The acronym "LAHSO" refers to what specific air traffic control procedure? (AIM 4-3-11)

LAHSO is an acronym for "Land and Hold Short Operations." At controlled airports, ATC may clear a pilot to land and hold short of an intersecting runway, an intersecting taxiway, or some other designated point on a runway. Such a clearance may be accepted provided that the pilot-in-command determines that the aircraft can safely land and stop within the Available Landing Distance (ALD). Student pilots or pilots not familiar with LAHSO should not participate in the program. Pilots are expected to decline a LAHSO clearance if they determine it will compromise safety or if weather is below basic VFR conditions (a minimum ceiling of 1,000 feet and 3 SM visibility).

12. Where can available landing distance (ALD) data be found? (AIM 4-3-11)

ALD data are published in the special notices section of the A/FD and in the U.S. Terminal Procedures Publications. Controllers will also provide ALD data upon request.

Additional Study Questions

1. **Can a 100-hour inspection be substituted for an annual inspection?** (14 CFR 91.409)

2. **For what length of time does an airworthiness certificate remain valid?** (FAA-H-8083-25)

3. **For what length of time does a temporary aircraft registration certificate remain valid?** (14 CFR 47.31)

4. **What is an aircraft equipment list and where is it found?** (FAA-H-8083-1)

5. **How can a pilot determine which placards are required to be displayed in a particular airplane?** (AFM/POH)

6. **Since a 100-hour inspection can be "overflown" under certain conditions, is it possible to "overfly" an annual inspection?** (14 CFR 91.409)

7. **How can a pilot determine which ADs apply to a particular aircraft?** (FAA-H-8083-25)

8. **Explain the differences between FAA-approved airplane flight manuals, pilot operating handbooks, and owner's manuals.** (14 CFR 21.5, 91.9, AFM, POH)

Takeoffs and Climbs

4

A. Normal Takeoff and Climb

1. Describe a normal takeoff and climb.

A normal takeoff and climb procedure is one in which the airplane is headed directly into the wind or the wind is very light, and the takeoff surface is firm with no obstructions along the takeoff path, and is of sufficient length to permit the airplane to gradually accelerate to normal climbing speed.

2. Discuss the importance of a thorough knowledge of normal takeoff and climb principles and procedures.

A thorough knowledge of takeoff and climb principles, both in theory and practice, will prove to be of great value throughout the pilot's career. It often may prevent an attempt to takeoff under critical conditions that would require performance beyond the capability of the airplane or skill of the pilot. The takeoff itself, though relatively simple, often presents the most hazards of any part of a flight.

3. What are the steps involved in performing a normal takeoff and climb procedure?

Although the takeoff and climb process is one continuous maneuver, it can be divided into three main steps in order to explain the process:

a. The takeoff roll:
   - Align the airplane with the runway centerline;
   - Apply throttle smoothly and continuously to maximum allowable power;
   - Maintain directional control with rudder; slight rudder pressure will be required to compensate for torque;
   - Glance at the engine instruments for any sign of malfunction.

b. The liftoff:
   - As soon as all flight controls become effective during the takeoff roll, back pressure should be applied gradually to lift the nose wheel off of the runway (rotation);
   - Adjust and maintain liftoff attitude for V_X or V_Y;
   - Keep the wings level and establish an initial heading.

Continued

c. The initial climb after becoming airborne:
 • Establish pitch attitude for V_X or V_Y as necessary;
 • Retrim aircraft for appropriate speed;
 • Maintain takeoff power until 500 AGL above surrounding terrain;
 • Adjust heading to maintain track of extended runway centerline.

4. What are the standards expected of a student for a normal takeoff and climb? (FAA-S-8081-12B)

The student:

a. Shows knowledge of the elements related to normal and cross-wind takeoff, climb operations, and rejected takeoff procedures.

b. Positions the flight controls for the existing wind conditions.

c. Clears the area, taxies onto the takeoff surface and aligns the airplane on the runway center/takeoff path.

d. Advances the throttle smoothly to takeoff power.

e. Lifts off at the recommended airspeed, and accelerates to V_Y.

f. Establishes a pitch attitude that will maintain V_Y ±5 knots*.

g. Retracts the landing gear if appropriate, and flaps after a positive rate of climb is established.

h. Maintains takeoff power and V_Y ±5* knots to a safe maneuvering altitude.

i. Maintains directional control, proper wind-drift correction throughout the takeoff and climb.

j. Complies with noise abatement procedures.

k. Completes appropriate checklists.

Private standard: Establish pitch attitude for V_Y, maintain V_Y +10/-5 knots during climb.

5. What are some common student errors when performing normal takeoffs and climbs?
(FAA-S-8081-6C and FAA-H-8083-3)

a. Improper runway incursion avoidance procedures.
  - Does not check for traffic before crossing runway hold line and before entering a taxiway.
  - Does not read back runway crossing and hold short instructions.
  - Unfamiliar with airport signage.

b. Improper initial positioning of flight controls and wing flaps. No aileron deflection for crosswind; flaps not set as recommended.

c. Improper power application—not applying full power or applying power too quickly or too slowly.

d. Inappropriate removal of hand from throttle. Hand should always remain on throttle during maneuvers such as takeoff, landing, slow flight, etc.

e. Poor directional control.
  - Not correcting for torque effect.
  - Overcorrecting or undercorrecting with rudder.

f. Improper use of ailerons.
  - In a crosswind, as speed increases aileron deflection should be reduced.
  - Allowing the upwind wing to rise causing airplane to skip sideways.

g. Improper pitch attitude during liftoff.
  - Forcing the airplane off the runway; too much pitch attitude too soon.
  - Airplane lifts off at too slow an airspeed causing it to stall back to the runway.
  - Allowing the takeoff roll to continue causing the airplane to remain on the runway too long.

h. Failure to establish and maintain proper climb configuration and airspeed.
  - Not establishing the pitch attitude for best rate-of-climb.
  - Not retracting flaps/gear as appropriate.

Continued

i. Drift during climb.
  • Allowing the airplane to drift away from the runway extended centerline.
  • Not clearing area directly in front of aircraft during climb.

j. Improper use of checklist.
  • Does not use checklist consistently.
  • Fails to complete checklist at appropriate time.

B. Crosswind Takeoff and Climb

1. Describe a crosswind takeoff and climb.

A crosswind takeoff is a takeoff performed when the wind direction is from other than directly in front of the airplane.

2. Discuss the importance of knowing crosswind takeoff and climb principles and techniques.

While it is usually preferable to take off directly into the wind whenever possible or practical, there will be many instances when circumstances or wisdom will indicate otherwise. Consequently, the pilot must be familiar with the principles and techniques involved in crosswind takeoffs as well as those for normal takeoffs.

3. What are the principles and procedures involved in a crosswind takeoff and climb?

a. Crosswind takeoff roll:
  • Taxi into takeoff position and check strength and direction of wind.
  • Start takeoff roll with full aileron control into the wind.
  • As the forward speed of the airplane increases and the crosswind becomes more and more of a relative headwind, the mechanical holding of full aileron into the wind should be reduced.

b. Crosswind liftoff:
  • If a significant crosswind exists, the main wheels should be held on the ground slightly longer than in a normal takeoff so that a smooth but very definite liftoff can be made.
  • As both main wheels leave the runway, adequate drift correction must be maintained by the pilot or the airplane will slowly be carried sideways with the wind.

c. Initial crosswind climb:
- If proper correction is being applied, as soon as the airplane becomes airborne it will be slipping into the wind sufficiently to counteract the drifting effect of the wind.
- This slipping should be continued until the airplane has climbed well above the ground. At that time the airplane should be headed toward the wind to establish just enough "crab" to counteract the wind and then the wings rolled level.
- The climb while in this crab should be continued so as to follow a ground track aligned with the runway direction.

4. What are the standards expected of a student for a crosswind takeoff and climb? (FAA-S-8081-12B)

The student:

a. Shows knowledge of the elements related to normal and crosswind takeoff, climb operations, and rejected takeoff procedures.

b. Positions the flight controls for the existing wind conditions.

c. Clears the area, taxies onto the takeoff surface and aligns the airplane on the runway center/takeoff path.

d. Advances the throttle smoothly to takeoff power.

e. Lifts off at the recommended airspeed, and accelerates to V_Y.

f. Establishes a pitch attitude that will maintain V_Y ±5 knots*.

g. Retracts the landing gear if appropriate, and flaps after a positive rate of climb is established.

h. Maintains takeoff power and V_Y ±5* knots to a safe maneuvering altitude.

i. Maintains directional control, proper wind-drift correction throughout the takeoff and climb.

j. Complies with noise abatement procedures.

k. Completes appropriate checklists.

Private standard: Establish pitch attitude for V_Y, maintain V_Y +10/-5 knots during climb.

5. What are some common student errors in performing crosswind takeoffs and climbs?
(FAA-S-8081-6C and FAA-H-8083-3)

a. Improper runway incursion avoidance procedures.
   • Does not check for traffic before crossing runway hold line and before entering a taxiway.
   • Does not read back runway crossing and hold short instructions.
   • Unfamiliar with airport signage.

b. Improper initial positioning of flight controls and wing flaps.
   • If a crosswind exists, full aileron into wind should be applied initially.
   • Flaps should be set as recommended by manufacturer.

c. Improper power application.
   • Not applying full power.
   • Applying power too quickly or too slowly.

d. Inappropriate removal of hand from throttle. The hand should always remain on throttle during maneuvers such as takeoff, landing, slow flight, etc.

e. Poor directional control.
   • Not correcting for torque effect.
   • Overcorrecting or undercorrecting with rudder.

f. Improper use of ailerons.
   • As speed increases aileron deflection should be reduced.
   • Allowing the upwind wing to rise causing the airplane to skip sideways.

g. Improper pitch attitude during liftoff.
   • Forcing the airplane off the runway; too much pitch attitude too soon.
   • Airplane lifts off at too slow an airspeed causing it to stall back to the runway.
   • Allowing takeoff roll to continue; airplane remains on the runway too long.

h. Failure to establish and maintain proper climb configuration and airspeed.
   - Not establishing pitch attitude for best rate-of-climb.
   - Not retracting flaps/gear as appropriate.

i. Drift during climb.
   - Allowing airplane to drift away from the runway extended centerline.
   - Not clearing area directly in front of aircraft during climb.

j. Improper use of checklist.
   - Does not use checklist consistently.
   - Fails to complete checklist at appropriate time.

C. Short-Field Takeoff and Climb

1. What is the purpose of short-field takeoff and climb procedures?

As the name implies, short-field takeoff procedures are used when an airplane must be operated out of an area with either a short runway or the available takeoff area is restricted by obstructions.

2. Why is it important that a pilot be familiar with these procedures?

A takeoff and climb from a field where the takeoff area is short or the available takeoff area is restricted by obstructions, requires that the pilot operate the airplane at the limit of its takeoff performance capabilities. The pilot must exercise positive and precise control of the airplane attitude and airspeed so that takeoff and climb performance results in the shortest ground roll and the steepest angle of climb. To takeoff and depart safely, the pilot must be well indoctrinated in the use and effectiveness of best-angle-of-climb speed and best-rate-of-climb speed for the specific airplane flown.

3. Describe the short-field takeoff and climb procedures.

a. Set flaps as recommended by manufacturer.

b. Taxi onto runway using all available runway length.

c. Momentarily apply brakes while applying maximum allowable power.

d. Check all engine instruments in the green and release brakes.

e. Adjust airplane pitch attitude/angle of attack for minimum drag and maximum acceleration.

f. Accelerate to recommended liftoff airspeed.

g. On liftoff, adjust pitch attitude for V_X (best angle) until obstacles cleared or if no obstacles an altitude at least 50 feet AGL is obtained.

h. Retract flaps and gear (if retractable) when well clear of obstacles and best rate-of-climb has been established.

4. What are the standards expected of a student for short-field takeoff and climb? (FAA-S-8081-12B)

The student:

a. Shows knowledge of the elements related to a short-field takeoff and maximum performance climb.

b. Positions the flight controls for the existing wind conditions, sets flaps as recommended.

c. Clears the area; taxies into takeoff position using maximum available takeoff area and aligns the airplane on the runway center/takeoff path.

d. Applies brakes (if appropriate) while advancing the throttle smoothly to takeoff power.

e. Lifts off at the recommended airspeed, and accelerates to recommended obstacle clearance airspeed, or V_X.

f. Establishes a pitch attitude that will maintain the recommended obstacle clearance airspeed, or V_X, +5/-0 knots, until the obstacle is cleared, or until the airplane is 50 feet (20 meters) above the surface*.

g. After clearing the obstacle, establishes the pitch attitude for V_Y, accelerates to V_Y, and maintains V_Y, ±5 knots, during the climb.

h. Retracts the landing gear, if appropriate and flaps after clear of any obstacles or as recommended by manufacturer.

i. Maintains takeoff power and V_Y ±5 knots to a safe maneuvering altitude.

j. Maintains directional control and proper wind-drift correction throughout the takeoff and climb.

k. Completes appropriate checklist.

* Private standard: Establishes a pitch attitude that will maintain the recommended obstacle clearance airspeed, or V_X, +10/-5 knots, until the obstacle is cleared, or until the airplane is 50 feet (20 meters) above the surface.

5. Describe some common errors for students performing short-field takeoff and climb.
(FAA-S-8081-6C and FAA-H-8083-3)

a. Improper runway incursion avoidance procedures.
   • Does not check for traffic before crossing runway hold line and before entering a taxiway.
   • Does not read back runway crossing and hold short instructions.
   • Unfamiliar with airport signage.

b. Failure to position the airplane for maximum utilization of available takeoff area.

c. Improper initial positioning of flight controls and wing flaps.
   • No aileron deflection for crosswind.
   • Flaps not set as recommended.

d. Improper power application.
   • Not applying full power.
   • Applying power too quickly or too slowly.

e. Inappropriate removal of hand from throttle. Hand should always remain on throttle during maneuvers such as takeoff, landing, slow flight, etc.

f. Poor directional control.
   • Not correcting for torque effect.
   • Overcorrecting or undercorrecting with rudder.

Continued

g. Improper use of brakes.
   • Failure to hold brakes until full power is developed and engine instruments are checked.
   • Failure to remove feet from brakes during takeoff roll.

h. Improper pitch attitude during liftoff.
   • Too much pitch attitude too soon.
   • Forcing the airplane off the runway; airplane lifts off at too slow an airspeed causing it to stall back to the runway.
   • Allowing takeoff roll to continue; airplane remains on the runway too long.

i. Failure to establish and maintain proper climb configuration and airspeed.
   • Retracting flaps/landing gear before clear of obstacle.
   • Not maintaining best angle of climb prior to flaps/gear retraction.

j. Drift during climb.
   • Allowing airplane to drift away from runway extended centerline.
   • Not clearing area directly in front of aircraft during climb.

k. Improper use of checklist.
   • Does not use checklist consistently.
   • Fails to complete checklist at appropriate time.

D. Soft-Field Takeoff and Climb

1. What is the purpose of soft-field takeoff and climb procedures?

They are used when operating an airplane off of an unimproved surface such as grass, soft sand, mud, snow, or rough terrain, etc.

2. Why is it important that a pilot be familiar with these procedures?

They require the use of operational techniques for getting the airplane airborne as quickly as possible. Soft surfaces such as tall grass, soft sand, mud, snow, etc. usually retard the airplane's acceleration during the takeoff roll so much that adequate takeoff speed might not be attained with normal techniques. Also useful when operating an airplane from a rough field where it is advisable to get the airplane off the ground as soon as possible to avoid damaging the landing gear.

3. Describe the soft-field takeoff and climb procedures.

a. Wing flaps should be lowered prior to starting the takeoff roll (if recommended by the manufacturer).

b. Taxi the airplane at as fast a speed as possible, consistent with safety and surface conditions. Avoid making sharp turns, using brakes, and any other action which might bog the airplane down.

c. The airplane should be kept in continuous motion with sufficient power while lining up for the takeoff roll.

d. As the airplane is aligned, apply power smoothly to maximum allowable power.

e. As the airplane accelerates, enough elevator back pressure should be applied to reduce the weight supported by the nose wheel.

f. Maintain a nose-high attitude throughout the takeoff run sufficient to relieve the main gear of progressively more and more weight. This will minimize drag caused by surface irregularities or adhesion.

g. As the airplane becomes airborne, lower pitch attitude slightly to gain additional airspeed while in ground effect.

h. Accelerate to V_X with obstacle or V_Y without obstacle before leaving ground effect.

i. Continue climb at V_X or V_Y as appropriate.

j. Retract the wing flaps and/or landing gear when clear of obstacles.

4. What are the standards expected of a student for soft-field takeoff and climb? (FAA-S-8081-12B)

The student:

a. Exhibits knowledge of the elements related to a soft-field takeoff and climb.

b. Positions the flight controls for existing conditions and to maximize lift as quickly as possible.

c. Clears the area; taxies onto takeoff surface at a speed consistent with safety without stopping while advancing the throttle smoothly to takeoff power.

d. Establishes and maintains a pitch attitude that will transfer the weight of the airplane from the wheels to the wings as rapidly as possible.

e. Lifts off at the lowest possible airspeed and remains in ground effect while accelerating to V_X or V_Y, as appropriate.

f. Establishes a pitch attitude for V_X or V_Y, as appropriate, and maintains selected airspeed ±5 knots*, during the climb.

g. Retracts the landing gear, if appropriate and flaps after clear of any obstacles or as recommended by the manufacturer.

h. Maintains takeoff power and V_X or V_Y ±5 knots* to a safe maneuvering altitude.

i. Maintains directional control and proper wind-drift correction throughout the takeoff and climb.

j. Completes appropriate checklist.

Private standard: Establishes a pitch attitude for V_X or V_Y, as appropriate, and maintains selected airspeed +10/-5 knots, during the climb.

5. What are some common errors for students performing soft-field takeoff and climb?
(FAA-S-8081-6C and FAA-H-8083-3)

a. Improper runway incursion avoidance procedures; does not read back runway crossing and hold short instructions; does not check for traffic before crossing runway hold line and before entering a taxiway; unfamiliar with airport signage.

b. Improper initial positioning of flight controls and wing flaps.
   • No aileron deflection for crosswind.
   • Flaps not set as recommended.

c. Hazards of allowing the airplane to stop on the takeoff surface prior to initiating takeoff—aircraft may not have enough power to begin takeoff roll again.

d. Improper power application.
   • Not applying full power.
   • Applying power too quickly or too slowly.

e. Inappropriate removal of hand from throttle. Hand should always remain on throttle during maneuvers such as takeoff, landing, slow flight, etc.

f. Poor directional control.
   • Not correcting for torque effect.
   • Overcorrecting or undercorrecting with rudder.

g. Improper use of brakes. Use of brakes should not be required in soft field operations.

h. Improper pitch attitude during liftoff.
   • Not applying full up elevator during the initial takeoff roll delaying liftoff.
   • Not reducing full up elevator during the takeoff roll delaying liftoff.
   • Allowing airplane to liftoff and then stall back onto runway.

i. Hazards of settling back to takeoff surface after becoming airborne. Excessive loads may be inflicted on the landing gear with possible loss of control of aircraft.

j. Failure to establish and maintain proper climb configuration and airspeed.
   • Not remaining in ground effect while accelerating to V_X or V_Y as appropriate.
   • Not maintaining V_X until clear of obstacle.
   • Retracting flaps before clear of obstacle.

k. Drift during climb.
   • Allowing airplane to drift away from runway extended centerline.
   • Not clearing areas directly in front of aircraft during climb.

l. Improper use of checklist—does not use checklist consistently or fails to complete checklist at appropriate time.

Additional Study Questions

1. What will you teach the student concerning when to lift-off (airspeed, runway distance) during the takeoff roll? (FAA-H-8083-3)

2. In the event of an engine failure on takeoff, what procedure will you teach your student to use? (FAA-H-8083-3)

3. How will you teach the student to establish and maintain proper crosswind correction prior to lift-off? (FAA-H-8083-3)

4. What procedure will you teach the student to use to correct for a crosswind after lift-off and during the initial climb? (FAA-H-8083-3)

5. How will you teach your student to determine the required takeoff distance for an aircraft on a given day? (FAA-H-8083-3)

6. What procedures should you instruct your student to follow, for when to retract flaps and landing gear (if applicable) during a short-field takeoff? (FAA-H-8083-3)

7. Explain the importance of ground effect as it relates to a soft-field takeoff. (FAA-H-8083-3)

8. What problems will be apparent if the student establishes a pitch attitude that is either too high or too low in a soft-field takeoff? (FAA-H-8083-3)

Fundamentals
of Flight

5

A. Straight-and-Level Flight

1. What is straight-and-level flight?

Flight in which a constant heading and altitude are maintained. It is accomplished by making immediate corrections for deviations in direction and altitude from unintentional slight turns, descents, and climbs.

2. What is the objective in learning straight-and-level flight maneuvers?

To learn the proper use of the controls for maneuvering the airplane, to attain the proper attitude in relation to the horizon by use of inside and outside references (the integrated flight instruction method), and to emphasize the importance of dividing attention and constantly checking all reference points.

3. How is straight-and-level flight achieved?

The pitch attitude for level flight (constant altitude) is usually obtained by selecting some portion of the airplane's nose as a reference point, and then keeping that point in a fixed position relative to the horizon. That position should be cross-checked occasionally against the altimeter and attitude indicator to determine whether or not the pitch attitude is correct.

To achieve straight flight (laterally level flight) the pilot should select two or more outside visual reference points directly ahead of the airplane (such as fields, towns, lakes), to form points along an imaginary line and keep the airplane's nose headed along that line. While using these references, an occasional check of the heading indicator and attitude indicator should be made to determine that the airplane is actually maintaining flight in a constant direction.

4. **What are some common student errors in the performance of straight-and-level flight?**
(FAA-S-8081-6C and FAA-H-8083-3)

   a. Failure to cross-check and correctly interpret outside and instrument references. Fixating on instruments inside instead of using a combination of inside and outside references.

   b. Application of control movements rather than pressures — use of jerky control movements instead of smooth control pressures.

   c. Uncoordinated use of flight controls — not applying right rudder to compensate for torque effect in straight-and-level flight.

   d. Faulty trim technique:
      • Failure to trim the aircraft.
      • Excessive use of trim.
      • Using trim as a primary flight control.
      • Trimming the aircraft before establishing pitch attitude and power setting.

B. Level Turns

1. Describe a level turn.

A turn is a basic flight maneuver used to change or return to a desired heading. It involves close coordination of all three flight controls — aileron, rudder, and elevator.

2. Discuss the importance of the level turn, as a basic maneuver.

Since turns are a part of almost every other flight maneuver, it is important that the pilot thoroughly understand the factors involved and learn to perform them well.

3. What are the steps involved in performing a level turn?

   a. Roll into the banked attitude by coordinated use of aileron and rudder in the direction of turn.

   b. When the desired angle of bank is obtained, neutralize the ailerons and rudder to maintain bank.

    c. Back pressure must be applied in the turn to compensate for the loss of vertical lift and to maintain altitude.

    d. Roll out of the turn by applying coordinated aileron and rudder pressure in the opposite direction of the turn until level attitude is reached. As the angle of bank is decreased the elevator should be released smoothly as necessary to maintain altitude.

4. What are some common student errors in performing level turns? (FAA-S-8081-6C and FAA-H-8083-3)

    a. Failure to cross-check and correctly interpret outside and instrument references. Fixating on instruments inside instead of using a combination of inside and outside references.

    b. Application of control movements rather than pressures— use of jerky control movements instead of smooth control pressures.

    c. Uncoordinated use of flight controls.
- Initially too much bank or rudder when establishing the turn.
- Slipping or skidding during the turn.

    d. Faulty altitude and bank control.
- Excessive or insufficient back pressure resulting in a gain or loss of altitude.
- Bank angle varies due to lack of division of attention between inside and outside references.

C. Straight Climbs and Climbing Turns

1. What is a straight climb? A climbing turn?

A straight climb is one in which the airplane gains altitude while traveling straight ahead. It is a basic flight maneuver in which an increase in both the pitch attitude and power result in a gain in altitude. Climbing turns are those in which the airplane gains altitude while turning.

2. What is the objective in learning the straight climb/climbing turn maneuver?

The objective of this maneuver, as with the other basic flight maneuvers, is to learn the proper use of the controls for maneuvering the airplane, to attain the proper attitude in relation to the horizon by use of inside and outside references, and to emphasize the importance of dividing attention and constantly checking all references points.

3. Describe how to achieve the straight climb/climbing turn maneuver.

a. Establish a climb by applying back pressure on the elevator to increase pitch attitude. Simultaneously establish the desired bank angle if performing a climbing turn.

b. Apply full power and establish a pitch attitude for the climbing airspeed (V_Y).

c. Cross-check the airspeed indicator with the position of the airplane's nose in relation to the horizon as well as the attitude indicator.

d. Trim the aircraft for this attitude/airspeed.

e. Use right rudder to correct for torque effect.

f. Maintain a constant heading by cross-checking visual references as well as instrument references. Maintain wings level while cross-checking heading indicator, attitude indicator, turn coordinator. If performing a climbing turn, maintain the desired bank angle by cross-checking visual references as well as instrument references.

4. What are some common student errors in performing straight climbs/climbing turns?
(FAA-S-8081-6C and FAA-H-8083-3)

a. Failure to cross-check and correctly interpret outside and instrument references—fixating on instruments inside instead of using a combination of inside and outside references.

b. Application of control movements rather than pressures—use of jerky control movements instead of smooth control pressures.

c. Uncoordinated use of flight controls.
- Not compensating for torque effect in climb.
- Slipping or skidding during the turn.

d. Faulty trim technique.
- Failure to trim the aircraft.
- Excessive use of trim.
- Using trim as a primary flight control.
- Trimming the aircraft before establishing pitch attitude and power setting.

D. Straight Descents and Descending Turns

1. Describe the straight descent and descending turn maneuvers.

A descent or a glide is a basic maneuver in which the airplane is losing altitude in a controlled descent with little or no engine power; forward motion is maintained by gravity pulling the airplane along an inclined path, and the descent rate is controlled by the pilot balancing the forces of gravity and lift. Descending turns are those in which the airplane loses altitude while turning.

2. Explain the objective in learning straight descents/ descending turns, and why these maneuvers are especially important.

Although power-off descents (glides) and descending turns are directly related to the practice of power-off accuracy landings, they have a specific operational purpose in normal landing procedures, and forced landings after engine failure. Therefore, it is necessary that they be performed more subconsciously than other maneuvers because, most of the time during their execution, the pilot will be giving full attention to details other than the mechanics of performing the maneuver. Since power-off descents and descending turns are performed relatively close to the ground, accuracy of their execution and the formation of proper technique and habits are of special importance.

3. How is a straight descent or descending turn maneuver performed?

a. Apply carburetor heat and reduce power to idle.

b. Maintain a level pitch attitude to reduce airspeed to the recommended glide speed.

c. Establish the desired bank angle if performing a descending turn.

d. Allow the pitch attitude to decrease as necessary to maintain best glide speed.

e. When airspeed is stabilized, the aircraft should be retrimmed.

4. What are some common errors in performing straight descents/descending turns?
(FAA-S-8081-6C and FAA-H-8083-3)

a. Failure to cross-check and correctly interpret outside and instrument references—fixating on instruments inside instead of using a combination of inside and outside references.

b. Application of control movements rather than pressures—use of jerky control movements instead of smooth control pressures.

c. Uncoordinated use of flight controls.
   • Initially too much bank or rudder when establishing the turn.
   • Slipping or skidding during the turn.

d. Faulty trim technique.
   • Failure to trim the aircraft.
   • Excessive use of trim.
   • Using trim as a primary flight control.
   • Trimming aircraft before establishing pitch attitude and power setting.

e. Failure to clear engine and use carburetor heat, as appropriate.

E. Practical Test Standards for the Basic Maneuvers

1. What are the practical test standards for teaching basic flight maneuvers? (FAA-S-8081-6C)

The flight instructor exhibits instructional knowledge of the elements of straight-and-level flight, level turns, straight climbs/climbing turns, and straight descents and descending turns by describing:

a. The effect and use of flight controls.

b. The integrated flight instruction method.

c. Outside and instrument references used for pitch, bank, and power control; the cross-check and interpretation of those references; and the control technique used.

d. Trim technique.

e. Methods of overcoming tenseness and overcontrolling.

2. What recommended standards should a flight instructor use to evaluate a student's performance of the basic flight maneuvers?

The student:

a. Maintains desired heading ±10°.

b. Maintains desired altitude ±100 feet.

c. Maintains desired airspeed ±10 knots.

d. Maintains desired bank angle.

Note: The four basic tasks in this chapter, when conducted visually and not by reference to instruments, are not specified in the Private or Commercial practical test standards. The above standards are recommended for evaluation purposes only.

Additional Study Questions

1. Define integrated flight instruction. (FAA-H-8083-3)

2. How is a change of airspeed accomplished during straight-and-level flight? (FAA-H-8083-3)

3. What is the difference between a shallow, medium, and steep turn? (FAA-H-8083-3)

4. What procedure will you teach your student to use when rolling out of a turn? (FAA-H-8083-3)

5. Explain how parallax error can affect a student when practicing right and left turns. (FAA-H-8083-3)

6. How can a pilot increase the rate-of-turn and decrease the radius at the same time? (FAA-H-8083-3)

7. What procedure will you teach your student to use when returning to straight-and-level flight from a climb? (FAA-H-8083-3)

8. What is the difference between a normal climb and a "cruise" climb? (FAA-H-8083-3)

9. Why is it necessary for the student to establish more right rudder in a right climbing turn than in a left climbing turn? (FAA-H-8083-3)

10. What is the glide ratio of an airplane? (FAA-H-8083-3)

11. What procedure will you teach your student to use to level-off from a descent? (FAA-H-8083-3)

12. How will you teach your student to establish a specific airspeed and rate-of-descent in a power-on descent? (FAA-H-8083-3)

Slow Flight, Stalls, and Spins   **6**

A. Power-On Stalls

1. What is a power-on stall?

Power-on stalls are, as the name implies, stalls in which full power is being developed as the aircraft stalls. They are intended to simulate the characteristics of an airplane that has stalled in a takeoff and departure configuration.

2. Explain the objective in learning the power-on stall.

The objectives in performing stalls are to familiarize the pilot with the conditions that produce stalls, to assist in recognizing a takeoff and departure stall, and to develop the habit of taking prompt preventive or corrective action.

3. What are the steps involved in performing a power-on stall?

a. Establish a specific heading and altitude (recovery by 1,500 feet AGL).

b. Perform clearing turns.

c. Establish the takeoff and departure configuration.

d. Slow the airplane to normal liftoff airspeed.

e. Apply takeoff power for a takeoff stall, or the recommended climb power for a departure stall.

f. Establish a climb attitude.

g. After the climb attitude is established, the nose should be brought smoothly upward to an attitude obviously impossible for the airplane to maintain and held at that attitude until a full stall occurs.

h. Recovery should be accomplished by immediately reducing the pitch attitude/angle of attack, applying maximum power (not necessary in a takeoff stall) and maintaining directional control through coordinated use of controls.

i. Control any yawing tendency with rudder.

j. Use ailerons to level wings as soon as possible.

Continued

k. Retract flaps to the recommended setting and retract landing gear (if retractable), after a positive rate of climb is established.

l. Accelerate to V_X or V_Y speed before the final flap retraction and return to initial altitude, heading, and airspeed.

4. What are the standards expected of a student for performing a power-on stall? (FAA-S-8081-12B)

The student:

a. Shows knowledge of the elements related to power-on stalls.

b. Selects an entry altitude that allows the task to be completed no lower than 1,500 feet (460 meters) AGL.

c. Establishes the takeoff or departure configuration. Sets power to no less than 65 percent available power.

d. Transitions smoothly from the takeoff or departure attitude to a pitch attitude that will induce a stall.

e. Maintains a specified heading ±5°, in straight flight;* maintains a specified angle of bank, not to exceed a 20°, ±10°, in turning flight, while inducing the stall.

f. Recognizes and recovers promptly as the stall occurs by simultaneously reducing the angle of attack, increasing power to maximum allowable, and leveling the wings to return to a straight-and-level flight attitude, with a minimum loss of altitude appropriate for the airplane.

g. Retracts flaps to the recommended setting, retracts the landing gear if retractable, after a positive rate of climb is established.

h. Accelerates to V_X or V_Y speed before the final flap retraction; returns to the altitude, heading, and airspeed specified by the examiner.

Private standard: Maintains a specified heading, ±10°, in straight flight.

Note: In some high performance airplanes, the power setting may have to be reduced below the practical test standards guideline power setting to prevent excessively high pitch attitudes (greater than 30° nose up).

5. What are some common student errors in the performance of a power-on stall?
(FAA-S-8081-6C and FAA-H-8083-3)

a. Failure to establish the specified landing gear and flap configuration prior to entry.

b. Improper pitch, heading, and bank control during straight ahead and turning stalls.
   - Not reducing power initially to slow the airplane to a typical takeoff and departure airspeed.
   - Increasing the pitch attitude too much, too quickly, resulting in an excessively steep nose-up attitude and an unrealistic situation.

c. Improper pitch and bank control during turning stalls.
   - Not reducing power initially to slow the airplane to a typical takeoff and departure airspeed.
   - Increasing the pitch attitude too much, too quickly, resulting in an excessively steep nose-up attitude and an unrealistic situation.
   - Not maintaining the specified bank angle.

d. Rough or uncoordinated control technique.
   - Not using rudder to assist in maintaining initial directional control.
   - All aileron and no rudder will only aggravate the situation, especially before the wings have had time to regain sufficient airflow.

e. Failure to recognize the first indications of a stall—not recognizing initial buffeting and lack of control effectiveness.

f. Failure to achieve a stall. Not increasing pitch attitude high enough to induce a stall or initiating recovery before stall occurs.

g. Improper torque correction—not correcting for torque effect with right rudder.

h. Poor stall recognition and delayed recovery—not reducing back pressure after stall has occurred.

i. Excessive altitude loss or excessive airspeed during recovery—pitch attitude is reduced to an excessive nose down attitude, or is maintained in a nose down attitude longer than necessary.

j. Secondary stall during recovery—student hastens recovery by increasing pitch attitude too quickly.

B. Power-Off Stalls

1. What is a power-off stall?

A power-off stall is a maneuver designed to simulate an accidental stall occurring during a segment of a landing approach. Airplanes equipped with flaps and/or retractable gear will be in the landing configuration. Power-off stalls are practiced from straight-ahead flight as well as from moderately banked turns to simulate an accidental stall during a turn from base leg to final.

2. Discuss the advantages of learning the power-off stall.

Power-off stalls are practiced to show what could happen if the controls are improperly used during a turn from the base leg to the final approach. The power-off straight ahead stall simulates the attitude and flight characteristics of a particular airplane during the final approach and landing. During the practice of intentional stalls, the real objective is not to learn how to stall the airplane but to learn how to recognize an incipient stall and take prompt corrective action. Practice of stalls is important because it simulates stall conditions that could occur during normal flight maneuvers.

3. How is a power-off stall performed?

a. Establish a specific heading and altitude (recovery by 1,500 feet AGL).

b. Perform clearing turns.

c. Extend landing gear (if applicable).

d. Carburetor heat ON.

e. Reduce power and maintain back pressure to slow aircraft to flap operating speed.

f. Extend approach flaps.

g. Reduce power to idle and establish approach airspeed.

h. Bring the nose smoothly upward until the full stall occurs.

i. Immediately reduce angle of attack to regain flying speed.

j. Simultaneously apply full power (carburetor heat off).

k. Retract flaps incrementally.

l. Control any yawing tendency with rudder.

m. Use ailerons to level wings as soon as possible.

n. As airspeed approaches V_X or V_Y, establish a climb attitude to maintain V_X or V_Y. After establishing V_X or V_Y positive rate climb, retract final flaps.

o. Return to cruise flight.

4. What are the standards expected of a student for performing a power-off stall? (FAA-S-8081-12B)

The student:

a. Shows knowledge of the elements related to power-off stalls.

b. Selects an entry altitude that allows the task to be completed no lower than 1,500 feet (460 meters) AGL.

c. Establishes a stabilized descent in the approach or landing configuration, as specified by the examiner.

d. Transitions smoothly from the approach or landing attitude to a pitch attitude that will induce a stall.

e. Maintains a specified heading, ±10° in straight flight; maintains a specified angle of bank, not to exceed 20°, ±5°*, in turning flight while inducing the stall.

f. Recognizes and recovers promptly as the stall occurs by simultaneously reducing the angle of attack, increasing power to maximum allowable, and leveling the wings to return to a straight-and-level flight attitude with a minimum loss of altitude appropriate for the airplane.

g. Retracts the flaps to the recommended setting, retracts the landing gear if retractable after a positive rate of climb is established.

h. Accelerates to V_X or V_Y speed before the final flap retraction; returns to the altitude, heading, and airspeed specified by the examiner.

Private standard: Maintains a specified heading, ±10°, in straight flight; maintains a specified angle of bank not to exceed 20°, ±10°, in turning flight, while inducing the stall.

5. List some common student errors in performing the power-off stall. (FAA-S-8081-6C and FAA-H-8083-3)

a. Failure to establish the specified landing gear and flap configuration prior to entry.

b. Improper pitch, heading, and bank control during straight-ahead stalls and improper pitch and bank control during turning stalls.
   • Not reducing power initially to slow the airplane to a typical takeoff and departure airspeed.
   • Increasing the pitch attitude too much, too quickly, resulting in an excessively steep nose-up attitude and an unrealistic situation.
   • Not maintaining the specified bank angle.

c. Rough or uncoordinated control technique.
   • Not using rudder to assist in maintaining initial directional control.
   • All aileron and no rudder will only aggravate the situation, especially before the wings have had time to regain sufficient airflow.

d. Failure to recognize the first indications of a stall—not recognizing the initial buffeting and lack of control effectiveness.

e. Failure to achieve a stall. Not increasing the pitch attitude high enough to induce a stall or initiating recovery before the stall occurs.

f. Improper torque correction. Not correcting for torque effect with right rudder.

g. Poor stall recognition and delayed recovery. Not reducing back pressure after the stall has occurred.

h. Excessive altitude loss or excessive airspeed during recovery. Pitch attitude is reduced to an excessive nose down attitude, or is maintained in a nose down attitude longer than necessary.

i. Secondary stall during recovery. Student hastens recovery by increasing pitch attitude too quickly.

C. Crossed-Control Stalls

1. What happens in a crossed-control stall?

A crossed-control stall occurs when the pilot allows the aircraft to be flown in uncoordinated flight with the flight controls crossed— that is, aileron pressure applied in one direction and rudder pressure in the opposite direction. If excessive back pressure is applied, a crossed-control stall may result.

2. Explain why the flight instructor should demonstrate the crossed-control stall to the student.

Demonstrating this maneuver shows the effect of improper control technique and emphasizes the importance of using coordinated control pressures when making turns. This type of stall is most likely to occur during a poorly planned and executed base to final approach turn and often is the result of overshooting the centerline of the runway during that turn.

3. How is the crossed-control stall demonstrated?

a. Establish a specific heading and altitude (recovery by 1,500 feet AGL).

b. Perform clearing turns.

c. Extend landing gear (if applicable).

d. Reduce power.

e. Maintain altitude until airspeed approaches normal glide speed.

f. Retrim aircraft.

g. Roll into a medium-banked turn.

h. During turn excessive rudder pressure should be applied in direction of turn but the bank held constant by applying opposite aileron pressure.

i. Increase back elevator pressure to keep nose from lowering.

j. Control pressures should be increased until airplane stalls.

k. When stall occurs, recover by releasing control pressures and increasing power as necessary.

Continued

l. Control any yawing tendency with rudder.

m. Use ailerons to level wings as soon as possible.

n. As airspeed approaches V_X establish climb attitude to maintain V_X and to establish a positive rate climb.

o. Return to cruise flight.

4. What are some common errors related to crossed-control stalls? (FAA-S-8081-6C and FAA-H-8083-3)

a. Failure to establish selected configuration prior to entry.

b. Failure to establish a crossed-control turn and stall condition that will adequately demonstrate the hazards of a crossed-control stall.
   - Not reducing power initially to slow the airplane to a typical approach speed.
   - Not increasing crossed-control pressures enough to induce a stall.
   - Not increasing back elevator pressure enough to induce a stall.

c. Improper or inadequate demonstration of the recognition of and recovery from a crossed-control stall.

d. Failure to present simulated student instruction that adequately emphasizes the hazards of a crossed-control condition in a gliding or reduced airspeed condition. Not explaining the "what, why, and how" of crossed-control stalls adequately.

Practical Test Standards (FAA-S-8081-6C)

The following is an excerpt from the Flight Instructor Practical Test Standards set by the FAA for demonstration of cross-controlled stalls:

The applicant exhibits instructional knowledge of the elements of crossed-control stalls, with the landing gear extended, by describing the:

a. Aerodynamics of crossed-control stalls.

b. Effects of crossed controls in gliding or reduced airspeed descending turns.

c. Flight situations where unintentional crossed-control stalls may occur.

d. Entry procedure and minimum entry altitude.

e. Recognition of crossed-control stalls.

f. Recovery procedure and minimum recovery altitude.

D. Elevator Trim Stalls

1. Describe an elevator trim stall.

Occurs when full power is applied to an airplane configured with excessive nose-up trim. Positive control of the airplane is not maintained, resulting in a stall. These type of stalls usually occur during a go-around procedure from a normal landing approach or a simulated forced landing approach, or immediately after takeoff.

2. Why should a flight instructor demonstrate an elevator trim stall?

This maneuver shows what can happen when full power is applied for a go-around and positive control of the airplane is not maintained. Therefore the objective is to show the importance of making smooth power applications, overcoming strong trim forces and maintaining positive control of the airplane to hold safe flight attitudes, and using proper and timely trim techniques.

3. How is an elevator trim stall demonstrated?

a. Establish a specific heading and altitude (recovery by 1,500 feet AGL).

b. Perform clearing turns.

c. Slowly retard the throttle and extend landing gear if retractable.

d. Extend one-half to full flaps.

e. Close throttle.

f. Maintain altitude until airspeed approaches normal glide speed.

Continued

g. When normal glide is established, the airplane should be retrimmed just as would be done during a normal landing approach.

h. Advance throttle to maximum power as in a go-around procedure. The combined forces of thrust, torque, and back elevator trim will tend to make the nose rise sharply and turn to the left. To demonstrate what could occur if positive control of the airplane were not maintained, no immediate attempt should be made to correct these forces.

i. When a stall is imminent, forward pressure must be applied to return the airplane to normal climbing attitude.

j. Trim should then be adjusted to relieve the heavy control pressures and the normal go-around and level-off procedures should be completed.

4. What are some common errors associated with elevator trim stalls? (FAA-S-8081-6C and FAA-H-8083-3)

a. Failure to present simulated student instruction that adequately emphasizes the hazards of poor correction for torque and up-elevator trim during go-around and other maneuvers. Not explaining the "what, why, and how" of elevator trim stalls adequately.

b. Failure to establish selected configuration prior to entry.

c. Improper or inadequate demonstration of the recognition of and the recovery from an elevator trim stall.
   • Not allowing the pitch attitude to increase above the normal climbing attitude.
   • Reducing power during recovery; not maintaining control of aircraft while retrimming and retracting flaps.

Practical Test Standards (FAA-S-8081-6C)

The following is an excerpt from the Flight Instructor Practical Test Standards set by the FAA for demonstration of the elevator trim stall:

The applicant exhibits instructional knowledge of the elements of elevator trim stalls, in selected landing gear and flap configurations, by describing the:

a. Aerodynamics of elevator trim stalls.

b. Hazards of inadequate control pressures to compensate for thrust, torque, and up-elevator trim during go-around and other related maneuvers.

c. Entry procedure and minimum entry altitude.

d. Recognition of elevator trim stalls.

e. Importance of recovering from an elevator trim stall immediately upon recognition.

E. Secondary Stalls

1. What is a secondary stall?

This stall is called a secondary stall since it may occur after a recovery from a preceding primary stall. It is caused by attempting to hasten the completion of a stall recovery before the airplane has regained sufficient flying speed.

2. What should the pilot be aware of regarding secondary stalls?

This stall usually occurs when the pilot becomes too anxious in returning to straight-and-level flight after a stall or spin recovery. Knowledge and proficiency in this maneuver will assist a pilot in avoiding secondary stalls.

3. How should a flight instructor demonstrate a secondary stall?

Secondary stalls can be demonstrated during the recovery phase of any of the basic stalls. The secondary stall can be induced by simply pulling the nose up more rapidly than necessary during the recovery from a full stall.

4. What are some common errors associated with secondary stalls? (FAA-S-8081-6C and FAA-H-8083-3)

a. Failure to establish selected configuration prior to entry.

b. Improper or inadequate demonstration of the recognition of and recovery from a secondary stall. Not applying sufficient back pressure to induce secondary stall.

c. Failure to present simulated student instruction that adequately emphasizes the hazards of poor procedure in recovering from a primary stall. Not explaining the "what, why, and how" of secondary stalls adequately.

Practical Test Standards (FAA-S-8081-6C)

The following is an excerpt from the Flight Instructor PTS set by the FAA for secondary stalls—

Exhibits instructional knowledge of the elements of secondary stalls, in selected landing gear and flap configurations by describing the:

a. Aerodynamics of secondary stalls.

b. Flight situations where secondary stalls may occur.

c. Hazards of secondary stalls during normal stall or spin recovery.

d. Entry procedure and minimum entry altitude.

e. Recognition of a secondary stall.

f. Recovery procedure and minimum recovery altitude.

F. Spins

1. Describe a spin. (FAA-H-8083-3)

A spin may be defined as an aggravated stall that results in what is termed "autorotation" wherein the airplane follows a downward corkscrew path. As the airplane rotates around a vertical axis, the rising wing is less stalled than the descending wing creating a rolling, yawing, and pitching motion. The airplane is basically being forced downward by gravity, rolling, yawing, and pitching in a spiral path.

2. Why is it important for the flight instructor to demonstrate spins and spin recovery?

Fear of and aversion to spins are deeply rooted in the public's mind and many pilots have an unconscious aversion to them. If one learns the cause of a spin and the proper techniques to prevent and/ or recover from the spin, mental anxiety and many causes of unintentional spins may be removed.

3. How should spins and spin recovery be demonstrated?

Entry:

a. Establish the appropriate altitude; recommended minimum altitude for recovery—3,500 feet AGL.

b. Perform clearing turns.

c. Apply carburetor heat and reduce the throttle to idle.

d. Configure the aircraft for a power-off stall (no flaps).

e. As the airplane approaches a stall, smoothly apply full rudder in the direction of the desired spin rotation and continue to apply back elevator to the limit of travel. The ailerons should be neutral.

f. Maintain full rudder deflection and elevator back pressure throughout the spin.

g. Allow the spin to develop (approximately 2 to 3 rotations).

Recovery:

a. Close the throttle (if not already accomplished).

b. Neutralize the ailerons.

c. Apply full opposite rudder.

d. Briskly move the elevator control forward to approximately the neutral position. (Some aircraft require merely a relaxation of back pressure; others require full forward elevator pressure.)

e. Once the stall is broken the spinning will stop. Neutralize the rudder when the spinning stops.

f. When the rudder is neutralized, gradually apply enough aft elevator pressure to return to level flight.

4. What are some common errors related to spin demonstration? (FAA-S-8081-6C and FAA-H-8083-3)

a. Failure to establish proper configuration prior to spin entry. Not establishing configuration recommended by manufacturer for intentional spins.

b. Failure to achieve and maintain a full stall during spin entry. Not maintaining elevator back pressure after entering the spin resulting in a steep spiral.

c. Failure to close throttle when a spin entry is achieved. Not closing throttle resulting in excessive loss of altitude.

d. Failure to recognize the indications of an imminent, unintentional spin. Uncoordinated flight combined with a fully stalled condition and use of incorrect aileron and rudder application for recovery are contributing factors to unintentional spins.

e. Improper use of flight controls during spin entry, rotation or recovery.
   • During entry not applying full rudder in direction of spin.
   • During rotation not applying full elevator back pressure, full rudder and neutralized ailerons.
   • During recovery, not applying full opposite rudder to stop rotation.
   • Not applying sufficient forward elevator to break the stalled condition.
   • Not using coordinated flight controls during recovery.

f. Disorientation during a spin. Loss of orientation with the outside reference point used to determine number of rotations.

g. Failure to distinguish between a high speed spiral and a spin. Not recognizing a high airspeed (increasing), high rate of descent (increasing), steep spiral condition; the nose of aircraft will not be as low in a steep spiral.

h. Excessive speed or accelerated stall during recovery.
   • After spin recovery, being too cautious in pulling out of dive resulting in excessive airspeed.
   • Applying too much back pressure when recovering, resulting in secondary stall.

i. Failure to recover with minimum loss of altitude.
  • Not using correct recovery procedures.
  • Hesitation in applying necessary control applications.

j. Hazards of attempting to spin an airplane not approved for spins — assuming all airplanes are capable of recovery from intentional spins.

Practical Test Standards (FAA-S-8081-6C)

The following is an excerpt from the flight instructor Practical Test Standards set by the FAA for spin aerodynamics and demonstration:

Exhibits instructional knowledge of the elements of spins by describing the:

a. Anxiety factors associated with spin instruction.

b. Aerodynamics of spins.

c. Airplanes approved for the spin maneuver based on airworthiness category and type certificate.

d. Relationship of various factors such as configuration, weight, center of gravity, and control coordination to spins.

e. Flight situations where unintentional spins may occur.

f. How to recognize and recover from imminent, unintentional spins.

g. Entry procedure and minimum entry altitude for intentional spins.

h. Control procedure to maintain a stabilized spin.

i. Orientation during a spin.

j. Recovery procedure and minimum recovery altitude for intentional spins.

G. Maneuvering During Slow Flight

1. What is slow flight? (FAA-H-8083-3)

In pilot training and testing, slow flight is broken down into two distinct elements: (1) the establishment, maintenance of, and maneuvering of the airplane at airspeeds and in configurations appropriate to takeoffs, climbs, descents, landing approaches and go-arounds, and (2) maneuvering at the slowest airspeed at which the airplane is capable of maintaining controlled flight without indications of a stall—usually 3 to 5 knots above stalling speed.

2. What is the objective in learning how to operate an airplane at slow flight?

To develop the pilot's sense of feel and ability to use the controls correctly, and to improve proficiency in performing maneuvers in which very low airspeeds are required. It is important to be able to determine the characteristic control responses of an airplane at different airspeeds. Pilots must develop this awareness in order to avoid stalls in airplanes they may fly at the slower airspeeds such as in of takeoff, climb, and landing approach.

3. Describe the procedure for operation at slow flight.

a. Establish a specific heading and altitude (recovery by 1,500 feet AGL).

b. Perform clearing turns.

c. Perform a pre-maneuver checklist (GUMPS).

d. Reduce power from cruise to slow airplane to gear and/or flap operating range.

e. Extend gear (if retractable); extend flaps and adjust pitch attitude to maintain altitude. Retrim aircraft.

f. As the airspeed approaches V_{SO}, use power to control altitude and pitch to control airspeed (area of reverse command).

g. Continually cross-check the heading indicator, altimeter, airspeed indicator and vertical airspeed indicator, as well as outside references, to ensure accurate control is maintained.

h. Right rudder should be applied to correct for left turning tendencies.

i. Establish left and right turns (15° bank), climbs and descents while in slow flight.

Recovery:

a. Apply full power.

b. Reduce flaps 10° at a time.

c. Maintain heading and altitude.

d. As airspeed increases, retract gear and any remaining flaps.

e. Retrim aircraft for cruise flight.

4. What are the standards expected of a student for maneuvering during slow flight? (FAA-S-8081-12B)

The student:

a. Shows knowledge of the elements related to maneuvering during slow flight.

b. Selects an entry altitude that will allow the task to be completed no lower than 1,500 feet (460 meters) AGL.

c. Establishes and maintains an airspeed at which any further increase in angle of attack, increase in load factor, or reduction in power, would result in an immediate stall.

d. Accomplishes coordinated straight-and-level flight, turns, climbs, and descents with landing gear and flap configurations specified by the examiner.

e. Divides attention between airplane control and orientation.

f. Maintains the specified altitude, ±50 feet (15 meters); specified heading, ±10°; airspeed +5/-0 knots, and specified angle of bank, ±5°.

Private PTS: Maintains the specified altitude, ± 100 feet (30 meters); specified heading, ± 10°; airspeed, + 10/-0 knots; and specified angle of bank, ± 10°.

5. What are some common student errors in flight at slow flight that a flight instructor should be aware of?
(FAA-S-8081-6C and FAA-H-8083-3)

a. Failure to establish specified gear and flap configuration.

b. Improper entry technique.
 • Difficulty in transition from cruise flight to slow flight.
 • Not increasing back pressure as power is reduced.
 • Increasing back pressure too quickly when power is reduced.
 • As airspeed slows, failure to apply pitch and power to control airspeed and altitude.

c. Failure to establish and maintain the specified airspeed—not applying correct pitch and power settings as required; airspeed is usually too high.

d. Excessive variations of altitude and heading when a constant altitude and heading are specified.
 • Not dividing attention as necessary.
 • Not cross-checking instruments and applying necessary control application.

e. Rough or uncoordinated control technique—overcontrolling the aircraft.

f. Improper correction for torque effect—not recognizing and compensating for torque effect.

g. Improper trim technique—not trimming aircraft as necessary.

h. Unintentional stalls.
 • Not recognizing imminent stall conditions.
 • Overcontrolling the aircraft resulting in a stall.

i. Inappropriate removal of hand from throttle(s). Not keeping hand on throttle(s) during maneuver.

H. Accelerated Maneuver Stalls

1. What is an accelerated maneuver stall? (FAA-H-8083-3)

At the same gross weight, airplane configuration, and power set-ting, a given airplane will consistently stall at the same indicated airspeed if no acceleration is involved. The airplane will, however, stall at a higher indicated airspeed when excessive maneuvering loads are imposed by steep turns, pull-ups, or other abrupt changes in its flightpath. Stalls entered from these flight situations are called "accelerated maneuver stalls," a term that does not refer to the airspeeds involved.

2. What is the objective of demonstrating an accelerated maneuver stall? (FAA-H-8083-3)

As with all stalls, it is not to develop competency in setting up the stall, but rather to learn how they may occur and to develop the ability to recognize them immediately and to take prompt, effective recovery action. It is important that recoveries are made at the first indication of a stall, or immediately after the stall has fully devel-oped; a prolonged stall condition should never be allowed. Failure to take immediate steps toward recovery when an accelerated stall occurs may result in a complete loss of flight control (notably, power-on spins).

3. Describe the procedure for demonstrating an accelerated maneuver stall. (FAA-H-8083-3)

a. Establish a specific heading and altitude (recovery by 1,500 feet AGL).

b. Perform clearing turns.

c. From straight-and-level flight at maneuvering speed or less, the airplane should be rolled into a steep level flight turn and back-elevator pressure gradually applied.

d. After the turn and bank are established, back-elevator pressure should be smoothly and steadily increased. The resulting appar-ent centrifugal force will push the pilot's body down in the seat, increase the wing loading, and decrease the airspeed.

Continued

e. After the airspeed reaches the design maneuvering speed or within 20 knots above the unaccelerated stall speed, back-elevator pressure should be firmly increased until a definite stall occurs. These speed restrictions must be observed to prevent exceeding the load limit of the airplane.

f. When the airplane stalls, recovery should be made promptly, by releasing sufficient back-elevator pressure and increasing power to reduce the angle of attack.

g. If an uncoordinated turn is made, one wing may tend to drop suddenly, causing the airplane to roll in that direction. If this occurs, the excessive back elevator pressure must be released, power added, and the airplane returned to straight-and-level flight with coordinated control pressure.

h. The pilot should recognize when the stall is imminent and take prompt action to prevent a completely stalled condition. It is imperative that a prolonged stall, excessive airspeed, excessive loss of altitude, or spin be avoided.

4. When explaining accelerated maneuver stalls to the student, what basic elements should be covered? (FAA-S-8081-6C)

a. Aerodynamics of accelerated maneuver stalls.

b. Flight situations where accelerated maneuver stalls may occur.

c. Hazards of accelerated stalls during stall or spin recovery.

d. Entry procedure and minimum entry altitude.

e. Recognition of the accelerated stall.

f. Recovery procedure and minimum recovery altitude.

5. What common instructional errors are associated with accelerated maneuver stall demonstrations? (FAA-S-8081-6C and FAA-H-8083-3)

a. Failure to establish proper configuration prior to entry.

b. Improper or inadequate demonstration of the recognition of and recovery from an accelerated maneuver stall.

c. Failure to present simulated student instruction that adequately emphasizes the hazards of poor procedures in recovering from an accelerated stall.

Additional Study Questions

1. Pilots must recognize the flight conditions that are conducive to stalls. Name several cues that indicate a stall may be imminent. (FAA-H-8083-3)

2. Explain the use of aileron and rudder in stall recovery. (FAA-H-8083-3)

3. Explain wing design as it relates to the stall characteristics of an airplane. (FAA-H-8083-3)

4. Why would the use of ailerons in stall recovery possibly result in an aggravated stall condition? (FAA-H-8083-3)

5. What are the four phases of a spin? (FAA-H-8083-3)

6. What will the indicated airspeed be in the incipient phase of a spin? (FAA-H-8083-3)

7. To determine if a spin maneuver is approved for a specific airplane, what sources should be checked? (FAA-H-8083-3)

8. Why are the weight and balance requirements of an aircraft important for safe performance and recovery of a spin maneuver? (FAA-H-8083-3)

9. When flying more slowly than minimum drag speed (LD/$_{MAX}$) the airplane will exhibit a characteristic known as "speed instability." Explain this characteristic. (FAA-H-8083-3)

10. Explain how to maintain a constant altitude and airspeed after establishing flight at minimum airspeed. (FAA-H-8083-3)

Basic Instrument
Maneuvers

7

A. General

1. Explain the value of learning basic maneuvers under simulated instrument conditions.

Developing the ability to maneuver an airplane for limited periods of time solely by reference to instruments and to follow radar instructions from ATC may become invaluable to a pilot when outside visual references are lost due to unexpected adverse weather. It must be emphasized to the student that this training does *not* prepare them for unrestricted operations in instrument weather conditions.

2. What are some common student errors in performance of the basic flight maneuvers? (FAA-S-8081-6C)

Students commonly commit errors of:

a. "Fixation," "omission," and "emphasis" errors during instrument cross-check.
   • Staring at one instrument and not cross-checking with other instruments.
   • Forgetting to include all instruments in scan.
   • Relying too heavily on one instrument for control of aircraft.

b. Improper instrument interpretation.
   • Not interpreting information provided correctly.
   • Not sure which instruments provide pitch, bank, and power information.

c. Improper control applications. If instrument interpretation is incorrect, then control application will be incorrect also.

d. Failure to establish proper pitch, bank, or power adjustments during altitude, heading, or airspeed corrections.
   • Not sure what instruments to look at when changing altitude, heading, or airspeed.
   • Not using the cross-check, interpret, and control method of attitude instrument flying.

e. Faulty trim technique. Not using trim; using trim as a primary flight control.

Continued

f. In performing straight, constant airspeed climbs, improper entry or level-off technique:
    • Not using a specific pitch attitude and power setting for climb;
    • Not planning level-off and under or overshooting altitude.

g. In performing turns to headings, improper entry or rollout technique:
    • Not rolling into the turn gradually;
    • Not adjusting the pitch attitude to compensate for the loss of vertical lift in turn;
    • Not planning the rollout.

B. Straight-and-Level Flight

1. What is involved in straight-and-level flight by reference to instruments only?

Straight-and-level flight by reference to instruments under simulated instrument conditions involves using the basic flight instruments to maintain a constant heading and altitude. This is accomplished by:

a. Establishing a definite altitude.

b. Establishing a definite heading.

c. Establishing a cruise power setting and airspeed.

d. Trimming aircraft for "hands off" flight.

e. Maintaining level flight by positioning the miniature aircraft in relation to the horizon bar on the attitude indicator. Cross-check with the altimeter and vertical speed indicator.

f. Maintaining straight flight by referencing the directional gyro occasionally for any indication of heading change. Cross-check with the attitude indicator and turn coordinator.

g. Cross-checking the instruments, interpreting what they are telling you, and controlling the aircraft.

2. What are the standards expected of a student for straight-and-level flight under simulated instrument conditions? (FAA-S-8081-14A)

The student:

a. Shows knowledge of attitude instrument flying during straight-and-level flight.

b. Maintains straight-and-level flight solely by reference to instruments using proper instrument cross-check and interpretation, coordinated control application.

c. Maintains altitude, ±200 feet (60 meters); heading ±20°; airspeed ±10 knots.

C. Constant Airspeed Climbs

1. Under simulated instrument conditions, what does a straight, constant airspeed climb involve?

A straight, constant airspeed climb involves a climb in which a constant heading is maintained at a predetermined airspeed. To accomplish this, the student should:

a. Raise the miniature aircraft to the approximate nose high indication appropriate to the predetermined climb speed.

b. Apply light back elevator pressure to initiate and maintain the climb attitude. The pressures will vary as the airplane decelerates.

c. Power may be advanced to the climb power setting simultaneously with the pitch change, or after the pitch change is established and the airspeed approaches climb speed.

d. Once the airplane stabilizes at a constant airspeed and attitude, the airspeed indicator is the primary instrument for pitch and the heading indicator is primary for bank.

2. What are the standards expected of a student for the performance of a constant airspeed climb by reference to instruments only? (FAA-S-8081-14A)

The student:

a. Shows knowledge of the elements related to attitude instrument flying during constant airspeed climbs.

b. Establishes climb configuration specified by examiner.

c. Transitions to climb pitch attitude and power setting on assigned heading using proper instrument cross-check and interpretation, and coordinated control application.

d. Demonstrates climbs solely by reference to instruments at a constant airspeed to specific altitudes in straight flight and turns.

e. Levels off at the assigned altitude and maintains that altitude, ±200 feet (60 meters); heading ±20°; airspeed ±10 knots.

D. Constant Airspeed Descents

1. Under simulated instrument conditions, what is involved in a constant airspeed descent?

A straight constant airspeed descent involves a descent in which a constant heading is maintained at a predetermined airspeed. To accomplish this, the student should:

a. Reduce power to a predetermined value.

b. Maintain back pressure until the airspeed slows to the desired descent airspeed.

c. Lower the miniature aircraft to the approximate nose-low indication appropriate to the predetermined airspeed/rate of descent.

d. Once the airplane stabilizes at a constant airspeed/rate of descent and attitude, retrim the aircraft.

e. Control airspeed with pitch and rate of descent with power.

2. What are the standards expected of a student for the performance of a constant airspeed descent by reference to instruments only? (FAA-S-8081-14A)

The student:

a. Shows knowledge of the elements related to attitude instrument flying during constant airspeed descents.

b. Establishes descent configuration specified by examiner.

c. Transitions to descent pitch attitude and power setting on assigned heading using proper instrument cross-check and interpretation, and coordinated control application.

d. Demonstrates descents solely by reference to instruments at a constant airspeed to specific altitudes in straight flight and turns.

e. Levels off at the assigned altitude and maintains that altitude, ±200 feet (60 meters); heading ±20°; airspeed ±10 knots.

E. Turns to Headings

1. What is involved in performing turns to headings by reference to instruments only?

Performing turns to headings solely by reference to instruments involves changing or returning the aircraft heading to a desired heading. The process is as follows:

a. Apply coordinated aileron and rudder pressure in the desired direction of turn.

b. On the roll-in, use the attitude indicator to establish the approximate angle of bank, then check the turn coordinator for a standard rate turn indication.

c. During the roll-in, check the altimeter, vertical speed indicator, and attitude indicator for pitch adjustments necessary as the vertical lift component decreases with an increase in bank.

d. When rolling out, apply coordinated aileron and rudder pressures opposite the direction of turn.

e. Lead the rollout by approximately 1/2 bank angle prior to the desired heading.

f. Anticipate a possible gain in altitude on rollout and adjust pitch attitude as appropriate.

2. **What are the standards expected of a student for performing turns to headings by reference to instruments only?** (FAA-S-8081-14A)

The student:

a. Shows knowledge of attitude instrument flying during turns to headings.

b. Transitions to level-turn attitude using proper instrument cross-check and interpretation, and coordinated control application.

c. Demonstrates turns to headings solely by reference to instruments; maintains altitude, ±200 feet (60 meters); maintains a standard rate turn and rolls out on the assigned heading, ±10°; maintains airspeed, ±10 knots.

F. Recovery From Unusual Flight Attitudes

1. What is meant by the term "unusual flight attitudes"?

When outside visual references are inadequate or lost, the VFR pilot is apt to unintentionally let the airplane enter a critical attitude (sometimes called an "unusual attitude"). In general, this involves an excessively nose-high attitude in which the airplane may be approaching a stall, or an extremely steep bank which may result in a steep downward spiral.

2. Discuss the importance of instrument training for recovery from an unusual attitude.

Since unusual attitudes are not intentional, they are often unexpected, and the reaction of an inexperienced or inadequately-trained pilot is usually instinctive rather than intelligent and deliberate. However, with practice the techniques for rapid and safe recovery from these critical attitudes can be learned.

3. Describe some techniques for recovery from unusual flight attitudes by reference to instruments.

Nose-high decreasing airspeed

a. Indicated by:
- Decreasing airspeed on airspeed indicator.
- Increasing altitude on altimeter and positive rate on vertical speed indicator.
- Bank on attitude indicator/heading indicator/turn coordinator.

b. Recover by:
- Reducing pitch attitude.
- Simultaneously increasing power.
- Leveling the wings as necessary.

Nose-low increasing airspeed

a. Indicated by:
- Increasing airspeed on airspeed indicator.
- Decreasing altitude on altimeter and negative rate on vertical speed indicator.
- Bank on attitude indicator/heading indicator/turn coordinator.

b. Recover by:
- Reducing power.
- Leveling the wings.
- Raising the nose gradually.

Note: The attitude indicator is normally the most useful instrument in determining the aircraft's attitude. However, extreme unusual attitudes may cause the gyros in the attitude indicator and heading indicator to tumble. In this situation the pitch attitude may be determined through combined use of the information provided by the airspeed indicator, altimeter, and vertical speed indicator. The turn coordinator may be used as the primary instrument in detecting bank angle.

4. What are the standards expected of a student for recovery from unusual flight attitudes by reference to instruments only? (FAA-S-8081-14A)

The student:

a. Shows knowledge of attitude instrument flying during unusual attitudes.

b. Recognizes unusual flight attitudes solely by reference to instruments; recovers promptly to a stabilized level flight attitude using proper instrument cross-check and interpretation and smooth, coordinated control application in correct sequence.

5. In simulated instrument conditions, what are some common student errors in recovering from unusual attitudes? (FAA-S-8081-6C)

Students commonly commit errors of:

a. Failure to recognize an unusual flight attitude.
   • Not interpreting the information provided correctly.
   • Not sure of which instruments provide pitch, bank, and power information.

b. Consequences of attempting to recover from an unusual flight attitude by feel rather than by instrument indications; not trusting instrument indications can lead to rapid altitude loss as a result of inadvertent steep spirals or power-on/power-off stalls.

c. Inappropriate control applications during recovery:
   • Not following the correct sequence of actions in recovery;
   • In descents: increasing back pressure before leveling the wings, not reducing power in descent; overcompensating on recovery by increasing pitch attitude past that for level flight.
   • In climbs: not lowering the nose fast enough; lowering the nose too far; not adding power.

d. Failure to recognize, from instrument indications, when the airplane is passing through a level flight attitude:
   • Not cross-checking instruments.
   • Not using the attitude indicator and/or airspeed indicator/altimeter to determine level flight.

Additional Study Questions

1. What are the three fundamental skills involved in all instrument flight maneuvers? (FAA-H-8083-15)

2. How will you teach your student the instrument cross-check skill? (FAA-H-8083-15)

3. What is "fixation" and why does it occur? (FAA-H-8083-15)

4. How will you teach your student the instrument interpretation skill? (FAA-H-8083-15)

5. Explain how instrument "emphasis" and "omission" occur. (FAA-H-8083-15)

6. How will you teach your student the aircraft control skill? (FAA-H-8083-15)

7. What are the four basic components of aircraft control? (FAA-H-8083-15)

8. What instruments are used for pitch, bank, and power information? (FAA-H-8083-15)

9. What are the two basic methods used for learning attitude instrument flying? (FAA-H-8083-15)

10. Why is trim technique so essential to smooth aircraft control when flying by reference to instruments? (FAA-H-8083-15)

Performance Maneuvers

8

A. Steep Turns

1. Describe a steep turn.

Steep turns result from a degree of bank (more than about 45°) at which the overbanking tendency of an airplane overcomes stability, and the bank tends to increase unless pressure is applied to the aileron controls to prevent it. Maximum turning performance is attained. It imposes relatively high load factors.

2. What is the objective of practicing a steep turn?

To develop smoothness, coordination, orientation, division of attention, and control techniques while executing a high-performance turn.

3. Describe how to perform a steep turn maneuver.

a. Establish a specific heading (and an outside reference) and altitude.

b. Perform clearing turns.

c. Roll into a 45- to 60-degree bank while maintaining altitude with necessary back pressure.

d. Complete a left and right 360° heading change. (It may be necessary to add additional power to maintain airspeed above a stall.)

e. Lead rollout to heading by one half the bank angle.

f. Use horizon and glare shield/cowling to maintain pitch attitude.

g. If loss of altitude occurs, decrease bank, add back pressure to regain altitude, and establish higher pitch attitude.

h. If gain of altitude occurs, increase bank (maximum 55°), decrease pitch attitude and or power.

4. What are the standards expected of a student for steep turns? (FAA-S-8081-12B)

The student:

a. Shows knowledge of the elements related to steep turns.

b. Establishes the manufacturers recommended airspeed or if one is not stated, a safe airspeed not to exceed V_A.

c. Rolls into a coordinated 360° steep turn with at least a 50° bank, followed by a 360° steep turn in the opposite direction.*

d. Divides attention between airplane control and orientation.

e. Maintains the entry altitude, ±100 feet (30 meters), airspeed, ±10 knots, bank, ±5°; and rolls out on the entry heading, ±10°.

* Private standards: Rolls into a coordinated 360° turn, maintains 45° bank, ±5°.

5. What are some common student errors in performing steep turns? (FAA-S-8081-6C and FAA-H-8083-3)

a. Improper pitch, bank, and power coordination during entry and rollout.
   • Increasing pitch attitude before establishing bank angle with resulting gain in altitude.
   • Not releasing back pressure in recovery with resulting gain in altitude.
   • Not enough or too much bank.
   • No use of power to assist in maintaining altitude.

b. Uncoordinated use of flight controls. Slipping or skidding through maneuver; a skid is common in turns to the right.

c. Inappropriate control applications—not making the necessary minor adjustments in altitude and bank throughout maneuver resulting in the need for major adjustments.

d. Improper technique in correcting altitude deviations—not reducing bank angle first before increasing back pressure when trying to correct for loss of altitude;

e. Loss of orientation—the initial heading from which the maneuver began is forgotten and/or the reference point outside can no longer be found.

f. Excessive deviation from desired heading during rollout.
- Not planning the rollout.
- Not leading the heading to be rolled-out on by half the amount of bank in degrees (i.e., 50° bank would require 25° of lead).

B. Steep Spirals

1. What is a steep spiral? (FAA-H-8083-3)

It is simply a constant gliding turn during which a constant radius around a point on the ground is maintained, similar to the turns around a point maneuver. The radius should be such that the steepest bank will not exceed 60°.

2. What is the objective of a steep spiral? (FAA-H-8083-3)

To improve pilot techniques for power-off turns, wind drift control, planning, orientation, and division of attention. Its most practical application is providing a procedure for dissipating altitude while remaining over a selected spot in preparation for landing, especially for emergency forced landings.

3. What are the standards expected of a student for steep spirals? (FAA-S-8081-12B)

The student:

a. Shows knowledge of the elements related to a steep spiral.

b. Selects an altitude sufficient to continue through a series of at least three 360° turns.

c. Selects a suitable ground reference point.

d. Applies wind-drift correction to track a constant radius circle around selected reference point with bank not to exceed 60° at steepest point in turn.

e. Divides attention between airplane control and ground track, while maintaining coordinated flight.

f. Maintains the specified airspeed, ±10 knots, rolls out toward object or specified heading, ±10°.

4. What are some common student errors in the performance of steep spirals?
(FAA-S-8081-6C and FAA-H-8083-3)

   a. Improper pitch, bank, and power coordination during entry or completion — not establishing appropriate pitch, airspeed, and power setting for glide; exceeding 60° of bank during turns; not clearing engine during maneuver.

   b. Uncoordinated use of flight controls — inadvertently slipping or skidding the airplane during turns.

   c. Improper planning and lack of maintenance of constant airspeed and radius — not maintaining constant airspeed as bank is increased and decreased in turns; not recognizing and correcting for wind drift. Failure to hold airspeed constant will cause the radius of turn and necessary angle of bank to vary excessively.

   d. Failure to stay orientated to the number of turns and the rollout heading — not remaining aware of number of turns and altitude remaining; not completing necessary three turns prior to 1,000 feet, or rollout to a definite object or specific heading.

C. Chandelles

1. What is a chandelle?

A "chandelle" is a maximum performance climbing turn beginning from approximately straight-and-level flight, and ending at the completion of 180° of turn in a wings-level, nose-high attitude at the minimum controllable airspeed.

2. What is the objective of the chandelle maneuver?

To develop the pilot's coordination, orientation, planning, feel for maximum-performance flight, and positive control techniques at varying airspeeds and attitudes. Maximum flight performance of the airplane is obtained. The airplane should gain the most amount of altitude possible for a given degree of bank and power setting without stalling.

3. Describe how to perform a chandelle.

a. Establish a specific heading and altitude (no lower than 1,500 feet AGL).

b. Perform clearing turns.

c. Pick a prominent reference point and plan to perform the maneuver into the wind to prevent drift from the training area.

d. Establish a coordinated 30°-bank turn and plan on maintaining this bank angle for the first 90° of turn.

e. Apply takeoff or climb power and begin a climbing turn by smoothly applying back pressure to increase pitch attitude at a constant rate and to attain the highest pitch attitude as 90° of turn is completed.

f. When the turn has progressed 90° from the original heading, begin rolling out of the bank at a constant rate while maintaining a constant pitch attitude.

g. As the wings are being leveled at the completion of 180° of turn, the pitch attitude should be held momentarily while the airplane is at minimum controllable speed.

Note: First 90°—constant bank, changing pitch
Second 90°—constant pitch, changing bank

4. What are the standards expected of a student for performing chandelles? (FAA-S-8081-12B)

The student:

a. Exhibits knowledge of the elements related to chandelles.

b. Selects an altitude that will allow the maneuver to be performed no lower than 1,500 feet AGL (460 meters).

c. Establishes the recommended entry configuration, power, and airspeed.

d. Establishes the angle of bank at approximately 30°.

e. Simultaneously applies power and pitch to maintain a smooth, coordinated climbing turn to the 90° point with a constant bank.

f. Begins a coordinated constant rate rollout from the 90° point to the 180° point maintaining power and a constant pitch attitude.

Continued

g. Completes rollout at the 180° point, ±10° just above a stall airspeed, and maintaining that airspeed momentarily avoiding a stall.

h. Resumes straight-and-level flight with minimum loss of altitude.

5. What are some common student errors in the performance of chandelles?
(FAA-S-8081-6C and FAA-H-8083-3)

a. Improper pitch, bank, and power coordination during entry and rollout.
   • Initial pitch-up attitude to quick resulting in the aircraft approaching stall speed before 180° of direction change has occurred.
   • Initial pitch-up attitude too slow resulting in completion of maneuver at an airspeed well above the stall speed.
   • Initial bank angle exceeded resulting in completion of maneuver at an airspeed well above the stall speed.
   • Initial bank angle too shallow resulting in the aircraft approaching stall speed before 180° of direction change has occurred.
   • Failure to add full power at the start of maneuver.

b. Uncoordinated use of flight controls—not using enough rudder to compensate for torque effect.

c. Improper planning and timing of pitch and bank attitude changes.

d. Factors related to failure in achieving maximum performance.
   • Not maintaining appropriate bank angles during the maneuver.
   • Not maintaining appropriate pitch attitudes during the maneuver.
   • Not planning ahead.

e. A stall during the maneuver.
   • Usually occurs in the last 90° of turn due to poor planning.
   • At the completion of the maneuver the airspeed should be just above the stall speed.

f. Excessive deviation from desired heading during completion; allowing the heading to drift due to lack of torque correction.

D. Lazy Eights

1. What is a lazy eight?

A lazy eight consists of two 180° turns in opposite directions, while making a climb and a descent in a symmetrical pattern during each of the turns.

2. Discuss the use and advantages of practicing lazy eights.

The objective of the lazy eight is to develop the pilot's feel for varying control forces, and the ability to plan and remain oriented while maneuvering the airplane with positive, accurate control. Constantly changing control pressures are needed due to changing combinations of climbing and descending turns at varying airspeeds. Often used to develop and demonstrate the pilot's mastery of the airplane in maximum performance flight situations.

3. Describe the steps involved in a lazy eight maneuver.

a. Establish a specific heading and altitude (no lower than 1,500 feet AGL).

b. Perform clearing turns.

c. Pick a prominent reference point and plan to perform the maneuver into the wind to prevent drift from the training area.

d. Establish maneuvering speed or manufacturer's recommended speed.

e. Start the maneuver from level flight with a gradual climbing turn toward reference points.

f. At 45°-point: maximum pitch up attitude, bank 15° (approximately).

g. At 90°-point: bank approximately 30°, minimum airspeed, maximum altitude; level pitch attitude.

h. At 135°-point: maximum pitch down, bank 15° (approximately).

i. At 180°-point: level flight, entry airspeed, altitude same as entry altitude.

4. What are the standards expected of a student for performing lazy eights? (FAA-S-8081-12B)

The student:

a. Shows knowledge of the elements related to lazy eights.

b. Selects an altitude that will allow the task to be performed no lower than 1,500 feet AGL (460 meters).

c. Establishes the recommended entry configuration, power, and airspeed.

d. Maintains coordinated flight throughout the maneuver.

e. Achieves the following throughout the maneuver—
   • approximately 30° bank at the steepest point.
   • constant change of pitch and roll rate.
   • altitude tolerance at 180° points, ±100 feet (30 meters) from entry altitude.
   • airspeed tolerance at the 180°-point, plus ±10 knots from entry airspeed.
   • heading tolerance at the 180°-point ±10°.

f. Continues the maneuver through the number of symmetrical loops specified and resumes straight-and-level flight.

5. What are some common student errors in the performance of lazy eights?
(FAA-S-8081-6C and FAA-H-8083-3)

a. Poor selection of reference points:
   • Not selecting a reference point that is readily seen.
   • Picking a reference point that is too close.

b. Uncoordinated use of flight controls:
   • Not correcting for torque effect.
   • Due to decreasing airspeed, considerable right rudder pressure must be gradually applied to counteract torque at the top of the eight in both right and left turns.
   • More right rudder pressure will be required during the climbing turn to the right than the turn to the left because more torque correction is needed to prevent yaw from decreasing the rate of turn.
   • In the left climbing turn the torque will tend to contribute to the turn consequently less rudder pressure is needed.

c. Non-symmetrical loops resulting from poorly planned pitch and bank attitude changes:
- Initial pitch attitude too quick in the climbing turn resulting in the airplane stalling before reaching the 90°-point.
- Initial pitch attitude too slow in the climbing turn resulting in the airplane reaching the 90°-point without attaining the minimum airspeed.
- Initial bank angle excessive resulting in the airplane reaching the 90°-point before minimum airspeed is reached.
- Allowing the pitch attitude in the last 90° of turn to become excessively low resulting in exceeding the initial entry airspeed and/or altitude.

d. Inconsistent airspeed and altitude at key points—not planning ahead.

e. Loss of orientation:
- Poorly selected reference point not readily seen.
- Student not looking outside enough; poor division of attention.

f. Excessive deviation from reference points—not planning ahead.

Additional Study Questions

1. **Why does an airplane have a tendency to overbank in a steep turn?** (FAA-H-8083-3)

2. **What effect will a steep turn have on an airplane's stall speed and load factor? Why?** (FAA-H-8083-3)

3. **Why must power be added to maintain altitude and airspeed in a steep turn?** (FAA-H-8083-3)

4. **Why is more rudder pressure required when rolling out of a chandelle to the left than a chandelle to the right?** (FAA-H-8083-3)

5. **When entering a lazy eight, will you establish the bank first, pitch first, or both at the same time?** (FAA-H-8083-3)

Continued

6. **Discuss reference point selection for the lazy eight maneuver.** (FAA-H-8083-3)

7. **When performing a lazy eight, why is more rudder required in a right turn than in a left turn?** (FAA-H-8083-3)

8. **While performing a steep spiral, how is a constant radius around the selected point maintained?** (FAA-H-8083-3)

9. **Failure to control airspeed in a steep spiral will cause several problems. What are they?** (FAA-H-8083-3)

10. **Explain the procedure for control of wind drift during a steep spiral.** (FAA-H-8083-3)

Ground Reference Maneuvers

9

A. Rectangular Course

1. Describe a rectangular course maneuver.

This a practice maneuver in which the ground track of the airplane is equidistant from all sides of a selected rectangular area on the ground. While performing the maneuver, the altitude and airspeed are held constant.

2. What are the advantages of practicing a rectangular course?

Like those of other ground track maneuvers, one of the objectives is to develop division of attention between the flightpath and ground references, while controlling the airplane at low altitudes and watching for other aircraft in the vicinity. Another objective is to develop recognition of drift toward or away from a line parallel to the intended ground track. This will be helpful in recognizing drift toward or from an airport runway during the various legs of the airport traffic pattern.

3. Describe the process of executing a rectangular course.

a. Establish an altitude 600 to 1,000 feet AGL (500 feet above obstructions).

b. Perform clearing turns.

c. Select a square or rectangular field, the sides of which are approximately 1 mile in length.

d. Enter a left or right pattern, 45° to the downwind leg, at an appropriate distance (approximately one-fourth mile) from field boundaries. Maneuver as necessary to maintain a uniform distance from field boundaries.

e. The bank in each of the turns should be adjusted to compensate for wind drift.

Note:
Upwind to crosswind: Shallow bank, increasing to medium, and less than 90° of turn.

Crosswind to downwind: Increasing to steepest bank necessary and more than 90° of turn.

Continued

Downwind to crosswind: Steepest bank necessary, decreasing to medium, and more than 90° of turn.

Crosswind to upwind: Medium bank, decreasing to shallow, and less than a 90° turn.

4. What are the standards expected of a student for a rectangular course? (FAA-S-8081-14A)

The student:

a. Shows knowledge of the elements related to a rectangular course.

b. Selects a suitable reference area.

c. Plans the maneuver so as to enter a left or right pattern, 600 to 1,000 feet AGL (180 to 300 meters) at an appropriate distance from the selected reference area, 45° to the downwind leg.

d. Applies adequate wind-drift correction during straight-and-turning flight to maintain a constant ground track around the rectangular reference area.

e. Divides attention between airplane control and the ground track while maintaining coordinated flight.

f. Maintains altitude, ±100 feet (30 meters); maintains airspeed, ±10 knots.

5. What are some common student errors in performing a rectangular course? (FAA-S-8081-6C and FAA-H-8083-3)

a. Poor planning, orientation, or division of attention:
   • Not planning ahead.
   • Fixating on the field and forgetting to look for other air traffic.
   • Not selecting a proper distance from the field boundary.

b. Uncoordinated flight control application:
   • Turns are uncoordinated due to preoccupation with maneuver.
   • Not dividing attention correctly.

 c. Improper correction for wind drift:
- Failure to recognize or not correcting for wind drift.
- No crab on straight-and-level segments, which results in drifting toward or away from field.
- Not using correct bank angles in turns.
- Not turning the airplane when abeam the corners; instead the student turns the airplane when the wingtip is abeam the corner.

 d. Failure to maintain selected altitude or airspeed. Loss or gain in altitude due to lack of division of attention.

 e. Selection of a ground reference where there is no suitable emergency landing area within gliding distance. Poor planning when selecting area for maneuver.

B. S-Turns

1. Describe an S-turn.

An S-turn is a practice maneuver in which the airplane's ground track describes semi-circles of equal radii on each side of a selected straight line on the ground. The straight line may be a road, fence, railroad, or section line which lies perpendicular to the wind, and should be of sufficient length for making a series of turns. The maneuver consists of crossing the road at a 90° angle and immediately beginning a series of 180° turns of uniform radius in opposite directions, recrossing the road at a 90° angle just as 180° of turn is completed. A constant altitude should be maintained throughout the maneuver. The altitude should be low enough to easily recognize drift but in no case lower than 500 feet above the highest obstruction.

2. What is the S-turn used for?

The objectives of this maneuver are to develop the ability to compensate for wind drift during turns, orient the flightpath with ground references, and divide the pilot's attention while controlling the airplane at a relatively low altitude.

3. How are S-turns executed?

a. Establish an altitude 600 to 1,000 feet AGL (500 feet above obstructions).

b. Perform clearing turns.

c. Select a straight ground reference line or road that lies 90° to the direction of the wind.

d. Approach the road from the upwind side on a downwind heading and when directly over the road, roll into the first turn which should be the steepest.

e. As the airplane gradually turns back into the wind, begin to shallow the bank angle so as to arrive over the road as the wings roll level.

f. When directly over the road roll into the next turn, using a shallow bank initially (upwind), then gradually increasing bank to the steepest (downwind).

4. What are the standards expected of a student for S-turns? (FAA-S-8081-14A)

The student:

a. Shows knowledge of the elements related to S-turns.

b. Selects a suitable ground reference line.

c. Plans the maneuver so as to enter at 600 to 1,000 feet (180 to 300 meters) AGL, perpendicular to the selected reference line.

d. Applies adequate wind-drift correction to track a constant radius turn on each side of the selected reference line.

e. Reverses the direction of turn directly over the selected reference line.

f. Divides attention between airplane control and the ground track while maintaining coordinated flight.

g. Maintains altitude, ±100 feet (30 meters); maintains airspeed, ±10 knots.

5. What are some common student errors in performing S-turns? (FAA-S-8081-6C and FAA-H-8083-3)

a. Faulty entry technique:
  • Entering upwind.
  • Not clearing the area.
  • Entering at an improper altitude.

b. Poor planning, orientation, or division of attention:
  • Appropriate bank angles used too soon or too late due to lack of planning.
  • Forgets wind direction in relation to location.
  • Not dividing attention inside and outside equally.

c. Uncoordinated flight control application. Not dividing attention inside and outside resulting in uncoordinated turns.

d. Improper correction for wind drift:
  • Forgetting where wind is in relation to the airplane;
  • Not sure when to use steep and shallow bank angles.

e. A non-symmetrical ground track: not compensating for the wind, especially on the upwind side.

f. Failure to maintain selected altitude or airspeed. Not dividing attention inside and outside resulting in a loss or gain in altitude.

g. Selection of a ground reference line where there is no suitable emergency landing area within gliding distance — not planning ahead.

C. Turns Around a Point

1. What are "turns around a point"?

This training maneuver involves flying the airplane in two or more circles of uniform radii or distance from a prominent ground reference point using a maximum bank of approximately 45° while maintaining a constant altitude.

2. What is the objective of practicing turns around a point?

The objective, as with other ground reference maneuvers, is to help the pilot develop the ability to subconsciously control the airplane while at relatively low altitudes, dividing attention between the flight path and ground references, and watching for other air traffic in the vicinity.

3. How are turns around a point executed?

a. Establish an altitude 600 to 1,000 feet AGL (500 feet above obstructions).

b. Perform clearing turns.

c. Select a prominent point on the ground.

d. Enter the maneuver downwind at a distance equal to the desired radius of turn.

e. Roll into a bank when abeam reference. If any significant wind is present this will be the steepest bank in the maneuver (highest ground speed).

f. Decrease the bank angle as the aircraft turns into the wind (low ground speed).

Note:

Downwind turn: Steepest bank.

Downwind to crosswind: Gradually decrease to medium bank.

Crosswind to upwind: Gradually decrease from medium to shallow bank.

Upwind to crosswind: Gradually increase from shallow to medium bank.

Crosswind to downwind: Increase from medium to steep bank.

4. What are the standards expected of a student for turns around a point? (FAA-S-8081-14A)

The student:

a. Shows knowledge of the elements related to turns around a point.

b. Selects a suitable ground reference point.

c. Plans the maneuver so as to enter left or right at 600 to 1,000 feet (180 to 300 meters) AGL, at an appropriate distance from the reference point.

d. Applies adequate wind-drift correction to track a constant radius turn around the selected reference point.

e. Divides attention between airplane control and the ground track while maintaining coordinated flight.

f. Maintains altitude, ±100 feet (30 meters); maintains airspeed, ±10 knots.

5. What are some common student errors in performing turns around a point? (FAA-S-8081-6C and FAA-H-8083-3)

a. Faulty entry technique:
- Entering upwind.
- Not clearing the area.
- Enters at improper altitude.
- Not using the steepest bank on the initial turn from downwind.

b. Poor planning, orientation, or division of attention:
- Appropriate bank angles used too soon or too late due to lack of planning.
- Forgets wind direction in relation to location.
- Not dividing attention inside and outside equally.

c. Uncoordinated flight control application. Not dividing attention inside and outside resulting in uncoordinated turns.

d. Improper correction for wind drift:
- Forgetting where the wind is in relation to the airplane.
- Not sure when to use steep and shallow bank angles.

e. Failure to maintain selected altitude or airspeed. Not dividing attention inside and outside resulting in a loss or gain in altitude/airspeed.

f. Selection of a ground reference point where there is no suitable emergency landing area within gliding distance—not planning ahead.

D. Eights-On-Pylons

1. Describe eights-on-pylons.

This is a training maneuver in which you fly the airplane in circular paths, alternately left and right, in the form of a figure-8 around two selected points or pylons on the ground. No attempt is made to maintain a uniform distance from the pylon. Instead, the airplane is flown at such an altitude and airspeed that a line parallel to the airplane's lateral axis, and extending from the pilot's eye, appears to pivot on each of the pylons.

2. What is the objective of the eights-on-pylons maneuver?

While not truly a ground track maneuver, the objective is similar: to develop the ability to maneuver the airplane accurately while dividing one's attention between the flight path and maintaining a pivotal position on selected pylons on the ground.

3. How are eights-on-pylons executed?

a. Establish an approximate pivotal altitude.

b. Perform clearing turns.

c. Select two points on the ground along a line that lies 90° to the wind. The points should be prominent and adequately spaced to provide planning for the turns (approximately 3 to 5 seconds straight-and-level flight).

d. Begin the maneuver by flying diagonally crosswind between the pylons to a point downwind from the first pylon so that the first turn can be made into the wind.

e. As the airplane approaches the pylon a turn should be started by lowering the wing to place the pilot's line of sight reference on the pylon.

f. As the airplane heads into the wind the groundspeed decreases, and consequently, the pivotal altitude is lower and the airplane must descend to hold the reference line on the pylon.

g. As the turn progresses on the upwind side of the pylon, the wind becomes more of a crosswind and drifts the airplane closer to the pylon. Since a constant distance is not required no correction should be applied.

h. With the airplane drifting closer to the pylon, the angle of bank must be increased to hold the reference line on the pylon.

i. If the reference line appears to move ahead of the pylon the pilot should increase altitude.

j. As the airplane turns toward a downwind heading, the rollout from the turn should be started to allow the airplane to proceed diagonally to a point on the downwind side of the second pylon.

k. The rollout must be completed in the proper crab angle to correct for wind drift so that the airplane will arrive at a point downwind from the second pylon the same distance it was from the first pylon.

l. Upon reaching second pylon a turn is started in the opposite direction by lowering the upwind wing to again place the pilot's line of sight reference on the pylon.

4. What are the standards expected of a student for performing eights-on-pylons? (FAA-S-8081-12B)

The student:

a. Shows knowledge of the elements related to eights-on-pylons.

b. Determines the approximate pivotal altitude.

c. Selects suitable pylons that will permit straight and level flight between the pylons.

d. Enters the maneuver at the appropriate altitude and airspeed and at a bank angle of approximately 30° to 40° at the steepest point.

e. Applies the necessary corrections so that the line-of-sight reference line remains on the pylon.

f. Divides attention between accurate coordinated airplane control and outside visual references.

g. Holds pylon using appropriate pivotal altitude avoiding slips and skids.

5. **What are some common student errors in performing eights-on-pylons?** (FAA-S-8081-6C and FAA-H-8083-3)

a. Faulty entry technique:
   • Poor pylon selection.
   • Not entering by flying diagonally crosswind between the pylons.
   • Not clearing the area; not entering at pivotal altitude.

b. Poor planning, orientation, and division of attention:
   • Not planning for changes in groundspeed.
   • Losing the pylon.
   • Forgetting wind direction in relation to location.
   • Not dividing attention inside and outside equally.

c. Uncoordinated flight control application:
   • Attempting to hold a pylon by use of rudder.
   • Not dividing attention inside and outside resulting in uncoordinated turns.

d. Use of an improper line of sight reference; not using a line of sight reference parallel to the lateral axis of the airplane.

e. Application of rudder alone to maintain the line of sight on pylon:
   • When reference line moves ahead of pylon, the pilot will tend to press the inside rudder to yaw the wing backward.
   • When the reference line moves behind the pylon, the pilot will press the outside rudder to yaw the wing forward.

f. Improper timing of turn entries and rollouts:
   • Rolling in too soon or rolling out too late.
   • Rolling in should be started just before the reference line reaches pylon.
   • The rollout should be started to allow the airplane to proceed diagonally to a point on the downwind side of the second pylon.

g. Improper correction for wind drift between pylons—not compensating for wind drift when between pylons. The distance from second pylon will not be equal to distance from first pylon.

h. Selection of pylons where there is no suitable emergency landing area within gliding distance—not planning ahead.

Additional Study Questions

1. Why should you instruct your student to practice rectangular courses using both left and right turns? (FAA-H-8083-3)

2. During practice of rectangular courses, what amount of bank should normally not be exceeded? (FAA-H-8083-3)

3. What will you teach your student about establishing the correct distance from the field boundaries in a rectangular course? (FAA-H-8083-3)

4. While practicing S-turns, your student is consistently rolling out, wings-level, prior to reaching the selected road. What is the problem and how can it be corrected? (FAA-H-8083-3)

5. While practicing S-turns, your student is consistently flying too far from the road and has established a ground track of excessive radius. What is the problem and how can it be corrected? (FAA-H-8083-3)

6. What will you teach your student concerning how to establish the correct distance from the point, in a turn-around-a-point maneuver? (FAA-H-8083-3)

7. What is the advantage to entering a turn-around-a-point maneuver directly downwind? (FAA-H-8083-3)

8. Will the pivotal altitude change when changing the angle of bank in an eights-on-pylons maneuver? (FAA-H-8083-3)

9. What is a "rule of thumb" for estimating pivotal altitude in an eights-on-pylons maneuver? (FAA-H-8083-3)

10. Explain why a pilot might incorrectly use the rudder during an eights-on-pylons maneuver. (FAA-H-8083-3)

Approaches and Landings

10

A. Normal or Crosswind Approach and Landing

1. Describe a normal approach and landing.

These are techniques for what is considered a "normal" situation; that is, when engine power is available, the wind is light and the final approach is made directly into the wind, the final approach path has no obstacles, and the landing surface is firm and of ample length to gradually bring the airplane to a stop.

2. What is the learning objective of a normal approach and landing?

The objective of a good stabilized approach and landing is to establish an angle of descent and airspeed that will permit the airplane to reach the desired touchdown point at an airspeed which will result in a minimum floating just before touchdown.

3. List the steps toward achieving a normal approach and landing.

a. Establish a normal traffic pattern.

b. At midfield, on downwind, complete a pre-landing checklist.

c. Abeam the touch down point on downwind, reduce power.

d. Maintain altitude and level pitch attitude momentarily to dissipate airspeed.

e. Retrim aircraft to establish airspeed within flap operating range (white arc).

f. Lower flaps to 10°.

g. Establish initial approach airspeed (1.4 x V_{SO}); retrim if necessary.

h. At an approximate 45°-point from the landing threshold, clear for traffic and turn base.

i. Extend flaps and retrim if necessary to maintain approach airspeed; apply wind drift correction.

j. Lead turn to final to roll out on runway extended centerline.

Continued

k. Once the field is assured extend final flaps.

l. Simultaneously adjust power and pitch attitude as necessary to control the airspeed and the descent angle, or to attain the desired altitudes along the approach path.

m. As airplane approaches runway and landing is assured slowly close the throttle and start the landing flare about 5 to 10 feet above the runway.

n. Continue applying back pressure as the airplane decelerates.

o. Land on the main wheels first.

p. Brake as necessary.

4. What is involved in a crosswind approach and landing?

A crosswind approach and landing involves techniques used when the wind is blowing across rather than parallel to the runway direction. Many runways or landing areas are such that landings must be made while the wind is blowing across rather than parallel to the landing direction; therefore, all pilots should be prepared to cope with these situations when they arise.

5. Describe the procedure used in a crosswind approach and landing (wing-low method).

a. Use the same procedures used for a normal approach.

b. On final, lower the upwind wing as necessary to control lateral drift over the extended runway centerline.

c. Use opposite rudder to align the longitudinal axis of the airplane with the extended runway centerline.

d. Maintain and adjust the control deflections as necessary to track the extended centerline.

e. As the airspeed slows during the roundout and flare, control deflections must be increased as necessary to obtain the desired effect.

f. After touchdown, slowly increase aileron deflection into the crosswind to assist in directional control.

6. **What are the standards expected of a student for a normal or crosswind approach and landing?** (FAA-S-8081-12B)

The student:

a. Shows knowledge of the elements related to normal and cross-wind approach and landing.

b. Considers the wind conditions, landing surface, obstructions, and selects a suitable touchdown point.

c. Establishes the recommended approach and landing configuration and airspeed and adjusts pitch attitude and power as required.

d. Maintains a stabilized approach and recommended airspeed, or in its absence, not more than 1.3 V_{SO}, ±5 knots, with wind gust factor applied.

Private PTS: Maintains a stabilized approach and recommended airspeed, or in its absence, not more than 1.3 V_{SO}, +10/-5 knots, with wind gust factor applied.

e. Makes smooth, timely, and correct control application during the roundout and touchdown.

f. Touches down smoothly at approximate stalling speed.

g. Touches down at or within 200 feet (60 meters) beyond a specified point, with no drift, and with the airplane's longitudinal axis aligned with and over the runway center/landing path.

Private PTS: Touches down at or within 400 feet (120 meters) beyond a specified point, with no drift, and with the airplane's longitudinal axis aligned with and over the runway center/landing path.

h. Maintains crosswind correction and directional control throughout the approach and landing sequence.

i. Completes appropriate checklist.

Note: If a crosswind condition does not exist, the applicant's knowledge of the crosswind elements shall be evaluated through oral testing.

7. What are some common student errors in performing normal or crosswind approach and landings?
(FAA-S-8081-6C and FAA-H-8083-3)

a. Improper use of landing performance data and limitations. Not calculating landing distances correctly.

b. Failure to establish the approach and landing configuration at the appropriate time or in the proper sequence. Not following established procedure.

c. Failure to establish and maintain a stabilized approach:
  • Not establishing correct airspeeds for downwind, base and final segments.
  • Not adjusting power and pitch attitude as necessary to control airspeed and rate of descent.
  • Not using flaps as necessary to control speed and rate of descent.
  • Not correcting for wind drift on downwind, base, and final.

d. Inappropriate removal of hand from throttle. Not keeping hand on throttle for power increases and reductions.

e. Improper techniques during roundout and touchdown:
  • Rounding out too late resulting in, if not corrected, a hard landing followed by a bounce and a stall and another hard landing.
  • Rounding out too high resulting in, if not corrected, an eventual loss in airspeed followed by a high sink rate and a hard landing.
  • Rounding out and "ballooning" down the runway; usually caused by misjudging the rate of descent and overcontrolling.
  • Rounding out and "floating" down the runway; usually caused by excessive airspeed on final approach.
  • Touchdown followed by a bounce as a result of an excessive rate of descent on final.
  • Touchdown with the aircraft drifting sideways as a result of not applying enough "wing low" into the crosswind.
  • Touchdown in a crab as a result of allowing a wing to rise on roundout or in the flare.

f. Poor directional control after touchdown:
- Allowing a wing to rise after touchdown.
- Allowing touchdown while in a crab.
- Overcontrolling with rudder.
- Ground loop: may be caused by a crosswind or overcontrolling airplane; this problem can be significant in tailwheel aircraft.

g. Improper use of brakes:
- Not using aerodynamic braking.
- Excessive use of brakes.
- Skidding the tires.

B. Forward Slip to a Landing

1. What is a forward slip? (FAA-H-8083-3)

A forward slip is one in which the airplane's direction of motion continues the same as before the slip was begun. The wing on the side toward which the slip is to be made is lowered and, simultaneously, the airplane's nose is yawed in the opposite direction by applying opposite rudder so that the airplane's longitudinal axis is at an angle to its original flightpath.

2. What is the purpose of a forward slip to a landing?

The primary purpose of forward slips is to dissipate altitude without increasing the airplane's speed, particularly in airplanes not equipped with flaps. There are many circumstances requiring the use of forward slips, such as in a landing approach over obstacles and in making forced landings, when it is always wise to allow an extra margin of altitude for safety in the original estimate of the approach.

3. How is a forward slip to a landing performed?

a. Reduce power to idle.

b. The wing on the side toward which the slip is to be made should be lowered by use of ailerons.

c. Simultaneously, the airplane's nose must be yawed in the opposite direction by applying opposite rudder so that the airplane's longitudinal axis is at an angle to its original flight path.

d. The degree to which the nose is yawed in the opposite direction from the bank should be such that the original ground track is maintained.

e. The pitch should be adjusted as necessary to maintain the appropriate airspeed.

f. Discontinuing the slip is accomplished by leveling the wings and simultaneously releasing rudder pressure while readjusting pitch attitude to the normal glide attitude.

4. What should a pilot be aware of regarding instrument error in a forward slip?

Because of the location of the pitot tube and static vents, airspeed indicators in some airplanes may have considerable error when the airplane is in a slip. The pilot must be aware of this possibility and recognize a properly performed slip by the attitude of the airplane, the sound of the airflow, and the feel of the flight controls. Forward slips with the wing flaps extended should not be done in airplanes wherein the manufacturer's operating instructions prohibit such operation.

5. What are the standards expected of a student in performing a forward slip to a landing? (FAA-S-8081-14A)

The student:

a. Shows knowledge of a forward slip to a landing.

b. Considers wind conditions, landing surface and obstructions, and selects the most suitable touchdown point.

c. Establishes slipping attitude at the point from which a landing can be made using recommended approach, landing configuration and airspeed; adjusts pitch attitude and power as required.

d. Maintains ground track aligned with runway centerline and airspeed which results in minimum float during roundout.

e. Makes smooth, timely, and correct control application during recovery from the slip, roundout, and touchdown.

f. Touches down smoothly at approximate stalling speed, at or within 400 feet (120 meters) beyond a specified point, with no side drift, and with the airplane's longitudinal axis aligned with and over runway centerline.

g. Maintains crosswind correction and directional control throughout approach and landing.

h. Completes appropriate checklist.

6. What are some common student errors in performing a forward slip to a landing?
(FAA-S-8081-6C and FAA-H-8083-3)

a. Improper use of landing performance data and limitations:
   • Not calculating landing distances correctly.
   • Performing a slip with flaps in an airplane in which this operation is prohibited.

b. Failure to establish approach and landing configuration at the appropriate time or in the proper sequence. Not following established procedure.

c. Failure to maintain a stabilized slip:
   • Not reducing power.
   • Not applying sufficient aileron and rudder to establish forward slip.
   • Not maintaining equal amounts of aileron and rudder input.
   • Not maintaining a safe airspeed while in the slip.

d. Inappropriate removal of hand from throttle. Not keeping hand on throttle for power increases and reductions.

e. Improper technique during transition from the slip to the touchdown:
   • The longitudinal axis of the airplane is not aligned with the runway centerline as a result of not allowing sufficient time between recovery from the slip and touch down.
   • Underestimating rate of sink during slip and landing hard.

f. Poor directional control after touchdown:
   • Allowing a wing to rise after touchdown.
   • Allowing touchdown while in a crab.
   • Overcontrolling with rudder.
   • Ground loop: may be caused by a crosswind or overcontrolling airplane; this problem can be significant in tailwheel aircraft.

g. Improper use of brakes:
   • Not using aerodynamic braking.
   • Excessive use of brakes.
   • Skidding the tires.

C. Go-Around

1. Describe a go-around.

A go-around is a procedure used when it may be advisable for safety reasons to discontinue the landing approach and make another approach under more favorable conditions. A go-around involves procedures including establishing full power, drag reduction and traffic pattern procedures.

2. Why is it important for the pilot to be ready for the go-around?

The earlier a dangerous situation is recognized and the sooner the landing is rejected and the go-around started, the safer the procedure will be. Extremely low base to final turns, overshot or low final approaches, the unexpected appearance of hazards on the runway, wake turbulence from a preceding airplane, or overtaking another airplane on the approach are hazardous conditions that would demand a go-around.

3. How is the go-around executed?

a. Make the decision to go-around as early as possible.

b. Simultaneously increase pitch attitude to stop the descent and apply takeoff power.

c. If the aircraft has been trimmed for the approach, expect to hold considerable forward elevator pressure to maintain a safe climb attitude.

d. After the descent has been stopped, the landing flaps may be partially retracted or placed in the takeoff position, as recommended by the manufacturer.

e. Roughly retrim the aircraft to relieve control pressure.

f. Establish a best angle (V_X) or best rate (V_Y) of climb as appropriate.

g. Retract the landing gear when a positive rate of climb has been established.

h. Retrim aircraft.

4. **What are the standards expected of a student for a go-around?** (FAA-S-8081-12B)

The student:

a. Shows knowledge of the elements related to a go-around/ rejected landing.

b. Makes a timely decision to discontinue the approach to landing.

c. Applies takeoff power immediately and transitions to climb pitch attitude for V_Y, and maintains V_Y ±5 knots.*

d. Retracts flaps as appropriate.

e. Retracts the landing gear if appropriate after a positive rate of climb is established.

f. Maneuvers to the side of runway/landing area to clear and avoid conflicting traffic.

g. Maintains takeoff power and V_Y ±5 knots to a safe maneuvering altitude.

h. Maintains directional control and proper wind-drift correction throughout the climb.

i. Completes the appropriate checklist.

Private PTS: Applies takeoff power immediately and transitions to climb pitch attitude for V_Y, and maintains V_Y +10/-5 knots.

5. **What are some common student errors in the performance of a go-around?**
(FAA-S-8081-6C and FAA-H-8083-3)

a. Failure to recognize a situation where a go-around/rejected landing is necessary. Not recognizing unsafe conditions that warrant a go-around.

b. Hazards of delaying a decision to go-around/rejected landing. Not making a decision until the last minute can make the go around an unsafe procedure.

c. Improper power application.
   • Not applying full power.
   • Failure to remove carburetor heat.
   • Failure to adjust propeller to low pitch/high RPM first.
   • Power application not smooth.

d. Failure to control pitch attitude.
  • On initial full power application, not controlling the sharp nose up attitude that will occur.
  • Not establishing the pitch attitude for best angle or best rate of climb.

e. Failure to compensate for torque effect: not correcting for torque effect in climb.

f. Improper trim procedure: not initially re-trimming aircraft to relieve heavy control pressure.

g. Failure to maintain recommended airspeeds; not establishing and maintaining best angle or best rate of climb as appropriate.

h. Improper wing flaps or landing gear retraction procedure:
  • Not retracting flaps, retracting flaps all at once or too soon, considering altitude.
  • Retracting the landing gear before a positive rate of climb has been established.

i. Failure to maintain proper track during climb-out; allowing aircraft to drift due to crosswind or poor heading control.

j. Failure to remain well clear of obstructions and other traffic; if a conflict with departing traffic exists, not banking away from runway and establishing a "parallel to runway" leg, to keep the traffic in sight. Not listening for and reacting to traffic advisories.

D. Short-Field Approach and Landing

1. Describe a short-field approach and landing.

The short-field approach and landing is a maximum performance operation that requires the use of procedures and techniques for the approach and landing at fields which have a relatively short landing area or where an approach must be made over obstacles which limit the available landing area. It is one of the most critical of the maximum performance operations, since it requires that the pilot fly the airplane at one of its crucial performance capabilities while close to the ground in order to safely land within confined areas.

2. Why is it important to practice short-field approaches and landings?

To land within a short field or confined area, the pilot must have precise, positive control of the rate of descent and airspeed to produce an approach that will clear any obstacles, result in little or no floating during the roundout, and permit the airplane to be stopped in the shortest possible distance.

3. How is a short-field approach and landing performed?

a. Establish a normal traffic pattern.

b. At midfield, on downwind, complete a prelanding checklist.

c. Abeam the touch down point on downwind, reduce power.

d. Maintain altitude and level pitch attitude momentarily to dissipate airspeed.

e. Retrim aircraft to establish airspeed within flap operating range (white arc).

f. Lower flaps to 10°.

g. Establish initial approach airspeed (1.4 x V_{SO}); retrim if necessary.

h. At an approximate 45°-point from the landing threshold (30°-point for a short field with obstacle), clear for traffic and turn base.

i. Extend flaps and retrim if necessary to maintain approach airspeed; apply wind drift correction.

j. Lead turn to final to roll out on runway extended centerline.

k. Extend full flaps on final.

l. Simultaneously adjust power and pitch attitude as necessary to control rate of descent and obtain an airspeed of 1.3 x V_{SO}.

m. If landing over a 50-foot obstacle, when clear, adjust pitch attitude slightly to establish rate of descent. Do not reduce power until in ground effect.

n. If landing with no obstacle, adjust descent angle to land just inside of the desired touchdown point.

o. After landing, identify and retract flaps, and apply maximum braking and full elevator back pressure.

4. **What are the standards expected of a student for short-field approaches and landings?** (FAA-S-8081-12B)

   a. Shows knowledge of the elements related to a short-field approach and landing.

   b. Considers the wind conditions, landing surface, obstructions, and selects the most suitable touchdown point.

   c. Establishes the recommended approach and landing configuration and airspeed; adjusts pitch attitude and power.

   d. Maintains a stabilized approach and recommended approach airspeed, or in its absence, not more than 1.3 V_{SO}, ±5 knots, with wind gust factor applied.

   Private PTS: Maintains a stabilized approach and recommended approach airspeed, or in its absence not more than 1.3 V_{SO}, +10/-5 knots, with wind gust factor applied.

   e. Makes smooth, timely, and correct control application during the roundout and touchdown.

   f. Touches down smoothly at minimum control airspeed.

   g. Touches down at or within 100 feet (30 meters) beyond a specified point, with no side drift, minimum float and with the airplane's longitudinal axis aligned with and over the runway center/landing path.

   Private PTS: Touches down at or within 200 feet (60 meters) beyond a specified point, with no side drift, minimum float and with the airplane's longitudinal axis aligned with and over the runway center/landing path.

   h. Maintains crosswind correction and directional control throughout the approach and landing sequence.

   i. Applies brakes, as necessary, to stop in the shortest distance consistent with safety.

   j. Completes appropriate checklist.

5. What are some common student errors in the performance of short-field approaches and landings? (FAA-S-8081-6C and FAA-H-8083-3)

a. Improper use of landing performance data and limitations — not calculating landing distances correctly.

b. Failure to establish the approach and landing configuration at the appropriate time or in the proper sequence. Not following established procedure.

c. Failure to establish and maintain a stabilized approach:
   • Not establishing the correct airspeeds for downwind, base and final segments.
   • Not reducing power as necessary to control rate of descent.
   • If short field over an obstacle: when clear of obstacle, reducing power resulting in possible stall; diving for runway resulting in excessive airspeed and floating.
   • Not using flaps as necessary to control speed and rate of descent.
   • Not correcting for wind drift on downwind, base, and final.

d. Improper technique in use of power, wing flaps, and trim:
   • Not using pitch and power to control airspeed and rate of descent.
   • Not extending flaps as necessary.
   • Not trimming aircraft for appropriate airspeed.

e. Inappropriate removal of hand from throttle — not keeping hand on throttle for power increases and reductions.

f. Improper techniques during roundout and touchdown:
   • Rounding out too late resulting in, if not corrected, a hard landing followed by a bounce and a stall and another hard landing.
   • Rounding out too high resulting in, if not corrected, an eventual loss in airspeed followed by a high sink rate and a hard landing.
   • Rounding out and "ballooning" down the runway; usually caused by misjudging the rate of descent and over-controlling.
   • Rounding out and "floating" down the runway; usually caused by excessive airspeed on final approach.
   • Touchdown followed by a bounce as a result of an excessive rate of descent on final.

g. Poor directional control after touchdown:
  • Allowing a wing to rise after touchdown.
  • Allowing touchdown while in a crab.
  • Overcontrolling with rudder.
  • Ground loop—may be caused by a crosswind or over-controlling airplane; this problem can be significant in tail-wheel aircraft.

h. Improper use of brakes:
  • Not using aerodynamic braking.
  • Excessive use of brakes.
  • Skidding the tires.

E. Soft-Field Approach and Landing

1. What is a soft-field approach and landing?

When landing on rough fields or those with soft surfaces such as snow, sand, mud, or tall grass, the pilot must control the airplane so that the wings support the weight of the airplane as long as is practical in order to minimize drag and stresses imposed on the landing gear by the surface. The approach for the soft-field landing is similar to the normal approach used for operating into long, firm landing areas, the major difference being that during the soft field landing, the airplane is held 1 to 2 feet off the surface as long as possible to dissipate the forward speed enough so the wheels touch down gently at minimum speed.

2. What is the objective for practicing soft-field approaches and landings?

Operations into and out of airports with paved runways will not always be possible. Soft-field approach and landing techniques are used when normal approach and landing procedures will not be effective or particularly safe.

3. How is a soft-field approach and landing performed?

a. Establish a normal traffic pattern.

b. At midfield, on downwind, complete a pre-landing checklist.

c. Abeam the touch down point on downwind, reduce power.

d. Maintain altitude and level pitch attitude momentarily to dissipate airspeed.

e. Retrim aircraft to establish airspeed within flap operating range (white arc).

f. Lower flaps to 10°.

g. Establish initial approach airspeed (1.4 x V_{SO}); retrim if necessary.

h. At an approximate 45°-point from the landing threshold (30°-point for a short field with obstacle), clear for traffic and turn base.

i. Extend flaps and retrim if necessary to maintain approach airspeed; apply wind-drift correction.

j. Lead turn to final to roll out on runway extended centerline.

k. Extend full flaps on final.

l. Simultaneously adjust power and pitch attitude as necessary to control rate of descent and obtain an airspeed of 1.3 x V_{SO}.

m. Touchdown at the lowest possible airspeed with the airplane in a nose-high pitch attitude.

n. After the main wheels touch the surface, hold sufficient back elevator pressure to keep the nose wheel off the ground until it can no longer aerodynamically be held off the field surface.

o. Gently lower the nose wheel to the surface.

p. A slight addition of power during and immediately after the touchdown will aid in easing the nose wheel down.

q. Avoid the use of brakes.

r. Increase power, as necessary, to keep the airplane moving and from becoming stuck in the surface.

4. **What are the standards expected of a student for soft-field approaches and landings?** (FAA-S-8081-12B)

The student:

a. Shows knowledge of a soft-field approach and landing.

b. Considers wind conditions, landing surface, and obstructions.

c. Selects the most suitable touchdown point.

d. Establishes recommended approach and landing configuration; and adjusts power and pitch attitude as required.

e. Maintains stabilized approach and recommended airspeed, or in its absence, not more than 1.3 V_{SO}, with gust factor applied, ±5 knots.*

f. Makes smooth, timely, and correct control application during roundout and touchdown.

g. Maintains crosswind correction and directional control throughout approach and landing.

h. Touches down softly, with no drift, and with the airplane's longitudinal axis aligned with the landing surface.

i. Maintains proper position of flight controls and sufficient speed to taxi on soft surface.

j. Completes appropriate checklists.

Private PTS: Maintains a stabilized approach and recommended approach airspeed, or in its absence not more than 1.3 V_{SO}, +10/-5 knots, with gust factor applied.

5. What are some common student errors in the performance of soft-field approaches and landings?
(FAA-S-8081-6C and FAA-H-8083-3)

a. Improper use of landing performance data and limitations. Not calculating landing distances correctly.

b. Failure to establish approach and landing configuration at the appropriate time or in the proper sequence. Not following established procedure.

c. Failure to establish and maintain a stabilized approach:
   - Not establishing correct airspeeds for downwind, base and final segments.
   - Not reducing power as necessary to control rate of descent.
   - Not using flaps as necessary to control speed and rate of descent.
   - Not correcting for wind drift on downwind, base, and final.

d. Failure to consider the effect of wind and landing surface:
   - Not inspecting area first to determine landing surface.
   - Not considering the effect of a headwind in slowing the airplane's forward speed on touchdown.

e. Improper technique in use of power, wing flaps or trim:
   - Not using pitch and power to control airspeed and rate of descent.
   - Not extending flaps as necessary.
   - Not trimming aircraft for appropriate airspeed.

f. Inappropriate removal of hand from throttle. Not keeping hand on throttle for power increases and reductions.

g. Improper techniques during roundout and touchdown:
   - Rounding out too late resulting in, if not corrected, a hard landing followed by a bounce and a stall and another hard landing.
   - Rounding out too high resulting in, if not corrected, an eventual loss in airspeed followed by a high sink rate and a hard landing.
   - Rounding out and "ballooning" down the runway; usually caused by misjudging the rate of descent and over-controlling.

- Rounding out and "floating" down the runway; usually caused by excessive airspeed on final approach.
- Touchdown followed by a bounce as a result of an excessive rate of descent on final.

h. Failure to hold back elevator pressure after touchdown. Not maintaining sufficient back elevator pressure to keep weight off of the nose wheel and prevent a heavy load on the nose gear causing the nose wheel to dig in.

i. Closing the throttle too soon after touchdown:
- Not maintaining some power to increase elevator effectiveness so the weight may be kept off of the nose wheel as long as possible.
- Not maintaining some power to keep aircraft moving and prevent it from becoming stuck.

j. Poor directional control after touchdown:
- Allowing a wing to rise after touchdown.
- Allowing touchdown while in a crab.
- Overcontrolling with rudder.
- Ground loop — may be caused by a crosswind or overcontrolling airplane; this problem can be significant in tailwheel aircraft.

k. Improper use of brakes:
- Not using aerodynamic braking.
- Excessive use of brakes.
- Skidding the tires.

F. Power-Off 180° Accuracy Approach and Landing

1. What is a power-off 180° accuracy approach and landing? (FAA-H-8083-3)

These are made by gliding with the engine idling from a specific point on downwind, to touchdown beyond and within 200 feet of a designated line or mark on the runway.

2. What is the objective of learning a power-off 180° accuracy approach and landing? (FAA-H-8083-3)

The objective is to instill in the pilot the judgment and procedures necessary for accurately flying the airplane *without power* to a safe landing.

3. What are the standards expected of a student when executing the power-off 180° accuracy approach and landing? (FAA-S-8081-12B)

The student:

a. Shows knowledge of the elements related to a power-off 180° accuracy approach and landing.

b. Considers the wind conditions, landing surface, obstructions, and selects an appropriate touchdown point.

c. Positions airplane on downwind leg, parallel to landing runway, and not more than 1,000 feet AGL.

d. Abeam the specified touchdown point, closes throttle and establishes appropriate glide speed.

e. Completes final airplane configuration.

f. Touches down in a normal landing attitude, at or within 200 feet (60 meters) beyond the specified touchdown point.

g. Completes the appropriate checklist.

4. What are some common student errors in performing power-off 180° approach and landings?
(FAA-S-8081-6C and FAA-H-8083-3)

a. Failure to establish approach and landing configuration at proper time or in proper sequence—not establishing pitch, power and trim at key points; prematurely extending flaps or delaying flap extension.

b. Failure to identify the key points in the pattern—not recognizing key point on downwind, or 45° key point on base leg.

c. Failure to establish and maintain a stabilized approach—airspeed too fast or too slow on final; not determining and establishing the necessary descent rate resulting in being too high or too low on final.

d. Failure to consider the effect of wind and landing surface—delaying turn to base resulting in excessively low final; turning base too early resulting in an excessively high final; no consideration of effect of runway surface (rough or soft).

e. Improper use of power, wing flaps, or trim—not reducing power; retracting or extending flaps to reach desired spot; neglecting use of trim after power reduction and configuration changes.

f. Improper procedure during roundout and touchdown—starting roundout too late in an effort to land on desired spot; pulling the elevator control back too early in an effort to stretch a glide to reach the desired spot.

g. Failure to hold back elevator pressure after touchdown—not using aerodynamic braking to shorten landing roll.

h. Poor directional control after touchdown—careless use of rudder (over or undercontrolling) excessive use of brakes control direction; no use of aileron.

i. Improper use of brakes—excessive use of braking to stop at desired point.

Additional Study Questions

1. Before you instruct your student on the process of approach and landing, in what maneuvers should that student be proficient? (FAA-H-8083-3)

2. What should your student learn about flaps during the approach and landing process? (FAA-H-8083-3)

3. What will you teach your student concerning where to look during the approach, roundout and touchdown? (FAA-H-8083-3)

4. What are the two methods of drift correction during crosswind landings? (FAA-H-8083-3)

5. While flying a crosswind approach to a landing, how will you teach your student to know when the existing crosswind is too strong to continue to a safe landing? (FAA-H-8083-3)

6. What are the two types of slips and what is each used for? (FAA-H-8083-3)

7. What is wheel-barrowing and why does it occur? (FAA-H-8083-3)

8. What is porpoising and why does it occur? (FAA-H-8083-3)

9. Explain how a ground loop might occur. (FAA-H-8083-3)

10. How will you teach your student to correct for ballooning during the roundout phase of landing? (FAA-H-8083-3)

11. Explain the correct course of action to take if the selected touchdown area will be missed during a normal landing. (FAA-H-8083-3)

Emergency
Operations

11

A. Emergency Approach and Landing (Simulated)

1. What are the different types of emergency approach and landing procedures? (FAA-H-8083-3)

a. Forced landing—an immediate landing, on or off an airport, necessitated by the inability to continue further flight.

b. Precautionary landing—a premeditated landing, on or off an airport, when further flight is possible but inadvisable.

c. Ditching—a forced or precautionary landing on water.

2. What is the objective of teaching simulated emergency approach and landing procedures to a student? (FAA-H-8083-3)

The objective is to instill in the pilot the knowledge that almost any terrain can be considered "suitable" for a survivable crash landing if the pilot knows how to use the airplane structure for self-protection and the protection of passengers.

3. What are the standards expected when practicing emergency approach and landings? (FAA-S-8081-12B)

a. Prompt establishment of the best glide airspeed and the recommended configuration.

b. How to select a suitable emergency landing area.

c. Planning and execution of approach to the selected landing area.

d. Use of emergency checklist.

e. Importance of attempting to determine reason for the malfunction.

f. Importance of dividing attention between flying the approach and accomplishing emergency checklist.

g. Procedures that can be used to compensate for undershooting or overshooting selected emergency landing area.

4. What are some common errors when practicing simulated emergency approach and landing procedures? (FAA-S-8081-6C)

a. Improper airspeed control.

b. Poor judgment in the selection of an emergency landing area.

c. Failure to estimate the approximate wind speed and direction.

d. Failure to fly the most suitable pattern for existing situation.

e. Failure to accomplish the emergency checklist.

f. Undershooting or overshooting selected emergency landing area.

B. Systems and Equipment Malfunctions

1. What are the various types of simulated system and equipment malfunctions you will be teaching? (FAA-S-8081-6C)

a. Smoke, fire, or both, during ground or flight operations.

b. Rough running engine or partial power loss.

c. Loss of engine oil pressure.

d. Fuel starvation.

e. Engine overheat.

f. Hydraulic malfunction.

g. Electrical malfunction.

h. Carburetor or induction icing.

i. Door or window opening in flight.

j. Inoperative or "runaway" trim.

k. Landing gear or flap malfunction.

l. Pressurization malfunction.

2. What is the objective of teaching simulated system and equipment malfunctions? (FAA-H-8083-3)

The objective is to develop the student's ability to detect, analyze and apply the appropriate procedure for a given system or equipment malfunction. The key to successful management of an emergency situation (or preventing a progression into a true emergency) is a thorough familiarity with, and adherence to, the procedures developed by the airplane manufacturer and contained in the FAA-approved AFM or POH.

3. What are the standards expected of a student when simulating system and equipment malfunctions? (FAA-S-8081-12B)

The student:

a. Exhibits knowledge of the elements related to systems and equipment malfunctions appropriate to the airplane provided for the practical test.

b. Analyzes the situation and takes appropriate action for simulated emergencies appropriate to the airplane provided for the practical test for at least five (5) of the following:
   - partial or complete power loss.
   - engine roughness or overheat.
   - carburetor or induction icing.
   - loss of oil pressure.
   - fuel starvation.
   - electrical malfunction.
   - vacuum/pressure, and associated flight instruments malfunction.
   - pitot/static.
   - landing gear or flap malfunction.
   - inoperative trim.
   - inadvertent door or window opening.
   - structural icing.
   - smoke/fire/engine compartment fire.
   - any other emergency appropriate to the airplane.

c. Follows the appropriate checklist or procedure.

4. What are some common errors associated with practice of system and equipment malfunction procedures?

a. Failure to recognize/detect the system or equipment malfunction.

b. Inadequate knowledge of aircraft systems and equipment.

c. Failure to accomplish the appropriate checklist or procedure.

C. Emergency Equipment and Survival Gear

1. What is the objective of teaching a student about emergency equipment and survival gear?
(FAA-H-8083-3)

To educate the student on the equipment and gear appropriate for operation in various climates, over various types of terrain, and over water as well as provide knowledge on the purpose, method of operation or use, servicing and storage of appropriate equipment.

2. What are the practical test standards for the emergency equipment and survival gear task? (FAA-S-8081-12B)

The student should:

a. Exhibit knowledge of the elements related to emergency equipment and survival gear appropriate to the airplane and environment encountered during flight.

b. Identify appropriate equipment that should be on board the airplane.

3. What are common errors for the emergency equipment and survival gear task? (FAA-S-8081-6C)

The student fails to exhibit knowledge—

a. Of when it would be prudent to carry emergency and survival equipment.

b. Of what type of emergency and survival equipment is appropriate for different climates and terrain.

c. On the purpose, method of operation or use, servicing and storage of appropriate equipment.

D. Emergency Descent

1. Describe an emergency descent procedure.
(FAA-H-8083-3)

An emergency descent is a maneuver for descending as rapidly as possible to a lower altitude or to the ground for an emergency landing. The need for this maneuver may result from an uncontrollable fire, a sudden loss of cabin pressurization, or any other situation demanding an immediate and rapid descent.

2. What is the objective when conducting an emergency descent procedure? (FAA-H-8083-3)

The objective of this maneuver is to descend the airplane as soon and as rapidly as possible within the structural limitations of the airplane.

3. Describe the procedure for conducting an emergency descent procedure. (FAA-H-8083-3)

a. Simulated emergency descents should be made in a turn to check for other air traffic below and to look around for a possible emergency landing area.

b. A radio call announcing descent intentions may be appropriate to alert other aircraft in the area.

c. When initiating the descent, a bank of approximately 30 to 45° should be established to maintain positive load factors (G forces) on the airplane.

d. Except when prohibited by the manufacturer, the power should be reduced to idle, and the propeller control (if equipped) should be placed in the low pitch (high rpm) position. This will allow the propeller to act as an aerodynamic brake to help prevent an excessive airspeed buildup during the descent.

e. The landing gear and flaps should be extended as recommended by the manufacturer. This will provide maximum drag so that the descent can be made as rapidly as possible, without excessive airspeed.

Continued

f. The pilot should not allow the airplane's airspeed to pass the never-exceed speed (V_{NE}), the maximum landing gear extended speed (V_{LE}), or the maximum flap extended speed (V_{FE}), as applicable. The descent should be made at the maximum allowable airspeed consistent with the procedure used.

g. The recovery from an emergency descent should be initiated at a high enough altitude to ensure a safe recovery back to level flight or a precautionary landing.

Note: Emergency descent training should be performed as recommended by the manufacturer, including the configuration and airspeeds.

4. What factors should be taken into consideration when selecting the appropriate airspeed for the emergency descent? (FAA-H-8083-3)

In the case of an engine fire, a high airspeed descent should be established to extinguish the fire. However, weakening of the airplane structure is a major concern and descent at a lower airspeed would place less stress on the airplane. If the descent is conducted in turbulent conditions, the pilot must also comply with the design maneuvering speed (V_A) limitations. This will provide increased drag and therefore loss of altitude as quickly as possible.

5. What are some of the common errors when conducting a practice emergency descent procedure? (FAA-S-8081-6C)

a. Failing to identify the reason for executing an emergency descent.

b. Improper use of the prescribed emergency checklist to verify accomplishment of procedures for initiating the emergency descent.

c. Improper use of clearing procedures before initiating and during the emergency descent.

d. Improper procedures for recovering from an emergency descent.

6. **What are the standards expected of a student performing an emergency descent procedure?** (FAA-S-8081-6C)

   a. Exhibits knowledge of the elements related to an emergency descent.

   b. Recognizes situations, such as depressurization, cockpit smoke and/or fire that require an emergency descent.

   c. Establishes the appropriate airspeed and configuration for the emergency descent.

   d. Exhibits orientation, division of attention, and proper planning.

   e. Maintains positive load factors during the descent.

   f. Completes appropriate checklists.

Additional Study Questions

1. **What are several factors that may interfere with a pilot's ability to act promptly and properly when faced with an emergency?** (FAA-H-8083-3)

2. **Explain the effect wind will have on an emergency approach and landing maneuver.** (FAA-H-8083-3)

3. **What will you teach your students concerning the position of retractable landing gear during an off-airport emergency landing?** (FAA-H-8083-3)

4. **Concerning terrain selection, what factors govern a pilot's choice of emergency landing sites?** (FAA-H-8083-3)

5. **Be capable of explaining the various system and equipment malfunctions, including the probable causes and recommended pilot actions for each.** (FAA-H-8083-3)

6. **What two factors should be considered when selecting appropriate survival equipment to carry for a flight over uninhabited terrain?** (AIM 6-2-7)

7. **Why should prolonged practice of emergency descent procedures be avoided?** (FAA-H-8083-3)

Appendix 1

Advisory Circular
61-65E

Subject: **Certification: Pilots, and Flight and Ground Instructors**

Date: 11/29/05   Initiated By: AFS-800

This advisory circular (AC) provides guidance for pilots, flight instructors, ground instructors, and examiners on the certification standards, knowledge test procedures, and other requirements in Title 14 of the Code of Federal Regulations (14 CFR) part 61. This revision provides guidance for those persons seeking sport pilot certification.

Original signed by John M. Allen for
James J. Ballough, Director
Flight Standards Service

Contents

1. **PURPOSE.** This advisory circular (AC) provides guidance for pilots, flight instructors, ground instructors, and examiners on the certification standards, knowledge test procedures, and other requirements in Title 14 of the Code of Federal Regulations (14 CFR) part 61.

2. **CANCELLATION.** AC 61-65D, Certification: Pilots and Flight and Ground Instructors, dated September 20, 1999, is canceled.

3. **RELATED READING MATERIAL (CURRENT EDITIONS).**
   a. AC 61-98, Currency and Additional Qualification Requirements for Certificated Pilots.
   b. AC 61-107, Operations of Aircraft at Altitudes Above 25,000 Feet MSL and/or MACH Numbers (MMO) Greater Than .75.
   c. FAA-G-8082-1, Airline Transport Pilot, Aircraft Dispatcher, and Flight Navigator Knowledge Test Guide.
   d. FAA-G-8082-5, Commercial Pilot Knowledge Test Guide.
   e. FAA-G-8082-7, Flight and Ground Instructor Knowledge Test Guide.
   f. FAA-G-8082-13, Instrument Rating Knowledge Test Guide.
   g. FAA-G-8082-17, Recreational Pilot and Private Pilot Knowledge Test Guide.
   h. FAA Order 8710.3, Designated Pilot and Flight Engineer Examiner's Handbook.
   i. FAA Order 8710.7, Sport Pilot Examiner's Handbook.
   j. Part 61 quality assurance (Q&A) and part 141 Q&As are located on the Federal Aviation Administration (FAA) General Aviation and Commercial Division (AFS-800) home page at http://www.faa.gov/

about/office_org/headquarters_offices/avs/offices/afs/afs800/ afs810/more/. These documents do not include information on sport pilots, flight instructors with a sport pilot rating, or private weight-shift-control or powered parachute ratings.

k. FAA Order 8080.6, Conduct of Airman Knowledge Tests.

4. **PILOT TRAINING AND TESTING.** Part 61 contains the aeronautical experience, certification requirements, responsibilities, privileges, and limitations for each grade of certificate: student pilot, sport pilot, recreational pilot, private pilot, commercial pilot, airline transport pilot, instrument rating, flight instructor, and ground instructor. Under the "total training concept," the areas of operation specified for each grade of certificate by part 61 encompasses the areas of operation and tasks contained in the practical test standards (PTS). Instructors are responsible for training applicants "…to acceptable standards in all subject matter areas, procedures, and maneuvers included in the tasks within the appropriate practical test standard." For example:

a. An applicant for a private pilot certificate must have logged the aeronautical experience as required by part 61 and have had his/her logbook endorsed by his/her certificated flight instructor (CFI) who determines that the applicant is proficient in the appropriate areas of operation listed in section 61.107(b).

b. The flight maneuvers associated with each of the areas of operation listed in section 61.107 are found under similar titles in the current editions of the appropriate PTS. The standards for successful completion of each maneuver and procedure are noted in the elements of each task in the appropriate PTS.

5. **KNOWLEDGE TESTS.** The knowledge tests for the sport pilot certificate, recreational pilot certificate, private pilot certificate, commercial pilot certificate, airline transport pilot (ATP) certificate, flight instructor certificate, ground instructor certificate, and ratings cover the subject areas in which aeronautical knowledge is required by part 61.

a. If required by section 61.35(a)(1), an appropriate knowledge test will only be administered to an applicant who presents acceptable evidence of completion of the required training.

b. Applicants are not required to show such evidence to take the ATP, CFI, certificated ground instructor (CGI), military competency, or foreign pilot instrument knowledge tests unless they are applying to retake a test after failing that test (per section 61.49).

c. The FAA computerized knowledge test program has been implemented to provide expeditious testing services for applicants at locations and times convenient to the public. For location of computerized testing centers, contact the nearest Flight Standards District Office (FSDO) or use the list of computerized testing

centers at http://www.faa.gov/education_research/testing/airmen/
media/test_centers.pdf.

6. **COMPLETION OF GROUND TRAINING OR A HOME STUDY
CURRICULUM.** Ground training courses to prepare for the aeronautical knowledge test may be offered by pilot schools, colleges, aviation
organizations, and individual flight or ground instructors. Home study
curriculums are available from representatives of the aviation industry.
Home study curriculums individually developed by students should be
compiled from material described in the applicable FAA knowledge
test guide. The student, to show evidence of a ground school or home
study curriculum completion, may use any one of the following
methods.

   a. A certificate of graduation from a pilot training course conducted
   by an FAA-certificated pilot school, appropriate to the certificate or
   rating sought, or a statement of accomplishment from the school
   certifying satisfactory completion of the ground school portion of
   the course;

   b. An endorsement from an appropriately rated FAA-certificated
   ground or flight instructor who has certified that the applicant has
   satisfactorily completed the ground training required for the certificate or rating sought and is prepared for the test;

   c. A certificate of graduation or statement of accomplishment from a
   ground school course, appropriate to the certificate and rating
   sought that was conducted by an agency such as a high school,
   college, adult education program, the Civil Air Patrol, or a Reserve
   Officer's Training Corps flight training program;

   d. A certificate of graduation from an industry-provided aviation
   home study course. The certificate must be developed by the
   aeronautical enterprise providing the study material. The certificate
   of graduation must correspond to the FAA knowledge test for the
   certificate or rating sought. The aeronautical enterprise providing
   the course of study must also supply a comprehensive knowledge
   test, which can be scored as evidence that the student has completed the course of study. The knowledge test must be sent to the
   course provider for scoring. Upon satisfactory completion of the
   examination, a graduation certificate signed by an authorized CFI
   of the course provider will be provided to the student; or

   e. Applicants are encouraged to obtain ground training from the
   sources described in paragraph 6a through 6d above. An applicant
   who is unable to provide any of the above documents when applying for a knowledge test may present an individually developed
   home study course to an appropriately rated flight or ground
   instructor. The instructor will review the course materials and may
   question the applicant to determine that the course was completed

and that the applicant does possess the knowledge required for the certificate or rating sought. The instructor will then complete an endorsement certifying that the applicant is prepared for the knowledge test.

7. **EVIDENCE OF IDENTITY AND AGE.** Applicants for knowledge tests and airman certificates must provide positive proof of identification, address, and age at the time of application.

    a. **Identification.** The identification presented must include a photograph of the applicant, the applicant's signature, and the applicant's actual residential address (if different from the mailing address). This information may be presented in more than one form of identification. Acceptable methods of identification include, but are not limited to drivers' licenses, government identification cards, passports, and military identification cards. Some applicants may not possess the identification documentation described. In the case of an applicant under the age of 16 years for a knowledge test or practical test for other than a glider or balloon rating (or 14 years of age for a knowledge test or practical test for a glider or balloon rating), the applicant's parent or guardian may accompany the applicant and present information attesting to the applicant's identity. If this is done, a statement to that effect will be submitted for enclosure in the airman's permanent record.

    b. **Address.** A temporary mailing address for delivery of the certificate may be indicated on a separate statement attached to the application. However, the address required for official record purposes as shown on an airman application for a certificate must represent the airman's actual permanent residential street address, including apartment number, etc., when appropriate. An alternate mail delivery service address (commercial mail box provider, flight school, airport office, etc.) is unacceptable. A post office box or rural route number is unacceptable as a permanent residence on an application unless unavoidable circumstances require such an address. An applicant residing on a rural route, in a boat or mobile (recreational) vehicle, or in some other like residence that requires the use of a post office box or rural route number for an address, must attest to the circumstances by signing a statement on a separate sheet of paper. The information provided must include sufficient details to ensure identification of the geographical location of the airman's residence. If necessary to positively identify the place of residence, the applicant may be required to provide a hand-drawn map or a typed or written explanation of directions to the residence that clearly shows or describes the location of the residence. When the residence is a boat or other mobile vehicle, the registration number, tag number, etc., and dock or park location must be provided. When applying for the practical test for an airman certificate, a post office address may be specified for use on the certificate issued. A signed request must be submitted with the application for this purpose. The permanent residence address must be shown in the manner specified above.

c. **Age.** Applicants applying to take a practical test must show they meet the minimum age requirement for the certificate sought. When applying to take a knowledge test, applicants must show that they will meet the minimum age requirement for the certificate sought within 24 calendar-months of the date of application for the knowledge test.

8. **PRACTICAL TESTS.**

a. A practical test is conducted to evaluate the applicant's knowledge and skill for the pilot certificate and rating sought. During a practical test, the examiner will quiz the applicant orally on knowledge elements and ask the applicant to perform the skill elements of the test. However, oral testing may be used at any time during the practical test. An examiner is responsible for determining whether the applicant meets the standards outlined in the objectives of each required task in the appropriate PTS.

b. For elements of a maneuver or procedure on the practical test in which the applicants are required to be tested orally or by written questions, the PTS uses the words "…The applicant exhibits knowledge of…" or "…the applicant exhibits instructional knowledge of…" in the area of each task noted as "Objective."

c. For elements of a maneuver or procedure on the practical test in which the applicants are required to demonstrate their piloting skills, the PTS uses words such as considers situations, maintains, utilizes, initiates, transitions to, arrives at, establishes and maintains, remains aware, avoids situations, selects, properly, makes a, recognizes, stops, completes, etc., in the area of each task noted as "Objective."

d. In accordance with section 61.45(a), a flight simulator or flight training device may be used for some elements of the practical test. Authorization and the extent of use of a flight simulator or flight training device during the practical test is addressed in the appropriate appendix section of the applicable PTS for the pilot certificate and rating sought.

9. LIGHT-SPORT AIRCRAFT WITH A SINGLE PILOT STATION.

a. In accordance with section 61.45(f), a practical test may be conducted in a light-sport aircraft that has a single pilot station. The FAA believes that with certain limitations, it is appropriate to allow the practical test, at the sport pilot certificate level only, to be conducted from the ground by a designated pilot examiner (DPE) or an aviation safety inspector (ASI). The examiner or ASI must agree to conduct the practical test in a single-seat aircraft and must ensure that the practical test is conducted in accordance with the sport pilot PTS for single-seat aircraft. Knowledge of all tasks applicable to the category/class of aircraft will be evaluated orally. Single-seat sport pilots must demonstrate competency in those specific tasks identified in the PTS and any other tasks selected by the examiner. The examiner must be in a position to observe the operation of the aircraft and evaluate the proficiency of the applicant from the ground.

b. The limitation "No passenger carriage and flight in a single-pilot station aircraft only" will be placed on the person's pilot certificate, which limits a pilot to operations in a single-seat light-sport aircraft, and no passenger carriage will be authorized. Only a DPE or an ASI is authorized to remove this limitation. This can be accomplished when the sport pilot takes a practical test in a two-place light-sport aircraft and conducts the additional tasks identified in the PTS. This practical test may be conducted in the same or additional category of aircraft.

c. Upon successful completion of the practical test, the limitation will be removed and the sport pilot is authorized to act as pilot-in-command (PIC) in all categories of light-sport aircraft for which he or she has a make and model endorsement within a set of aircraft to operate. The limitation can also be removed if the sport pilot completes the certification requirements in an aircraft with a minimum of two places, for a higher certificate or rating.

d. A sport pilot who is issued a certificate with a single-seat limitation must complete a flight review, as required by section 61.56. If the flight review is conducted in an aircraft, it must be in an aircraft with a minimum of two pilot stations, in which the pilot is rated, and with an authorized instructor who is current and qualified to act as PIC.

e. An instructor may perform a proficiency check for an additional category or privilege in accordance with section 61.321 to be added to a sport pilot certificate or higher using a single-seat light-sport aircraft, provided the instructor is also a DPE or an ASI.

f. The instructor or ASI must agree to conduct the practical test in a single-seat light-sport aircraft and must ensure that the proficiency check is conducted in accordance with the sport pilot PTS for single-seat aircraft. Knowledge of all tasks applicable to the category or class of aircraft will be evaluated orally. Those pilots seeking sport pilot privileges in a single-seat light-sport aircraft must demonstrate competency in those specific tasks identified in the PTS and any other tasks selected by the instructor.

g. The instructor or ASI must have radio contact and be in a position to observe the operation of the light-sport aircraft and evaluate the proficiency of the applicant from the ground.

h. On successful completion of proficiency check, the instructor or ASI will issue an endorsement with the following limitation: "No passenger carriage and flight in a single-pilot station aircraft only (add category/class/make and model)" limiting the pilot's operations to a single-seat aircraft in this category, class, make, and model. The instructor must sign this endorsement with his or her CFI and examiner number.

i. This limitation can be removed by the pilot having successfully completed a proficiency check involving the additional tasks identified in the PTS in a two-pilot station light-sport aircraft for the specific category and class rating sought and in accordance with section 61.321. The proficiency check must be conducted in the same category and class of light-sport aircraft. Upon successful completion of the proficiency check, the pilot will be issued an endorsement for the light-sport aircraft privilege sought.

j. A recreational pilot or higher, when exercising sport pilot privileges, is required to have an endorsement for only the category and/or class of light-sport aircraft for which he/she is authorized to act as PIC. A sport pilot is required to have an endorsement for the category, class, make, and model within a set of aircraft (see section 61.1(b)(14) for the definition of "set of aircraft") in which he/she is authorized to act as PIC.

10. **PREREQUISITES FOR PRACTICAL TESTS.** Except as provided by section 61.39(c), each applicant must have received an endorsement from an authorized instructor who certified that the applicant received and logged the required flight time/training in preparation for the practical test within 60 days preceding the date of the test and has been found proficient to pass the practical test.

> **NOTE: The endorsement must also state that the applicant has satisfactory knowledge of the subject areas in which he/she was shown to be deficient by the FAA airman knowledge test report, if required.**

a. All applicants must have the required endorsements specified in part 61 for the aircraft category, class, rating, or privilege of certification sought.

b. All applicants who reapply for a retest for a practical test must present another endorsement from their instructor that states the applicant has been given the necessary training and is prepared for the practical test.

c. A practical test, whether or not satisfactorily completed, "uses up" the instructor's endorsement for that test. An instructor's recommendation on FAA Form 8710-1, Airman Certificate and/or Rating Application, is required for each retest conducted for a certificate or rating.

d. Except for a practical test for a sport pilot certificate, flight instructor certificate with a sport pilot rating, glider category rating, or a balloon class rating, applicants must hold at least a current third class medical certificate. If the practical test/proficiency check is being administered in a flight simulator/flight training device, the applicant is not required to hold a medical certificate (see section 61.23(b)(8)).

e. The ability to read, speak, write, and understand the English language is an eligibility requirement that applies to all pilot certificates, ratings, and privileges. No certificate, rating, or privilege will be issued if the applicant cannot meet this requirement, except when such inability to read, speak, write, and understand the English language is due to medical reasons and as permitted under section 61.13(b), and as allowed by other CFR sections.

11. **STUDENT PILOT CERTIFICATION.** Specific knowledge, flight proficiency, flight experience, and endorsement requirements for the student pilot certificate are located in part 61, subpart C.

a. A student pilot certificate can be issued by a designated aviation medical examiner as part of a medical certificate. However, an ASI and DPE can also issue student pilot certificates. Whenever a student pilot certificate (other than a student pilot seeking a sport pilot certificate) is issued by an ASI or DPE, the applicant must hold a current medical certificate for performing solo privileges in an airplane, rotorcraft, powered-lift, weight-shift-control aircraft, powered parachute, or airship. Glider and balloon student pilots are not required to hold a medical certificate (see section 61.23(b)(3)).

(1) Use the following table to determine how to apply for a student pilot certificate for applicants other than those seeking a sport pilot certificate:

If ...	Then ...
(a) An applicant operates a balloon or glider, or has a current and valid medical certificate issued under 14 CFR part 67,	(a) The applicant must apply using FAA Form 8710-1 with a FSDO or an FAA DPE to receive a student pilot certificate (FAA Form 8710-2).
(b) An applicant is not operating a balloon or a glider, and does not have a current and valid medical certificate issued under part 67,	(b) The applicant must apply for a student medical certificate (FAA Form 8420-2, Medical Certificate _____ Class and Student Pilot Certificate), with at least a third class medical certificate issued under part 67 with an FAA aviation medical examiner.

(2) Use the following table to determine how to apply for a student pilot certificate for applicants seeking a sport pilot certificate:

If ...	Then ...
(a) An applicant operates a balloon or glider, or has a current and valid medical certificate issued under part 67, or a current and valid U.S. driver's license,	(a) The applicant must apply for a student pilot certificate with a FSDO or an FAA DPE.
(b) An applicant is not operating a balloon or a glider, and has neither a current and valid medical certificate issued under part 67, nor a current and valid U.S. driver's license,	(b) The applicant must apply for a student medical certificate with at least a third class medical certificate issued under part 67 with an FAA aviation medical examiner.

b. Additional information on the eligibility requirements for student pilots can be found in section 61.83 and the general limitations for student pilots can be found in section 61.89.

12. PRESOLO REQUIREMENTS.

a. The "90-day" solo endorsement that goes in the student pilot's logbook is required every 90 days for the student to be afforded continuing solo privileges, per section 61.87(n).

b. Although section 61.19(b) establishes, in a pertinent part, that a student pilot certificate expires 24 calendar-months from the month in which it is issued, the endorsements on that student pilot certificate are a matter of record indefinitely. The endorsements are required to be updated from "time-to-time" in the student pilot's logbook to retain solo privileges.

c. The following pre-solo requirements must be met:

    (1) Before being authorized to conduct a solo flight, a student pilot must have demonstrated satisfactory aeronautical knowledge by completion of a knowledge test (see §61.87(b)). Before being authorized to conduct a solo flight, a student pilot must have received and logged the flight training required by sections 61.87(c) and (d) through (m), as appropriate. Satisfactory aeronautical knowledge and an acceptable performance level must have been demonstrated to an authorized instructor, per section 61.87(b).

    (2) Prior to solo flight, a student pilot is required to have his or her student pilot certificate and logbook endorsed for the specific make and model aircraft to be flown. Thereafter, the student pilot's logbook must be endorsed every 90 days to retain solo flight privileges. These endorsements must be given by an authorized flight instructor who has flown with the student (per section 61.87(p)).

13. ADDITIONAL SOLO PRIVILEGES. The following additional student solo privileges may be authorized:

NOTE: The student pilot certificate only provides for listing the aircraft's category for the solo cross-country privilege endorsement. Per section 61.93(c)(1), the solo cross-country endorsement on the student pilot certificate must be "...for the specific category of aircraft to be flown." However, per section 61.93(c)(2)(i), the solo cross-country endorsement in the student pilot's logbook must be "...for the specific make and model of aircraft to be flown."

a. A student pilot may operate an aircraft in solo flight at night provided that student has received the required flight training at night and the appropriate endorsements as required by section 61.87(o). A student pilot seeking a sport pilot certificate is not authorized to operate a light-sport aircraft at night, per section 61.89(c).

    (1) A student pilot may operate an aircraft on a solo cross-country flight provided that student has received the training required by sections 61.93(e) through (m), as appropriate, has demonstrated acceptable skills, abilities, and competency to his/her instructor who then would endorse the person's student pilot certificate and logbook. Additionally, before each solo cross-country flight, an instructor must endorse the student's logbook.

NOTE: This endorsement does not need to be made by the instructor who normally provides training to the student.

(2) The instructor who makes the endorsement to authorize this solo cross-country flight will personally review the student's preflight planning and preparation and attest to the correctness and preparedness of the student's cross-country planning under the known circumstances. The instructor may add limitations to the endorsement to ensure an accurate written understanding between the student and the instructor to better ensure the safety of the flight.

b. When an instructor permits his or her student to make a solo cross-country flight, any solo flight greater than 25 nautical miles (nm) (or 15 nm in the case of a powered parachute) from the airport from where the flight originated, or make any solo flight and landing at any location other than the airport of origination, that student must have received the solo cross-country training and endorsements requirements of section 61.93. Additionally, unless there is an emergency, no student may make a solo flight landing at any point other than the airport where the student pilot normally receives cross-country training and endorsements of section 61.93.

c. A flight instructor may authorize a student to practice solo takeoffs and landings at an airport within 25 nm (or 15 nm in the case of a powered parachute) from the airport at which the student pilot is normally receiving training after meeting the requirements of section 61.93(b)(1).

d. A student pilot may be authorized to make repeated, specific solo cross-country flights that are not greater than 50 nm from the point of departure if the student meets the requirements of section 61.93(b)(2). The authorized instructor should specify in the student's logbook endorsement, the conditions under which the flights may be made.

e. A student pilot who seeks a sport pilot certificate or a recreational pilot certificate and wants to obtain privileges to operate in Class B, C, and D airspace, at an airport located in Class B, C, or D airspace, and to, from, through, or at an airport having an operational control tower, must receive and log ground and flight training from an authorized instructor on the aeronautical knowledge areas listed in section 61.94(a) and have received a logbook endorsement in accordance with section 61.94(b).

f. A student pilot may NOT operate an aircraft in solo flight in Class B airspace or on a solo flight to, from, or at an airport located in Class B airspace unless that student pilot has received the ground and flight training and instructor endorsements required by section 61.95(a) and (b).

14. **SPORT PILOT CERTIFICATION.** Specific knowledge, flight proficiency, flight experience, and endorsement requirements for the sport pilot certificate are located in part 61, subpart J.

   a. An applicant for a sport pilot certificate, except those meeting the requirements of section 61.329, must possess at least a student pilot certificate that is current and valid.

   b. The flight instructor is given discretion in developing a training program to meet the requirements of section 61.309. The regulation spells out the specific minimum aeronautical experience requirements that must be met.

   c. A sport pilot certificate is issued without a specific category or class listed. An endorsement is required for each category, class, make, and model of light-sport aircraft a sport pilot is qualified to fly.

   d. Sport pilots will require an endorsement to fly at least one make and model of light-sport aircraft within the same set of aircraft. Once an endorsement is obtained for a specific make and model of light-sport aircraft, the sport pilot can fly any other make and model in the same set without any additional endorsements. The FAA has established a list of sets of light-sport aircraft, which is available online at http://www.faa.gov/licenses_certificates/airmen_certification/sport_pilot/media/aircraft_sets.pdf. (See section 61.1(b)(14) for the definition of "set of aircraft.")

   e. An appropriately authorized flight instructor must supervise the training and experience required in obtaining additional sport pilot privileges. Additional training requirements and endorsements are established for the following additional privileges:

   (1) Category or class of light-sport aircraft (section 61.321).

   (2) Make and model of light-sport aircraft (section 61.323).

   (3) Operate a light-sport aircraft in Class B, C, or D airspace, at an airport located in Class B, C, or D airspace, or to, from, through, or on an airport having an operational control tower (section 61.325).

   (4) Operate a light-sport aircraft that has a V_H greater than 87 knots (kts) calibrated airspeed (CAS) (section 61.327).

   f. Any pilot exercising sport pilot privileges (and applicants for the certificate) must understand and comply with all sport pilot privileges and limitations, particularly the applicable operating limits and endorsement requirements in subpart J. Section 61.303 establishes which operating limits and endorsement requirements apply to the operation of a light-sport aircraft, depending on the type of certificate or rating a pilot holds and the medical eligibility requirements the pilot meets. For example, a pilot holds a recreational pilot certificate, but not a medical certificate, and wishes to exercise sport pilot privileges. The pilot must comply with cross-country requirements in section 61.101(c), even if the flight does not exceed 50 nm from the departure airport (reference section 61.303). The pilot must also comply with the additional training requirements and endorsements established in paragraph 14c. See also paragraph 13.

g. Each pilot exercising sport pilot privileges must carry his or her logbook and other evidence of the required authorized instructor endorsements on all flights. Other evidence of the required authorized instructor endorsements may be a preprinted card or record that includes the endorsements. See section 61.51(i)(3).

15. **RECREATIONAL PILOT CERTIFICATION.** Specific knowledge, flight proficiency, flight experience, and endorsement requirements for the recreational pilot certificate are located in part 61, subpart D.

a. Section 61.101 contains all limitations that pertain to the recreational pilot certificate and outlines procedures for obtaining additional certificates or ratings. An appropriately authorized flight instructor must supervise the training and experience required in furtherance of a higher level of certificate. Each flight conducted by the recreational pilot under those provisions must be authorized by the flight instructor's endorsement in the recreational pilot's logbook.

b. Recreational pilots may act as PIC on a flight that is in Class B, C, and D airspace, at an airport located in Class B, C, or D airspace, and to, from, through, or on an airport having an operational control tower after having received the required training and endorsement (per section 61.101(d)). Recreational pilots must have their logbook in their personal possession during flight (per section 61.101(d)(3)).

c. Recreational pilots who want to fly beyond 50 nm from the departure airport where training was received must receive additional ground and flight training on the private pilot cross-country training requirements of part 61, subpart E, and must receive an instructor endorsement (per section 61.101(c)). Recreational pilots must have their logbook in their personal possession when operating an aircraft (per section 61.101(c)(3)).

16. **PRIVATE PILOT CERTIFICATION.** Specific knowledge, flight proficiency, flight experience, and endorsement requirements for the private pilot certificate are located in part 61, subpart E.

a. An applicant for a private pilot certificate must possess at least a student pilot certificate, sport pilot certificate, or a recreational pilot certificate that is current and valid.

b. The flight instructor is given discretion in developing a flight training program to meet the requirements of part 61, subpart E. The regulation spells out the specific minimum aeronautical experience requirements that must be met.

c. Applicants must meet night experience requirements regardless of medical qualification considerations. The only exception is in accordance with section 61.110.

d. The 3 hours of flight training in a single-engine or multiengine airplane on the control and maneuvering of an airplane solely by reference to instruments (see sections 61.109(a)(3) and (b)(3)) and the 3 hours of flight training in a powered-lift on the control and maneuvering of a powered-lift solely by reference to instruments (see section 61.109(e)(3)) do not have to be conducted by a certificated flight instructor—instrument (CFII). However, the training must be in an aircraft and not in a flight simulator or a flight training device unless it was performed in accordance with a 14 CFR part 142 approved training program.

e. Except as in accordance with section 61.110, a person who does not meet the night flying requirements in a gyroplane, powered parachute, or weight-shift-control aircraft (section 61.109(d)(2), (i)(2), or (j)(2)) may be issued a private pilot certificate with the limitation "Night Flying Prohibited." This limitation may only be removed by an examiner or ASI if the holder complies with the requirements of section 61.109(d)(2), (i)(2), or (j)(2), as appropriate.

f. Private pilots (and applicants for the certificate) must understand and comply with all private pilot privileges and limitations, including compensation or hire and expense sharing, in accordance with section 61.113 through section 61.117.

17. **COMMERCIAL PILOT CERTIFICATION.** Specific knowledge, flight proficiency, flight experience, and endorsement requirements for the commercial pilot certificate is located in part 61, subpart F.

a. An applicant for a commercial pilot certificate must hold at least a private pilot certificate issued under part 61.

NOTE: This may be a standard U.S. pilot certificate, or a section 61.75 pilot certificate that is based on a foreign pilot license or meets the requirements of section 61.73. The person may be able to apply for a commercial pilot certificate by being able to meet the requirements of section 61.73 (meaning, able to qualify for the commercial pilot certificate under the special rules for military pilots or former military pilots). If a person is basing application for a commercial pilot certificate on a

> section 61.75 pilot certificate, the authenticity of the foreign pilot license must be verified through the person's foreign civil aviation authority.

b. An applicant for a commercial pilot certificate with an airplane or powered-lift category rating must hold or concurrently obtain the appropriate instrument rating.

18. **AIRLINE TRANSPORT PILOT (ATP) CERTIFICATION.** Specific knowledge, flight proficiency, flight experience, and endorsement requirements for an ATP certificate is located in part 61, subpart G.

   a. An applicant for an ATP certificate must possess one of the following:

   (1) A commercial pilot certificate and an instrument (airplane, helicopter, or powered-lift) rating issued under part 61;

   (2) A foreign ATP license or a foreign commercial pilot license and an instrument (airplane, helicopter, or powered-lift) rating, without limitations, issued by a contracting state to the Convention on International Civil Aviation. If applying for an ATP certificate based on holding a foreign pilot license and ratings, the authenticity of that foreign pilot license must be verified through the foreign civil aviation authority; or

   (3) Be a military pilot or former military pilot and have met the requirements of section 61.73 that qualifies the applicant for a commercial pilot certificate with an instrument (airplane, helicopter, or powered-lift) rating.

   b. An instructor recommendation is not required, unless the applicant has failed the practical test and this is a retest (per section 61.49). Applicants for retest must comply with the appropriate retest requirements of section 61.49. In addition, the instructor must sign the applicant's FAA Form 8710-1 application for the retest.

19. **FLIGHT INSTRUCTORS OTHER THAN FLIGHT INSTRUCTORS WITH A SPORT PILOT RATING.** Specific knowledge, flight proficiency, flight experience, and endorsement requirements for the flight instructor certificate, other than flight instructors with a sport pilot rating, is located in part 61, subpart H. To be eligible for a flight instructor certificate, an applicant must:

   a. Hold a commercial pilot certificate or an ATP certificate with an aircraft rating appropriate to the flight instructor rating sought and that was issued under part 61.

   b. Hold an instrument rating/instrument privileges (e.g., instrument privileges, as on an ATP certificate the instrument privileges are conferred) on the applicant's pilot certificate, if the applicant is seeking a flight instructor certificate with an airplane category, powered-lift rating, or instrument rating, and was issued under the pertinent certification requirements of part 61.

c. Have a logbook endorsement certifying that the applicant has been given the required ground and flight training and has been found competent to pass the practical test. An instructor who meets the requirements of section 61.195(h) must make the endorsement.

d. Have logged at least 15 hours as PIC in the category and class of aircraft that is appropriate to the flight instructor rating sought.

e. For applicants applying for a flight instructor certificate with airplane and glider category ratings, the applicant must have received a logbook endorsement that attests to satisfactory demonstration of instructional proficiency of stall awareness, spin entry, spins, and spin recovery procedures in airplanes or gliders, as appropriate. A logbook endorsement that attests to satisfactory demonstration of instructional proficiency of stall awareness, spin entry, spins, and spin recovery procedures is required for the initial flight instructor certificate (for a rating in airplanes or gliders). This means, even if the applicant were to initially seek a flight instructor certificate with an airplane multiengine rating, the applicant would still be required to receive a logbook endorsement that attests to satisfactory demonstration of instructional proficiency of stall awareness, spin entry, spins, and spin recovery procedures. However, the training would be required to be performed in an airplane (most likely a single-engine land airplane) that does not contain any restrictions from spins.

20. **FLIGHT INSTRUCTORS WITH A SPORT PILOT RATING.** Specific knowledge, flight proficiency, flight experience, and endorsement requirements for the flight instructor certificate with a sport pilot rating is located in part 61, subpart K. To be eligible for a flight instructor certificate with a sport pilot rating an applicant must:

a. Hold a current and valid sport, recreational, or private pilot certificate with category and class ratings or privileges, as applicable that are appropriate to the flight instructor privileges sought.

b. Have a logbook endorsement certifying that the applicant has met the aeronautical experience required by section 61.411, for the category and class privileges, as applicable, that are appropriate to the flight instructor privileges sought.

c. Have a logbook endorsement certifying that the applicant has been given the ground and flight training required by section 61.409 and has been found competent to pass the practical test. An instructor who meets the requirements of section 61.415 or section 62.429 must make the endorsement.

d. The training and experience required to obtain additional sport pilot flight instructor privileges must be supervised by an appropriately authorized flight instructor. Additional training requirements and endorsements are established for the following additional privileges:

(1) To provide training in an additional category or class of light-sport aircraft, an applicant must meet the training requirements and endorsements required in section 61.419. The applicant must successfully complete a proficiency check from an authorized instructor other than the instructor who trained him or her, and provide a completed FAA Form 8710-11, Airman Certificate and/or Rating Application—Sport Pilot, to the authorized instructor.

(2) To provide training in an additional make and model of light-sport aircraft, an applicant must have at least 5 hours of flight time in a make and model of light-sport aircraft within the same set of aircraft in which he or she provides training.

(3) To provide training to operate a light-sport aircraft in Class B, C, and D airspace, at an airport located in Class B, C, or D airspace, and to, from, through, or on an airport having an operational control tower, an applicant must have the endorsement specified in section 61.325, or be otherwise authorized to conduct operations in this airspace.

(4) To provide training in a light-sport aircraft with a V_H greater than 87 kts CAS, an applicant must have the endorsement specified in section 61.327, or be otherwise authorized to operate a light-sport aircraft with a V_H greater than 87 kts CAS.

e. For applicants applying for a flight instructor certificate with sport pilot rating with airplane or glider category privileges, the applicant must have received a logbook endorsement that attests he/she is competent and possesses instructional proficiency in stall awareness, spin entry, spins, and spin recovery procedures after receiving flight training in those training areas in an airplane or glider, as appropriate, that is certificated for spins.

(1) An applicant who seeks additional category and class privileges to be added to his/her flight instructor certificate with sport pilot rating in an airplane or glider would be required to receive the same training and logbook endorsement.

(2) This training would be required to be performed in a single-engine airplane or glider (preferably a light-sport aircraft) that does not contain any restrictions from spins.

f. For single place aircraft, pre-solo flight training must be provided in an aircraft that has two pilot stations and is of the same category and class applicable to the certificate, rating, or privilege sought.

g. To provide ground or flight training for a private pilot certificate with a powered parachute or weight-shift-control aircraft rating, an applicant must hold at least a private pilot certificate with the applicable category and class rating; a flight instructor certificate with a sport pilot rating or privileges, and the applicable flight instructor category and class privileges.

h. All flight instructors with a sport pilot rating or privileges must carry his or her logbook or other evidence of the required authorized instructor endorsements on all flights. Other evidence of the required authorized instructor endorsements may be a preprinted card or record that includes the endorsements. See section 61.51(i)(5).

21. **GOLD SEAL FLIGHT INSTRUCTOR CERTIFICATES (EXCEPT THOSE WITH A SPORT PILOT RATING).** The specific requirements for the gold seal flight instructor certificate (except those with a sport pilot rating) are contained in FAA Order 8700.1, General Aviation Operations Inspector's Handbook, volume 2, chapter 13 and FAA Order 8710.3, Designated Pilot and Flight Engineer Examiner's Handbook, chapter 14. Flight instructor certificates bearing distinctive gold seals are issued to flight instructors who have maintained a high level of flight training activity and who meet special criteria. Once issued, a gold seal flight instructor certificate will be reissued each time the instructor's certificate is renewed. Applicants for gold seal flight instructor certificates must meet the following requirements:

a. The flight instructor must hold a commercial pilot certificate with an instrument rating (glider flight instructors need not hold an instrument rating) or an ATP certificate;

b. The flight instructor must hold a ground instructor certificate with an advanced or instrument ground instructor rating; and

c. The flight instructor must have accomplished the following within the previous 24 calendar-months:

    (1) Trained and recommended at least 10 applicants for a practical test, and at least 80 percent of the applicants passed their tests on the first attempt;

    (2) Conducted at least 20 practical tests as a designated pilot examiner, or graduation tests as chief instructor of a 14 CFR part 141 approved pilot school course; or

    (3) A combination of the above requirements. (Two practical tests conducted equal the credit given for one applicant trained and recommended for a practical test.)

22. **GOLD SEAL FLIGHT INSTRUCTOR CERTIFICATES (WITH A SPORT PILOT RATING).** The specific requirements for the gold seal flight instructor certificate (with a sport pilot rating) are contained in FAA Order 8700.1, vol. 2, ch. 13, and FAA Order 8710.7, Sport Pilot Examiner's Handbook. Flight instructor certificates bearing distinctive gold seals are issued to flight instructors who have maintained a high level of flight training activity and who meet special

criteria. Once issued, a gold seal flight instructor certificate will be reissued each time the instructor's certificate is renewed. Applicants for gold seal flight instructor certificates (with a sport pilot rating) must meet the following requirements:

a. The flight instructor must hold at least a sport pilot certificate;

b. The flight instructor must hold a ground instructor certificate with a basic ground instructor rating;

c. The flight instructor must have accomplished one of the following within the previous 24 months:

(1) Trained and recommended at least 10 applicants for an original certificate with at least 80 percent of those applicants recommended passing the practical test on his or her first attempt;

(2) Conducted at least 20 certification practical tests as an examiner or conducted 20 certification graduation tests as a chief flight instructor for an approved pilot school course; or

(3) A combination of the requirements in paragraphs 22c(1) and (2). (Two certification practical tests/certification graduation tests equate to one trained and recommended applicant.)

23. **RENEWAL OF A FLIGHT INSTRUCTOR CERTIFICATE.** The renewal requirements for a flight instructor certificate are located in section 61.197. Renewal of a flight instructor certificate may be accomplished at any time.

a. A flight instructor certificate that has not expired may be renewed in accordance with section 61.197(a) by:

(1) Passing a practical test for one of the ratings listed on the person's current flight instructor certificate or passing a practical test for an additional flight instructor rating;

(2) Presenting to an ASI the appropriate records that verify the requirements of section 61.197(a)(2)(i) or (ii) were accomplished;

(3) Presenting to an ASI evidence of having graduated from an FAA-approved flight instructor refresher course (FIRC) within the preceding 3 calendar-months. The instructor's FIRC graduation certificate should be presented to an ASI at the time of application for renewal.

b. For individuals who wish to comply with section 61.197(a)(2)(ii), the FAA offers the following examples of "a position involving the regular evaluation" of pilots:

(1) Persons who regularly give aircraft checkouts at a fixed-base operator and the ASI are acquainted with the applicant's duties, responsibilities, and quality of instruction.

(2) Part 121 or 135 airline captains who regularly evaluate pilots and have satisfactory knowledge of part 61 pilot training,

certification, and standards. The ASI must be acquainted with the duties and responsibilities of those pilot positions.

(3) Company check pilots for 14 CFR part 133 operations who regularly evaluate pilots and have satisfactory knowledge of part 61 pilot training, certification, and standards. The ASI must be acquainted with the duties and responsibilities of those pilot positions.

c. Provided that the certificate is renewed within 3 calendar-months before the expiration month of a current flight instructor certificate, the renewed certificate will be valid for an additional 24 calendar-months beyond the expiration date shown on the current certificate. For example:

(1) If a flight instructor renewal applicant's current flight instructor certificate expires in August, then that applicant must accomplish one of the flight instructor renewal actions in the months of May, June, July, or August to retain the month of August as the expiration month (per section 61.197(b)(2)(i)).

(2) For example, assume a flight instructor renewal applicant has August 31, 2005, showing on her current flight instructor certificate. The applicant completes an FIRC on June 1, 2005, and presents her current flight instructor certificate and FIRC graduation certificate to a FSDO on June 1, 2005. The flight instructor certificate is renewed with a new expiration date of August 31, 2007 (per section 61.197(b)(2)(ii)).

d. If the flight instructor certification renewal action occurs outside the 3 calendar-month period of the expiration month on the flight instructor certificate, the renewed flight instructor certificate will be valid for an additional 24 calendar-months from the month the renewal requirements of section 61.197 were accomplished. A FIRC graduation certificate must be presented to a FSDO within 90 days of completion of the FIRC. The renewal action of section 61.197(a) must be accomplished before the expiration date shown on the applicant's flight instructor certificate.

e. There have been several inquires asking about the intent of the phrase "or other documentation acceptable to the Administrator" in section 61.3(d). During the flight instructor certification renewal process, when an FIRC graduation certificate is used for renewal and the applicant's flight instructor certificate is being processed for renewal, a copy of the FIRC graduation certificate is considered "acceptable documentation to the Administrator" until the applicant receives his or her permanent flight instructor certificate. Another example of other "acceptable documentation to the Administrator" is a copy of the flight instructor renewal application that the applicant has completed and signed FAA Form 8710-1.

f. Regardless of what has been explained in the paragraphs above, it should be understood that the FAA has the prerogative to require any applicant to complete a part or the entire applicable flight instructor practical test. A practical test may be required if there is reason to believe that it will correct some deficiency in the applicant's instructing abilities or it has been determined necessary to introduce new training procedures or certification requirements.

24. **EXPIRED FLIGHT INSTRUCTOR CERTIFICATE.** The requirements for holders of an expired flight instructor certificate to obtain new certificates are located in section 61.199. A practical test is required in the exchange of an expired flight instructor certificate. A DPE or an ASI will not reinstate expired flight instructor certificates unless the applicant passes a practical test.

a. The holder of an expired flight instructor certificate (i.e., a flight instructor certificate that conforms to section 61.5(c)) may exchange that certificate for a new certificate (except for a flight instructor certificate with a sport pilot rating) by passing one practical test, per section 61.183(h), for one of the aircraft ratings held on that person's expired flight instructor certificate.

> **NOTE: If the practical test is for a flight instructor certificate with a sport pilot rating, the examiner may only issue that rating and provide endorsements for the category and class privileges tested.**

b. Flight instructor ratings or limited flight instructor ratings on a pilot certificate are no longer valid. To reinstate instructor privileges, all requirements for initial issuance of a flight instructor certificate must be met.

25. **INSTRUMENT RATING.** Specific knowledge, flight proficiency, flight experience, and endorsement requirements for the instrument rating are located in section 61.65.

26. **ADDITIONAL AIRCRAFT RATINGS (OTHER THAN ATP).** Specific knowledge, flight proficiency, flight experience, and endorsement requirements for additional category, class, or type rating (for other than at the ATP level) are located in section 61.63.

a. Category and Class Ratings. Applicants adding a category and/or class rating to a recreational pilot certificate or higher must have an instructor's recommendations and appropriate endorsements. An applicant need not take an additional knowledge test, provided the person holds an airplane, powered-lift, rotorcraft, powered parachute, weight-shift-control aircraft, or airship rating at or above the pilot certificate level sought. An applicant must pass the required practical test appropriate to the pilot certificate for the aircraft category and, if applicable, class rating sought. Additionally, applicants must comply with the requirements of section 61.63, as noted below:

(1) **Category Ratings.** Applicants must receive the training and have the aeronautical experience required by part 61 that applies to the pilot certificate level for the category, and if applicable, class rating sought.

(2) **Class Ratings.** Applicants must be found competent in the knowledge areas and proficient in the areas of operation for the class rating sought.

(3) **Type Ratings.** Applicants must have the required training time, logbook, or training record endorsements, and pass the required practical test in accordance with the ATP/type rating PTS (see section 61.63(d)).

b. **Experimental Category and Class Rating—Section 61.31(k)(2)(iii)(B) for the Carriage of Passengers.** An applicant holding at least a recreational pilot certificate may apply for the issuance of a category and class rating limited to a specific make and model of experimental aircraft in accordance with the provisions of section 61.63(k), with the limitation "Authorized Experimental Aircraft: [Category] and [Class] rating [Make] and [Model]." The applicant is required to receive a logbook endorsement from an authorized flight instructor who has determined that the applicant is proficient to act as PIC of the same category, class, make, and model of experimental aircraft for which the application was made. The 5 hours of flight experience must have been logged between September 1, 2004, and August 31, 2005. Once the pilot complies with the provisions of section 61.63(k), that pilot may be issued the appropriate category and class rating limited to a specific make and model of experimental aircraft.

27. **ADDITIONAL CATEGORY/CLASS RATINGS AT THE ATP CERTIFICATION LEVEL.**

a. Specific knowledge, flight proficiency, flight experience, and endorsement requirements for additional category, class, or type rating (at the ATP certification level) are located in section 61.165.

b. Applicants for a type rating on the ATP certification level must have the required training time, logbook, or training record endorsements, and pass the required practical test in accordance with the ATP/type rating PTS (see section 61.157(b)).

c. An instructor recommendation is not required, unless the applicant has failed the practical test and this is a retest (per section 61.49). Applicants for retest must comply with the appropriate retest requirements of section 61.49. In addition, the instructor must sign the applicant's FAA Form 8710-1 application for the retest.

d. Experimental category and class rating—§61.31(k)(2)(iii)(B). An applicant holding an ATP certificate may apply for the issuance of a category and class rating limited to a specific make and model of experimental aircraft in accordance with the provisions of section 61.165(f) with the limitation "Authorized Experimental Aircraft: [Category] and [Class] rating [Make] and [Model]." The applicant is required to receive a logbook endorsement from an authorized flight instructor who has determined that the applicant is proficient to act as PIC of the same category, class, make, and model of experimental aircraft for which the application was made. The 5 hours of flight experience must have been logged between September 1, 2004, and August 31, 2005. Once the pilot complies with the provisions of section 61.165(f), that pilot may be issued the appropriate category and class rating limited to a specific make and model of experimental aircraft.

28. **OTHER INSTRUCTOR ENDORSEMENTS.** Specific requirements for knowledge, aeronautical experience and, as appropriate, testing for the complex airplane, high performance airplane, tailwheel airplane, high altitude/pressurized airplane, and type specific training are found in section 61.31.

29. **GROUND INSTRUCTOR CERTIFICATION.** The applicability, eligibility, privileges, and recency requirements for the ground instructor certificate is located in part 61, subpart I.

30. **AUTHORIZED INSTRUCTORS.** Section 61.1 defines an "authorized instructor" as any instructor who holds a valid and current flight or ground instructor certificate with the applicable privileges and limitations appropriate to the type of instruction provided. Section 61.41 authorizes instructors who are not certificated by FAA to provide training. However, only instructors who are certificated by FAA are allowed to provide the required endorsements toward the requirements for a pilot certificate, rating, or privilege issued under part 61.

31. **ADDITIONAL TRAINING FOR GLIDERS.** Specific knowledge, flight proficiency, and endorsement requirements for the ground tow, aerotow, and self-launch procedures for gliders are located in section 61.31(j).

   a. Pilots who desire to use ground-tow launch procedures must have satisfactorily accomplished ground and flight training on ground-tow procedures and operations. The pilot must have received an endorsement from a CFI–Glider instructor who certifies, in the pilot's logbook, that the pilot has been found proficient in ground-tow procedures and operations.

   b. Pilots who desire to use aerotow procedures must have satisfactorily accomplished ground and flight training on aerotow procedures and operations. The pilot must have received an endorsement from a CFI–Glider instructor who certifies, in the pilot's logbook, that the pilot has been found proficient in aerotow procedures and operations.

c. Pilots who desire to use self-launch procedures must have satisfactorily accomplished ground and flight training on self-launch procedures and operations. The pilot must have received an endorsement from a CFI–Glider instructor who certifies, in the pilot's logbook, that the pilot has been found proficient in self-launch procedures and operations.

d. As per section 61.31(j)(2), the holder of a glider rating issued prior to August 4, 1997, is considered to be in compliance with the training and logbook endorsement requirements of this paragraph for the specific operating privilege for which the holder is already qualified.

e. Prior to September 1, 2004, some weight-shift-control aircraft had been issued an experimental certificate in the glider category. In these cases only, initial pilot certification for the issuance of at least a private pilot certificate with a glider rating limited to weight-shift control or glider-trike privileges was authorized.

NOTE: After September 1, 2004, issuance of at least a private pilot certificate with a glider rating limited to weight-shift control or glider-trike privileges is no longer authorized, nor necessary, now that there are established training and certification requirements for weight-shift control category aircraft under part 61.

f. Effective January 15, 2005, airmen who conducted their initial pilot certification in a weight-shift control aircraft that was certificated as an experimental aircraft in the glider category and received a private pilot certificate or higher with a glider rating limited to weight-shift control or glider-trike privileges can apply using FAA Form 8710-11 at a FSDO for a weight-shift-control category and/or class rating to be added to their airman certificate with no further showing of competency.

32. AERONAUTICAL EXPERIENCE CREDIT—ULTRALIGHT VEHICLES. A person may use aeronautical experience obtained in an ultralight vehicle while a registered ultralight pilot with an FAA-recognized ultralight organization, as required by section 61.52, to meet the requirements for the following certificates and ratings issued under this part:

a. A sport pilot certificate.

b. A flight instructor certificate with a sport pilot rating.

c. A private pilot certificate with a weight-shift control or powered parachute category rating.

d. To meet the provisions of section 61.69 and section 61.415(e).

33. HOW TO OBTAIN ELECTRONICALLY. This AC is available online at http://www.airweb.faa.gov/rgl and can also be found at http://www.faa.gov/pilots/ under the Advisory Circulars link.

Appendix 1. Instructor Endorsements

The following examples are recommended sample endorsements for use by authorized instructors when endorsing logbooks for airmen applying for a knowledge or practical test, or when certifying accomplishment of requirements for pilot operating privileges. Each endorsement must be legible and include the instructor's signature, date of signature, certificated flight instructor (CFI) or certificated ground instructor (CGI) certificate number, and certificate expiration date, if applicable. The purpose for this advisory circular is to provide guidance and to encourage standardization among instructors.

Student Pilot Endorsements

1. **Presolo aeronautical knowledge: section 61.87(b).**

   I certify that (*First name, MI, Last name*) has satisfactorily completed the presolo knowledge exam of section 61.87(b) for the (*make and model aircraft*).

   /s/   [date]   J.J. Jones   987654321 CFI   Exp. 12-31-05

2. **Presolo flight training: section 61.87(c).**

   I certify that (*First name, MI, Last name*) has received the required presolo training in a (*make and model aircraft*). I have determined he/she has demonstrated the proficiency of section 61.87(d) and is proficient to make solo flights in (*make and model aircraft*).

   /s/   [date]   J.J. Jones   987654321 CFI   Exp. 12-31-05

3. **Presolo flight training at night: section 61.87(c) and (o).**

   I certify that (*First name, MI, Last name*) has received the required presolo training in a (*make and model aircraft*). I have determined he/she has demonstrated the proficiency of section 61.87(o) and is proficient to make solo flights at night in a (*make and model aircraft*).

   /s/   [date]   J.J. Jones   987654321 CFI   Exp. 12-31-05

4. **Solo flight (each additional 90-day period): section 61.87(p).**

   I certify that (*First name, MI, Last name*) has received the required training to qualify for solo flying. I have determined he/she meets the applicable requirements of section 61.87(p) and is proficient to make solo flights in (*make and model*).

   /s/   [date]   J.J. Jones   987654321 CFI   Exp. 12-31-05

5. **Solo takeoffs and landings at another airport within 25 nm: section 61.93(b)(1).**

   I certify that (*First name, MI, Last name*) has received the required training of section 61.93(b)(1). I have determined that he/she is proficient to practice solo takeoffs and landings at (*airport name*). The takeoffs and landings at (*airport name*) are subject to the following conditions: (*List any applicable conditions or limitations.*)

   /s/   [date]   J.J. Jones   987654321 CFI   Exp. 12-31-05

6. **Initial solo cross-country flight: section 61.93(c)(1).**

I certify that (*First name, MI, Last name*) has received the required solo cross-country training. I find he/she has met the applicable requirements of section 61.93, and is proficient to make solo cross-country flights in a (*make and model aircraft*).

/s/   [date]   J.J. Jones   987654321 CFI   Exp. 12-31-05

7. **Solo cross-country flight: section 61.93(c)(2).**

I have reviewed the cross-country planning of (*First name, MI, Last name*). I find the planning and preparation to be correct to make the solo flight from (*location*) to (*destination*) via (*route of flight*) with landings at (*name the airports*) in a (*make and model aircraft*) on (*date*). (*List any applicable conditions or limitations.*)

/s/   [date]   J.J. Jones   987654321 CFI   Exp. 12-31-05

8. **Repeated solo cross-country flights not more than 50 nm from the point of departure: section 61.93(b)(2).**

I certify that (*First name, MI, Last name*) has received the required training in both directions between and at both (*airport names*). I have determined that he/she is proficient of section 61.93(b)(2) to conduct repeated solo cross-country flights over that route, subject to the following conditions: (*List any applicable conditions or limitations.*)

/s/   [date]   J.J. Jones   987654321 CFI   Exp. 12-31-05

9. **Solo flight in Class B airspace: section 61.95(a).**

I certify that (*First name, MI, Last name*) has received the required training of section 61.95(a). I have determined he/she is proficient to conduct solo flights in (*name of Class B*) airspace. (*List any applicable conditions or limitations.*)

/s/   [date]   J.J. Jones   987654321 CFI   Exp. 12-31-05

10. **Solo flight to, from, or at an airport located in Class B airspace: section 61.95(a) and section 91.131(b)(1).**

I certify that (*First name, MI, Last name*) has received the required training of section 61.95(a)(1). I have determined that he/she is proficient to conduct solo flight operations at (*name of airport*). (*List any applicable conditions or limitations.*)

/s/   [date]   J.J. Jones   987654321 CFI   Exp. 12-31-05

Student Pilot Seeking Sport Pilot Certificate Endorsements

11. **Presolo aeronautical knowledge: section 61.87(b).**

I certify that (*First name, MI, Last name*) has satisfactorily completed the presolo knowledge exam of section 61.87(b) for the (*make and model aircraft*).

/s/   [date]   J.J. Jones   987654321 CFI   Exp. 12-31-05

12. **Presolo flight training: section 61.87(c).**

    I certify that (*First name, MI, Last name*) has received the required presolo training in a (*make and model aircraft*). I have determined he/she has demonstrated the proficiency of section 61.87 (*(d) through (m), as appropriate*) and is proficient to make solo flights in (*aircraft category*: make and model aircraft*).

    /s/   [date]   J.J. Jones   987654321 CFI   Exp. 12-31-05

    * Use the following letters to indicate the category of aircraft: (**d**) Airplane (**g**) Gyroplane (**i**) Glider (**j**) Airship (**k**) Balloon (**l**) powered parachute (**m**) weight-shift-control

13. **Solo flight (first 90-day period): section 61.87(n)(2).**

    I certify that (*First name, MI, Last name*) has received the required training to qualify for solo flying. I have determined he/she meets the applicable requirements of section 61.87(n) and is proficient to make solo flights in (*make and model*).

    /s/   [date]   J.J. Jones   987654321 CFI   Exp. 12-31-05

14. **Solo flight (each additional 90-day period): section 61.87(p)(v).**

    I certify that (*First name, MI, Last name*) has received the required training to qualify for solo flying. I have determined he/she meets the applicable requirements of section 61.87(p) and is proficient to make solo flights in (*make and model*).

    /s/   [date]   J.J. Jones   987654321 CFI   Exp. 12-31-05

15. **Solo takeoffs and landings at another airport within 25 nm: section 61.93(b)(1).**

    I certify that (*First name, MI, Last name*) has received the required training of section 61.93(b)(1). I have determined that he/she is proficient to practice solo takeoffs and landings at (*airport name*). The takeoffs and landings at (*airport name*) are subject to the following conditions: (*List any applicable conditions or limitations.*)

    /s/   [date]   J.J. Jones   987654321 CFI   Exp. 12-31-05

16. **Initial solo cross-country flight training: section 61.93(c)(1).**

    NOTE: The *instructor who provided the training* places an endorsement in the student's logbook before the first solo cross-country and endorses the back of the student pilot certificate.

    I certify that (*First name, MI, Last name*) has received the required solo cross-country training. I find he/she has met the applicable requirements of section 61.93, and is proficient to make solo cross-country flights in a (*make and model aircraft*).

    /s/   [date]   J.J. Jones   987654321 CFI   Exp. 12-31-05

17. **Solo cross-country flight: section 61.93(c)(2).**

    NOTE: This is done before each solo cross-country flight and may be accomplished by *any instructor* who reviews the flight planning. This endorsement is made in the student's logbook.

    I have reviewed the cross-country planning of (*First name, MI, Last name*). I find the planning and preparation to be correct to make the solo flight from (*location*) to (*destination*) via (*route of flight*) with landings at (*name the airports*) in a (*make and model aircraft*) on (*date*). (*List any applicable conditions or limitations.*)

    /s/   [date]   J.J. Jones   987654321 CFI   Exp. 12-31-05

18. **Repeated solo cross-country flights not more than 50 nm from the point of departure: section 61.93(b)(2).**

    I certify that (*First name, MI, Last name*) has received the required training in both directions between and at both (*airport names*). I have determined that he/she is proficient of section 61.93(b)(2) to conduct repeated solo cross-country flights over that route, subject to the following conditions: (*List any applicable conditions or limitations.*)

    /s/   [date]   J.J. Jones   987654321 CFI   Exp. 12-31-05

19. **Solo flight in Class B, C, and D airspace: section 61.94(a).**

    NOTE: Required each additional 90-day period.

    I certify that (*First name, MI, Last name*) has received the required training of section 61.94(a). I have determined he/she is proficient to conduct solo flights in (*name of Class B, C, or D*) airspace and authorized to operate to, from through and at _____ airport. (*List any applicable conditions or limitations.*)

    /s/   [date]   J.J. Jones   987654321 CFI   Exp. 12-31-05

20. **Solo flight to, from, or at an airport located in Class B, C, or D airspace or on an airport having an operational control tower: section 61.94(a) and section 91.131(b)(1).**

    NOTE: Required each additional 90-day period.

    I certify that (*First name, MI, Last name*) has received the required training of section 61.94(a)(1). I have determined that he/she is proficient to conduct solo flight operations at (*name of airport*) located in Class B, C, or D airspace or on an airport having an operational control tower. (*List any applicable conditions or limitations.*)

    /s/   [date]   J.J. Jones   987654321 CFI   Exp. 12-31-05

21. **Presolo flight training at night: section 61.87(c) and (o).**

    I certify that (*First name, MI, Last name*) has received the required presolo training in a (*make and model aircraft*) and determined he/she has demonstrated the proficiency of section 61.87(o) and is proficient to make solo flights at night in a (*make and model aircraft*).

    /s/   [date]   J.J. Jones   987654321 CFI   Exp. 12-31-05

Sport Pilot Endorsements

22. **Taking aeronautical knowledge test: section 61.35(a)(1) and section 61.309.**

    I certify that (*First name, MI, Last name*) has received the required aeronautical knowledge training of section 61.309. I have determined that he/she is prepared for the (*name the knowledge test*).

    /s/   [date]   J.J. Jones   987654321 CFI   Exp. 12-31-05

23. **Taking flight proficiency check for different category or class of aircraft: section 61.309 and section 61.311.**

    I certify that (*First name, MI, Last name*) has received the required training required in accordance with sections 61.309 and 61.311 and have determined that he/she is prepared for the (*name the proficiency check*).

    /s/   [date]   J.J. Jones   987654321 CFI   Exp. 12-31-05

24. **Passing flight proficiency check for different category or class of aircraft: section 61.309 and section 61.311.**

    I certify that (*First name, MI, Last name*) has met the requirements of sections 61.309 and 61.311 and I have determined him/her proficient to act as PIC of (*category and class*) of light-sport aircraft.

    /s/   [date]   J.J. Jones   987654321 CFI   Exp. 12-31-05

25. **Flight proficiency in same category and class within a different make and model of aircraft: section 61.323.**

    I certify that (*First name, MI, Last name*) has received the required training of section 61.323 in (*make and model aircraft*) and have determined him/her proficient to act as PIC of that light-sport aircraft.

    /s/   [date]   J.J. Jones   987654321 CFI   Exp. 12-31-05

26. **Taking sport pilot practical test: section 61.309, section 61.311, and section 61.313.**

    I certify that (*First name, MI, Last name*) has received the training required in accordance with section 61.309 and section 61.311 and met the aeronautical experience requirements of section 61.313. I have determined that he/she is prepared for the (*type of practical test*).

    /s/   [date]   J.J. Jones   987654321 CFI   Exp. 12-31-05

27. **Passing a sport pilot practical test: section 61.309, section 61.311, and section 61.313.**

    NOTE: Required by section 61.317, issued by a designated pilot examiner (DPE).

    I certify that (*First name, MI, Last name*) has met the requirements of section 61.309, section 61.311, and section 61.313, and I have determined him/her proficient to act as PIC of (*category and class of light sport aircraft*) aircraft.

    /s/   [date]   J.J. Jones   987654321 CFI   Exp. 12-31-05

28. **Class B, C, or D airspace, at an airport located in Class B, C, or D airspace, or to, from, through, or on an airport having an operational control tower: section 61.325.**

    I certify that (*First name, MI, Last name*) has received the required training of section 61.325. I have determined he/she is proficient to conduct operations in Class B, C, or D airspace, at an airport located in Class B, C, or D airspace, or to, from, through, or on an airport having an operational control tower.

    /s/   [date]   J.J. Jones   987654321 CFI   Exp. 12-31-05

29. **Light-sport aircraft that has a V_H greater than 87 knots CAS: section 61.327.**

    I certify that (*First name, MI, Last name*) has received the required training required in accordance with section 61.327 in a (*make and model aircraft*). I have determined him/her proficient to act as PIC of a light-sport aircraft that has a V_H greater than 87 knots (kts) CAS.

    /s/   [date]   J.J. Jones   987654321 CFI   Exp. 12-31-05

Recreational Pilot Endorsements

30. **Aeronautical knowledge test: section 61.35(a)(1), section 61.96(b)(3), and section 61.97(b).**

    I certify that (*First name, MI, Last name*) has received the required training of section 61.97(b). I have determined that he/she is prepared for the (*name the knowledge test*).

    /s/   [date]   J.J. Jones   987654321 CFI   Exp. 12-31-05

31. **Flight proficiency/practical test: section 61.96(b)(5), section 61.98(a) and (b), and section 61.99.**

    I certify that (*First name, MI, Last name*) has received the required training of section 61.98(b) and section 61.99. I have determined that he/she is prepared for the (*name the practical test*).

    /s/   [date]   J.J. Jones   987654321 CFI   Exp. 12-31-05

32. **Recreational pilot to operate within 50 nm of the airport where training was received: section 61.101(b).**

I certify that (*First name, MI, Last name*) has received the required training of section 61.101(b). I have determined he/she is competent to operate at the (*name of airport*).

/s/ [date] J.J. Jones 987654321 CFI Exp. 12-31-05

33. **Recreational pilot to act as PIC on a flight that exceeds 50 nm of the departure airport: section 61.101(c).**

I certify that (*First name, MI, Last name*) has received the required cross-country training of section 61.101(c). I have determined that he/she is proficient in cross-country flying of part 61, subpart E.

/s/ [date] J.J. Jones 987654321 CFI Exp. 12-31-05

34. **Recreational pilot with less than 400 flight hours and not logged PIC time within the preceding 180 days: section 61.101(g).**

I certify that (*First name, MI, Last name*) has received the required 180-day recurrent training of section 61.101(g) in a (*make and model aircraft*). I have determined him/her proficient to act as PIC of that aircraft.

/s/ [date] J.J. Jones 987654321 CFI Exp. 12-31-05

35. **Recreational pilot to conduct solo flights for the purpose of obtaining an additional certificate or rating while under the supervision of an authorized flight instructor: section 61.101(i).**

I certify that (*First name, MI, Last name*) has received the required training of section 61.87 in a (*make and model aircraft*). I have determined he/she is prepared to conduct a solo flight on (*date*) under the following conditions: (*List all conditions which require endorsement, e.g., flight which requires communication with air traffic control, flight in an aircraft for which the pilot does not hold a category/class rating, etc.*).

/s/ [date] J.J. Jones 987654321 CFI Exp. 12-31-05

36. **Class B, C, or D airspace, at an airport located in Class B, C, or D airspace, or to, from, through, or on an airport having an operational control tower: section 61.101(d).**

I certify that (*First name, MI, Last name*) has received the required training of section 61.101(d). I have determined he/she is proficient to conduct operations in Class B, C, or D airspace, at an airport located in Class B, C, or D airspace, or to, from, through, or on an airport having an operational control tower.

/s/ [date] J.J. Jones 987654321 CFI Exp. 12-31-05

Private Pilot Endorsements

37. Aeronautical knowledge test: sections 61.35(a)(1), 61.103(d), and 61.105.

I certify that (*First name, MI, Last name*) has received the required training in accordance with section 61.105. I have determined he/she is prepared for the (*name the knowledge test*).

/s/   [date]   J.J. Jones   987654321 CFI   Exp. 12-31-05

38. Flight proficiency/practical test: sections 61.103(f), 61.107(b), and 61.109.

I certify that (*First name, MI, Last name*) has received the required training in accordance with sections 61.107 and 61.109. I have determined he/she is prepared for the (*name the practical test*).

/s/   [date]   J.J. Jones   987654321 CFI   Exp. 12-31-05

Commercial Pilot Endorsements

39. Aeronautical knowledge test: section 61.35(a)(1), section 61.123(c), and section 61.125.

I certify that (*First name, MI, Last name*) has received the required training of section 61.125. I have determined that he/she is prepared for the (*name the knowledge test*).

/s/   [date]   J.J. Jones   987654321 CFI   Exp. 12-31-05

40. Flight proficiency/practical test: section 61.123(e), section 61.127, and section 61.129.

I certify that (*First name, MI, Last name*) has received the required training of section 61.127 and section 61.129. I have determined he/she is prepared for the (*name the practical test*).

/s/   [date]   J.J. Jones   987654321 CFI   Exp. 12-31-05

Instrument Rating Endorsements

41. Aeronautical knowledge test: section 61.35(a)(1) and section 61.65(a) and (b).

I certify that (*First name, MI, Last name*) has received the required training of section 61.65(b). I have determined that he/she is prepared for the (*name the knowledge test*).

/s/   [date]   J.J. Jones   987654321 CFI   Exp. 12-31-05

42. Flight proficiency/practical test: section 61.65(a)(6).

I certify that (*First name, MI, Last name*) has received the required training of section 61.65(c) and (d). I have determined he/she is prepared for the Instrument—(*airplane, helicopter, or powered-lift*) practical test.

/s/   [date]   J.J. Jones   987654321 CFI   Exp. 12-31-05

Flight Instructor (Other Than Flight Instructors with a Sport Pilot Rating) Endorsements

43. **Fundamentals of instructing knowledge test: section 61.183(d) and section 61.185(a)(1).**

    I certify that (*First name, MI, Last name*) has received the required fundamentals of instruction training of section 61.185(a)(1).

    /s/   [date]   J.J. Jones   987654321 CFI   Exp. 12-31-05

44. **Flight instructor ground and flight proficiency/practical test: section 61.183(g) and section 61.187(a) and (b).**

    I certify that (*First name, MI, Last name*) has received the required training of section 61.187(b). I have determined he/she is prepared for the CFI—(*aircraft category and class*) practical test.

    /s/   [date]   J.J. Jones   987654321 CFI   Exp. 12-31-05

45. **Flight instructor certificate with instrument—(category/class) rating/practical test: section 61.183(g) and section 61.187(a) and (b)(7).**

    I certify that (*First name, MI, Last name*) has received the required CFII training of section 61.187(b)(7). I have determined he/she is prepared for the CFII—(*airplane, helicopter, or powered-lift*) practical test.

    /s/   [date]   J.J. Jones   987654321 CFI   Exp. 12-31-05

46. **Spin training: section 61.183(i)(1).**

    I certify that (*First name, MI, Last name*) has received the required training of section 61.183(i). I have determined that he/she is competent in instructional skills for training stall awareness, spin entry, spins, and spin recovery procedures.

    /s/   [date]   J.J. Jones   987654321 CFI   Exp. 12-31-05

    NOTE: The above spin training endorsement is required of flight instructor applicants for the airplane and glider ratings only.

Flight Instructor with a Sport Pilot Rating Endorsements

47. **Taking the fundamentals of instructing knowledge test: section 61.405(a)(1).**

   I certify that (*First name, MI, Last name*) has received the required training in accordance with section 61.405(a)(1). I have determined that he/she is prepared for the Fundamentals of Instruction Knowledge Test.

   /s/   [date]   J.J. Jones   987654321 CFI   Exp. 12-31-05

48. **Taking sport pilot flight instructor aeronautical knowledge test: section 61.35(a) (1) and section 61.405(a).**

   I certify that (*First name, MI, Last name*) has received the required training of section 61.405(a)(2). I have determined that he/she is prepared for the (*name the knowledge test*).

   /s/   [date]   J.J. Jones   987654321 CFI   Exp. 12-31-05

49. **Taking the flight instructor flight proficiency check to provide training if a different category or class of aircraft—(additional category/class): section 61.419 and section 61.409.**

   I certify that (*First name, MI, Last name*) has received the required training in accordance with section 61.419 and section 61.409 and have determined he/she is prepared for a proficiency check for the flight instructor with a sport pilot rating in a (*aircraft category and class*).

   /s/   [date]   J.J. Jones   987654321 CFI   Exp. 12-31-05

50. **Passing the flight instructor flight proficiency check to provide training in a different category or class of aircraft—(additional category/class): section 61.419 and section 61.409.**

   I certify that (*First name, MI, Last name*) has met the requirements in accordance with section 61.419 and section 61.409. I have determined that he/she is proficient and authorized for the additional (*aircraft category and class*) flight instructor privilege.

   /s/   [date]   J.J. Jones   987654321 CFI   Exp. 12-31-05

51. **Taking the flight instructor practical test: section 61.409 and section 61.411.**

   I certify that (*First name, MI, Last name*) has received the required training of section 61.409 and met the aeronautical experience requirements of section 61.411. I have determined he/she is prepared for the flight instructor with a sport pilot rating practical test in a (*aircraft category and class*).

   /s/   [date]   J.J. Jones   987654321 CFI   Exp. 12-31-05

52. **Passing the flight instructor practical test: section 61.409 and section 61.411.**

   NOTE: Required by section 61.417, issued by a DPE.

   I certify that (*First name, MI, Last name*) has met the requirements in accordance with section 61.409 and section 61.411. I have determined that he/she is proficient and authorized for the (*aircraft category and class*) flight instructor privilege.

   /s/   [date]   J.J. Jones   987654321 CFI   Exp. 12-31-05

53. **Spin training: section 61.405(b)(1)(ii).**

   I certify that (*First name, MI, Last name*) has received the required training of section 61.405(b)(1)(ii). I have determined that he/she is competent and possess instructional proficiency in stall awareness, spin entry, spins, and spin recovery procedures.

   /s/   [date]   J.J. Jones   987654321 CFI   Exp. 12-31-05

   NOTE: This spin training endorsement is only required of flight instructor applicants for the airplane and glider ratings.

Ground Instructor Endorsement

54. **Ground instructor who does not meet the recent experience requirements: section 61.217(b).**

   I certify that (*First name, MI, Last name*) has demonstrated satisfactory proficiency on the appropriate ground instructor knowledge and training subjects of section 61.213(a)(3) and (a)(4).

   /s/   [date]   J.J. Jones   987654321 CFI   Exp. 12-31-05

   NOTE: Signed by CFI or CGI, as appropriate; the expiration date would apply only to a CFI.

Additional Endorsements

55. **Completion of a flight review: section 61.56(a) and (c).**

   I certify that (*First name, MI, Last name*), (*pilot certificate*), (*certificate number*), has satisfactorily completed a flight review of section 61.56(a) on (*date*).

   /s/   [date]   J.J. Jones   987654321 CFI   Exp. 12-31-05

   NOTE: No logbook entry reflecting unsatisfactory performance on a flight review is required.

56. **Completion of a phase of an FAA-sponsored pilot proficiency award program (WINGS): section 61.56(e).**

   I certify that (*First name, MI, Last name*), (*pilot certificate*), (*certificate number*), has satisfactorily completed Phase No. ___ of a WINGS program on (*date*).

   /s/   [date]   J.J. Jones   987654321 CFI   Exp. 12-31-05

57. **Completion of an instrument proficiency check: section 61.57(d).**

I certify that (*First name, MI, Last name*), (*pilot certificate*), (*certificate number*), has satisfactorily completed the instrument proficiency check of section 61.57(d) in a (*list make and model of aircraft*) on (*date*).

/s/ [date] J.J. Jones 987654321 CFI Exp. 12-31-05

NOTE: No logbook entry reflecting unsatisfactory performance on an instrument proficiency check is required.

58. **To act as PIC in a complex airplane: section 61.31(e).**

I certify that (*First name, MI, Last name*), (*pilot certificate*), (*certificate number*), has received the required training of section 61.31(e) in a (*make and model of complex airplane*). I have determined that he/she is proficient in the operation and systems of a complex airplane.

/s/ [date] J.J. Jones 987654321 CFI Exp. 12-31-05

59. **To act as PIC in a high performance airplane: section 61.31(f).**

I certify that (*First name, MI, Last name*), (*pilot certificate*), (*certificate number*), has received the required training of section 61.31(f) in a (*make and model of high performance airplane*). I have determined that he/she is proficient in the operation and systems of a high performance airplane.

/s/ [date] J.J. Jones 987654321 CFI Exp. 12-31-05

60. **To act as PIC in a pressurized aircraft capable of high altitude operations: section 61.31(g).**

I certify that (*First name, MI, Last name*), (*pilot certificate*), (*certificate number*), has received the required training of section 61.31(g) in a (*make and model of pressurized aircraft*). I have determined that he/she is proficient in the operation and systems of a pressurized aircraft.

/s/ [date] J.J. Jones 987654321 CFI Exp. 12-31-05

61. **To act as PIC in a tailwheel airplane: section 61.31(i).**

I certify that (*First name, MI, Last name*), (*pilot certificate*), (*certificate number*), has received the required training of section 61.31(i) in a (*make and model of tailwheel airplane*). I have determined that he/she is proficient in the operation of a tailwheel airplane.

/s/ [date] J.J. Jones 987654321 CFI Exp. 12-31-05

62. **To act as PIC of an aircraft in solo operations when the pilot does not hold an appropriate category/class rating: section 61.31(d)(3).**

    I certify that (*First name, MI, Last name*) has received the training as required by section 61.31(d)(3) to serve as a PIC in a (*category and class of aircraft*). I have determined that he/she is prepared to serve as PIC in that (*make and model of aircraft*).

    /s/   [date]   J.J. Jones   987654321 CFI   Exp. 12-31-05

63. **Retesting after failure of a knowledge or practical test: section 61.49.**

    I certify that (*First name, MI, Last name*) has received the additional (*flight and/or ground, as appropriate*) training as required by section 61.49. I have determined that he/she is prepared for the (*name the knowledge/practical test*).

    /s/   [date]   J.J. Jones   987654321 CFI   Exp. 12-31-05

    NOTE: In the case of a failed knowledge test, the instructor may complete the endorsement in the space provided at the bottom of the applicant's airman knowledge test report. The instructor must sign the block provided for the instructor's recommendation on the reverse side of FAA Form 8710-1 application for each retake of a practical test.

64. **Additional aircraft category or class rating (other than ATP): section 61.63(b) or (c).**

    I certify that (*First name, MI, Last name*), (*pilot certificate*), (*certificate number*), has received the required training for an additional (*name the aircraft category/class rating*). I have determined that he/she is prepared for the (*name the practical test*) for the addition of a (*name the aircraft category/class rating*).

    /s/   [date]   J.J. Jones   987654321 CFI   Exp. 12-31-05

65. **Type rating only, already holds the appropriate category or class rating (other than ATP): section 61.63(d)(2) and (3).**

    I certify that (*First name, MI, Last name*) has received the required training of section 61.63(d)(2) and (3) for an addition of a (*name the type rating*).

    /s/   [date]   J.J. Jones   987654321 CFI   Exp. 12-31-05

66. **Type rating concurrently with an additional category or class rating (other than ATP): section 61.63(d)(2) and (3).**

    I certify that (*First name, MI, Last name*) has received the required training of section 61.63(d)(2) and (3) for an addition of a (*name the category/class/type rating*). I have determined that he/she is prepared for the (*name the practical test*) for the addition of a (*name the aircraft category/class/type rating*).

    /s/   [date]   J.J. Jones   987654321 CFI   Exp. 12-31-05

67. Type rating only, already holds the appropriate category or class rating (at the ATP level): section 61.157(b)(1).

I certify that (*First name, MI, Last name*) has received the required training of section 61.157(b)(1) for an addition of a (*name the type rating*).

/s/   [date]   J.J. Jones   987654321 CFI   Exp. 12-31-05

68. Type rating concurrently with an additional category or class rating (at the ATP level): section 61.157(b)(1).

I certify that (*First name, MI, Last name*) has received the required training of section 61.157(b)(1) for an addition of a (*name the cat-egory/class/type rating*).

/s/   [date]   J.J. Jones   987654321 CFI   Exp. 12-31-05

69. Launch procedures for operating a glider: section 61.31(j).

I certify that (*First name, MI, Last name*), (*pilot certificate*), (*certifi-cate number*), has received the required training in a (*list the glider make and model*) for (*list the launch procedure*). I have determined that he/she is proficient in (*list the launch procedure*).

/s/   [date]   J.J. Jones   987654321 CFI   Exp. 12-31-05

70. Review of a home study curriculum: section 61.35(a)(1).

I certify I have reviewed the home study curriculum of (*First name, MI, Last name*). I have determined he/she is prepared for the (*name the knowledge test*).

/s/   [date]   J.J. Jones   987654321 CFI   Exp. 12-31-05

71. Experimental aircraft only—additional aircraft category or class rating (other than ATP): section 61.63(k).

I certify that (*First name, MI, Last name*), (*pilot certificate*), (*certifi-cate number*), as required by section 61.63(k) is proficient to act as PIC in a (*category, class, make, and model*) of experimental aircraft and has logged at least 5 hours flight time logged between September 1, 2004 and August 31, 2005 while acting as PIC in (*name the aircraft category/class rating and make and model*) that has been issued an experimental certificate.

/s/   [date]   J.J. Jones   987654321 CFI   Exp. 12-31-05

72. **Experimental aircraft only—additional aircraft category or class rating (ATP): section 61.165(f).**

I certify that (*First name, MI, Last name*), (*pilot certificate*), (*certificate number*), as required by section 61.165(f) is proficient to act as PIC in a (*category, class, make, and model*) of experimental aircraft and has logged at least 5 hours flight time logged between September 1, 2004 and August 31, 2005 while acting as PIC in (*name the aircraft category/class rating and make and model*) that has been issued an experimental certificate.

/s/   [date]   J.J. Jones   987654321 CFI   Exp. 12-31-05

73. **Aeronautical experience credit—ultralight vehicles: section 61.52.**

I certify, I have reviewed the records of (*First name, MI, Last name*), as required by section 61.52(c). I have determined he/she may use (*number of hours*) aeronautical experience obtained in an ultralight vehicle to meet the requirements for (*certificate/rating/privilege*).

/s/   [date]   J.J. Jones   987654321 CFI   Exp. 12-31-05

Applicant's Practical Test Checklist

Appendix 2

Appendix 2

Applicant's Practical Test Checklist

Appointment with Examiner _____

Examiner's Name _____

Date/Time _____

Acceptable Aircraft

Aircraft Documents

___ Airworthiness Certificate

___ Registration Certificate

___ Operating Limitations

Aircraft Maintenance Records

___ Logbook Record of Airworthiness Inspections and AD Compliance

___ Pilot's Operating Handbook, FAA-Approved Airplane Flight Manual

___ Current Weight and Balance Data

Personal Equipment

___ View Limiting Device

___ Current Aeronautical Charts

___ Computer and Plotter

___ Flight Plan Form

___ Flight Logs

___ Current AIM, Current Airport Facility Directory and Appropriate Publications

Personal Records

___ Identification—Photo/Signature

___ Pilot Certificate

___ Current and Appropriate Medical Certificate

___ Completed FAA Form 8710-1, Airman Certificate and/or Rating

___ Application with Instructor's Signature (if applicable)

___ Computer Test Report

___ Pilot Logbook with Appropriate Instructor Endorsements

___ FAA Form 8060-5, Notice of Disapproval (if applicable)

___ Approved School Graduation Certificate (if applicable)

___ Examiner's Fee (if applicable)

Notes

Notes

Notes